T0336333

NETWORKS OF POWER

NETWORKS OF POWER

Political Relations in the Late Postclassic Naco Valley, Honduras

Edward Schortman and Patricia Urban

UNIVERSITY PRESS OF COLORADO

© 2011 by the University Press of Colorado

Published by the University Press of Colorado
5589 Arapahoe Avenue, Suite 206C
Boulder, Colorado 80303

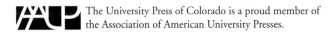 The University Press of Colorado is a proud member of
the Association of American University Presses.

The University Press of Colorado is a cooperative publishing enterprise supported, in part, by
Adams State College, Colorado State University, Fort Lewis College, Mesa State College, Metropolitan State College of Denver, University of Colorado, University of Northern Colorado,
and Western State College of Colorado.

∞ The paper used in this publication meets the minimum requirements of the American
National Standard for Information Sciences—Permanence of Paper for Printed Library Materials. ANSI Z39.48-1992

Library of Congress Cataloging-in-Publication Data

Schortman, Edward M.
    Networks of power : political relations in the late postclassic Naco Valley / Edward Schortman
and Patricia Urban.
       p. cm.
    Includes bibliographical references and index.
    ISBN 978-1-60732-062-3 (hardcover : alk. paper) — ISBN 978-1-60732-063-0 (e-book :
alk. paper)
       1. Mayas—Honduras—Naco Valley—Kings and rulers. 2. Mayas—Honduras—Naco
Valley—Politics and government. 3. Mayas—Honduras—Naco Valley—Antiquities. 4. Power
(Social sciences)—Honduras—Naco Valley. 5. Elites (Social sciences)—Honduras—Naco
Valley. 6. Excavations (Archaeology)—Honduras—Naco Valley. 7. Social archaeology—
Honduras—Naco Valley. 8. Naco Valley (Honduras)—Antiquities. I. Urban, Patricia A.
(Patricia Ann), 1950– II. Title.
    F1505.1.N33S36 2011
    972.83'01—dc22
                                                                          2011005674

Design by Daniel Pratt

20 19 18 17 16 15 14 13 12 11   10 9 8 7 6 5 4 3 2 1

To don Luis Nolasco

for his companionship and sincere
commitment to Naco and its prehistory.

Contents

Figures

Tables

Foreword

Ever since 1943, when Paul Kirchhoff gave us the first general description of Mesoamerica as a culturally integrated region, archaeologists and scholars have been excavating the territory and filling in the map using new combinations of methods and theories. This work of expanding and deepening our knowledge of Mesoamerican peoples has been carried out by, among other publications, the expansive *Handbook of Middle American Indians, The Oxford Encyclopedia of Mesoamerican Cultures*, numerous journals, articles, and scores of monographs revealing the history and structure of city-states, cultural regions, and regional interactions while also exploring ways to construct more useful chronologies and find effective methods of reading and interpreting the ever-growing evidence of social integration.

This new volume, *Networks of Power: Political Relations in the Late Postclassic Naco Valley*, meticulously researched and well written by Edward Schortman and Patricia Urban, takes us into a long-neglected part of Mesoamerican space and time and offers a fresh model of how to understand processes of social interaction within Southeast Mesoamerica and beyond. Arguing that the Naco valley has "suffered from benign neglect by archaeologists, especially when compared with the much better studied Maya lowlands immediately to the west," the authors explore archaeological and written evidence suggesting that Naco was "both a major population center and an entrepôt within exchange networks linking lower Central America with central Mexico" and was therefore important in understanding wider trading practices and social history. Instead of a more traditional archaeological approach of focusing on the single supreme ruler, structure, or city-state or emphasizing the category of the agency of individuals, the authors carry out "an experiment in using a 'network perspective' on interpersonal relations to describe political structures . . . concentrating on the ways people actually wage political contests close to the ground." Schortman and Urban's model seeks to give a new interpretive space to "local processes as products of human actions taken within distinctive historical streams that were *affected, but not determined,* by long-distance interactions, such as trade and inter-elite alliances" (italics added). This means a new light is thrown on power relations constructed by the people of Naco, who appear as "participants with diverse viewpoints who actively construed their relations with other peoples, including the Maya, in ways that made sense to them."

As the authors show, Naco's cosmopolitan nature is evident in numerous kinds of data, including archaeological patterns and early colonial ethnohistories, that show linguistic and economic diversity beyond what was previously understood. Readers of this book will learn how different towns and wider communities were integrated into dynamic social configurations in which non-elites played very effective roles in contesting the dominant structures and classes for material and symbolic assets—through effective networking. The result of these networking alliances was that centralized political structures were constantly responding to localized pressures that made them vulnerable to change and variation.

If the authors are correct in their interpretations, then Mesoamerican worlds were more fluid, "perpetually unresolved," unstable, and inwardly dynamic than previously thought. At the least, we learn to focus on and appreciate more than before how non-elites organized themselves in effective arrangements that enabled them to participate in and influence the power competitions that permeated their lives. The peoples of Naco struggled productively to ensure wider access to the gods and the goods by using social systems of cooperation *and* competition. We learn that even within a world topped by royal families, subordinates continued to hold important degrees of power to "articulate, accomplish, and legitimize goals." These subordinates manipulated subsets of resources, enabling them to play effective roles in the power contests that determined, to varying degrees, their quality of life.

One of this book's real values will depend on how its readers test against and apply this networking model and the new picture of Naco and its neighbors to other regions of Mesoamerica. At the least, we feel certain that Paul Kirchhoff would appreciate the way his original vision of Mesoamerica has been filled in over the years and how this book in particular makes that vision more dynamic and enigmatic at the same time.

DAVÍD CARRASCO AND EDUARDO MATOS MOCTEZUMA

Acknowledgments

We are very grateful to the many people and agencies who made the research reported herein possible. It is difficult to decide where to begin in extending our thanks. As nothing happens without funding, we express our gratitude for the generous support provided by the National Science Foundation (in 1996), the National Endowment for the Humanities (in 1990), the Fulbright Foundation (in 1988), and Kenyon College (for all three field seasons). The work reported in these pages was conducted by a large number of fine young scholars, of whom we single out for special thanks Laura Aldrete, Marne Ausec, Peggy Caldwell, Victoria Clarke, Sam Connell, Helen Henderson, Sonya Kane, Michael Kneppler, Jamie and Suzanne Mooney, Mary Morrison, T. Louis Neff, Neil Ross, David Schafer, Colleen Siders, Sylvia Smith, and Matthew Turek.

Our institutional host in Honduras for over three decades has been the Instituto Hondureño de Antropología e Historia (IHAH). We have been very fortunate to work closely and fruitfully with the directors of the IHAH (Lic. Victor Cruz, Arq. Jose Maria Casco, and Dra. Olga Hoya over the period covered here); the late Juan Alberto Duran, then chief of archaeology for the northern zone; and Ildefonso Orellano, who collaborated directly with us as our IHAH representative. Of the many people who provided valuable advice and insights concerning the ideas expressed in these pages, we are especially grateful to Wendy Ashmore, the late Dr. George Hasmeann, Dra. Gloria Lara Pinto, Christian Wells, and Anthony Wonderley with whom we shared a house and the travails and pleasures of the 1979 field season in the Naco valley.

The people of the Naco valley worked indefatigably and with great skill in a wide array of arenas to make this research possible. We cannot list all of our many fine Honduran collaborators, so we have to be content to single out our foreman, the late Sr. Luis Nolasco, and our chief of household staff, Sra. Margarita Posas, for thanks. Local landowners were generally approving of our work; the members of the Brisas del Valle Agricultural Cooperative were especially energetic in support of our efforts.

There are several drawbacks to delaying publication for so long after the completion of field research. One of those involves the loss of so many of our colleagues since the last time we put down our shovels in the Naco valley. Far too many of our former comrades are no longer here to take satisfaction in, or wince at, what has come of their labors. Luis Nolasco, long our foreman and friend, has passed away, as have Juan Alberto Duron of the IHAH; Jennifer Ehret, who was our student and colleague; our great friend Dr. George Hasemann; and dons Eulofio Paz, Jesus Zelaya, and Manuel Nolasco, who worked long and diligently to help us understand the Naco valley's prehistory. Words cannot express our gratitude for their companionship and support; we miss them all to this day and always will.

Needless to say, any errors of omission or commission this book contains are solely our responsibility.

NETWORKS OF POWER

ONE

Introduction

PURPOSES OF THE BOOK

This volume deals with Late Postclassic (AD 1300–1523) developments in the Naco valley, northwestern Honduras, based on studies carried out at Sites PVN 144 and PVN 306. Consideration of this material is designed to redress three imbalances. The first two are spatial and temporal in scope, whereas the third pertains to the realm of archaeological concepts. Southeast Mesoamerica (adjoining portions of Guatemala, Honduras, and El Salvador), we argue, has suffered from benign neglect by archaeologists, especially when compared with the much better studied Maya lowlands immediately to the west. This is especially the case for the last Precolumbian centuries, which comprise the least understood portion of the entire sequence. The research reported herein is intended to help fill in these gaps in our knowledge, although it is no more than a step in that direction.

The conceptual issue we consider relates to how that culture history might be profitably understood. In this instance we contend that traditional approaches to explanation in archaeology have stressed the causal importance of processes related to such structural variables as the physical environment, power relations, and ideology. People have generally been viewed as pushed along by historical forces they do not control or fully understand. When questions of agency are addressed in Southeast Mesoamerica in particular, they are generally limited to the machinations of elites. The actions taken by rulers of Classic period (AD 200–900) lowland Maya states, in particular those centered on Quirigua and Copan, are especially highlighted for their causal significance throughout the region.

Structural forces certainly do play roles in channeling human action, and elites can exercise outsized influence on the lives of those they rule. Nevertheless, we propose that these actors and processes by themselves do not account for the sequence of events reconstructed for the Naco valley or for the diverse trajectories of culture change, the details of which are emerging from ongoing studies throughout Southeast Mesoamerica. The goal-seeking behaviors of diverse actors, including but not restricted to elites, must be taken into account in explaining these events. We offer suggestions as to how this might be accomplished and then apply these ideas to the study of power contests in the Late Postclassic Naco valley.

This chapter summarizes briefly how the Naco valley investigations fit within, and contribute to, our evolving understanding of Southeast Mesoamerican prehistory. Of particular concern is establishing how we assigned the materials covered here to the Late Postclassic phase. This discussion is followed by a brief synopsis of the theoretical perspective we are espousing and the way it will be used to interpret Late Postclassic developments in the basin. The conceptual and culture-historical arguments offered here are meant as hypotheses that might profitably be applied in future studies both within Southeast Mesoamerica and beyond its borders. As will be made clear, we began our study of the Naco valley's late prehistory unprepared for what we would find (notwithstanding Anthony Wonderley's excellent published account [1981] of his research at the site of Naco itself). The ad hoc, sometimes stumbling course of these investigations followed from our unfamiliarity with Late Postclassic material and cultural forms, as well as assumptions we had about developments pertaining to that phase. We hope the information provided herein will help dispel some of those unwarranted presuppositions while alerting others to the exciting possibilities of studying the Late Postclassic in Southeast Mesoamerica.

LATE POSTCLASSIC POLITICAL
FORMATIONS IN SOUTHERN MESOAMERICA

Southern Mesoamerica, including the Maya highlands and lowlands along with bordering areas to the southeast, is generally characterized during the fourteenth through sixteenth centuries as a politically balkanized landscape situated on the margins of the expanding Mexica empire (e.g., Sharer and Traxler

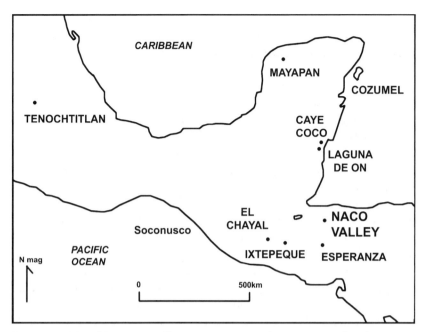

FIGURE 1.1 *Map of Mesoamerica showing major sites and areas mentioned in the text*

2006; figure 1.1). Efforts to create centralized, hierarchically structured realms here were variously successful, but the results were always fragile. By 1462 the sizable domain focused on Mayapan in northeastern Yucatan had fragmented into roughly sixteen variably well-defined and well-structured diminutive political units (Kepecs and Masson 2003: 41–42; Milbrath and Peraza Lope 2009). The contemporary, relatively small Quiche and Cakchiquel realms in the Guatemalan highlands were threatened by combinations of internal struggles and external threats (Braswell 2003a; Carmack 1981).

Leaders of these fractious polities participated in shared symbolic systems that facilitated cross-border interactions and the exchange of goods, ideas, and people (Smith 2003b). One of the most prominent of these widespread conceptual structures is glossed as the "Quetzalcoatl cult." This religion apparently originated at Chichen Itza in the Epiclassic (AD 700–900) and had spread throughout most of the Maya region by the Late Postclassic (Ringle, Gallareta Negron, and Bey 1998). As the name implies, the cult was centered on the eponymous, multifaceted deity. Widespread participation in this and other religious systems (Freidel and Sabloff 1984; Rathje and Sabloff 1973) encouraged the development of an overarching cultural framework expressed through a repertoire of ubiquitous symbols that united at least elites and their agents spread over numerous distinct, often warring realms (Boone 2003;

Boone and Smith 2003; Freidel and Sabloff 1984; Masson 2003a; Rathje and Sabloff 1973). Itinerant traders also penetrated political boundaries that linked populations in different portions of southern Mesoamerica both to each other and to people living to the south in lower Central America and north into the Mexica empire (Berdan 2003b).

Where Southeast Mesoamerica in general, and Naco in particular, fit within this pattern remains unclear. The little information available on the area during the last prehistoric centuries suggests that populations in the Southeast were relatively small and divided among diminutive realms riven by few hierarchical distinctions (Black 1995; Chamberlain 1966; Dixon 1989; Fowler 1989; Pinto 1991; Weeks, Black, and Speaker 1987; Wonderley 1985). Late Postclassic occupation seems so dispersed throughout Southeast Mesoamerica for several reasons, many of which have to do with the nature of the material remains and modern research priorities. The little work done on the area and the time period strongly suggests that most Late Postclassic habitations and outbuildings were made largely of perishable materials and raised directly on ancient ground surface (Andres and Pyburn 2004). Evidence of these occupations is therefore very difficult to identify during survey save in areas that have been recently plowed and where ground surface is not obscured by vegetation (e.g., Voorhies and Gasco 2004). Even the relatively sizeable buildings at political capitals are largely made of earth and are modest in comparison to their counterparts at earlier centers. These constructions are particularly vulnerable to such modern processes as plowing and house construction, disappearing rapidly in the face of economic development.

The situation is not helped by continuity in occupation from the Late Postclassic into the modern era. Many late Precolumbian centers support colonial and later occupations, resulting in the obliteration of Late Postclassic remains. Naco is a case in point. Although much of the settlement was still visible when first investigated by William Duncan Strong and his colleagues in 1936 (1938), by the time Wonderley returned to work there in 1977–1979, most of the site core was covered by modern edifices (1981). By 2008, portions of the town not buried beneath houses had been largely transformed by mechanized plowing for tobacco cultivation and construction of a military base. Very little of the ancient site is still visible.

These difficulties have conspired to direct archaeological attention to earlier time periods with more prominent surviving remains. The Late Classic (AD 600–800) and Terminal Classic (AD 800–950) have been particularly singled out for attention. During these intervals, even the smallest settlements are commonly marked by low stone-faced platforms discernible from ground surface. It is far easier, therefore, to reconstruct settlement patterns and political forms when working with such physically salient materials than it is when dealing with more elusive Late Postclassic remains. This was certainly the case in our investigations within the Naco valley (1975–1979, 1988–1996), which focused primarily on developments transpiring from the seventh through the tenth centuries. In the course of that work, we did locate ten sites outside Naco itself with evidence of Late Postclassic occupation, of which two—Sites PVN 306 and PVN 144—still boasted surface-visible architecture and were of considerable size. Nevertheless, these settlements were found largely in the course of work focused on understanding earlier intervals (see discussion later in this chapter).

There is good reason, therefore, to believe that populations in Southeast Mesoamerica were larger, and their political centers more numerous, than current archaeological reports indicate. Still, the scant ethnohistoric accounts available for the area are consistent in their description of western Honduras and neighboring zones as divided among small-scale political units, or *caci-cazgos* (Chamberlain 1966). To be sure, these chronicles are spotty at best and are more concerned with advancing the claims and counterclaims of Spanish conquerors to land and tribute than with describing indigenous cultures and practices. Still, the Iberian interlopers were positively motivated to find and exploit realms encompassing large, well-organized populations. The fact that none are mentioned in even a cursory manner and that western Honduras was treated largely as an area for slaving rather than for systematic exploitation through the use of Indian labor strongly indicates that indigenous political systems across the area were small and simply structured (Sherman 1978).

The site of Naco stands out against this backdrop as both a major popula-tion center and an entrepôt within exchange networks linking lower Central America with central Mexico (Chamberlain 1966; Wonderley 1981). Naco was sufficiently important that it attracted the first Spanish conquerors in the area, who sought from the town sustenance and allies in their internecine struggles (Chamberlain 1966). Population estimates for Naco at the time of first Spanish contact range from 8,000 adult men (Sherman 1978: 49) to 10,000 to 200,000 total people (Strong, Kidder, and Paul 1938: 27). The last of these is almost cer-tainly a great exaggeration, although it is difficult to say what the Spanish meant when referring to "Naco": was it the settlement that still bears that name, several closely related sites, or the entire "province" of which the Spanish thought Naco was the capital (Bancroft 1886(2): 61; Henderson 1979: 371; see also Chapter 6 of this volume)? The latter may have extended into the Sula Plain lying 15 km northeast of the valley (Bancroft 1886(2): 161; Diaz del Castillo 1916: 58; Henderson 1979: 371). In general, it seems likely that the town of Naco housed somewhere between 8,000 and 10,000 individuals by 1523.

The relatively few references to Naco in Spanish accounts return consistent-ly to its importance as a center of long-distance trade. Goods moving through this entrepôt are thought to have arrived along routes that combined seaborne with overland transport and stretched perhaps as far south as the Pacific Coast of Central America (Wonderley 1981: 27–29). Items involved in these trans-actions included such preciosities as gold, cacao beans, and feathers (Roys 1972: 55), although how and by whom the transactions were organized are unclear. There is a general sense that Maya merchants based along the shores of the Yucatan peninsula played significant roles in the aforementioned eco-nomic networks. These entrepreneurs apparently maintained resident agents in "Honduras" (Scholes and Roys 1948: 84) and sent fifty war canoes to aid their trade partners in an abortive effort to oust Spanish interlopers from the lower Ulua valley early in the Spanish conquest (Chamberlain 1966: 53–57). Naco's cosmopolitan nature is further suggested by the fact that some of its residents were able to converse directly with the Spaniards' indigenous central Mexican allies who accompanied the conquerors on their initial forays into the valley (Henderson 1979: 369; Pagden 1971: 607). Such linguistic facility may point to a foreign origin for at least part of the basin's population (Henderson 1979: 369; Wonderley 1981, 1985) or to a familiarity with languages used widely to conduct trade across much of southern Mesoamerica (Henderson 1979; Wonderley 1981: 28).

Written references to Naco and its commercial significance are more tan-talizing than definitive. What little is available on this point suggests that the valley's Late Postclassic inhabitants were integrated within networks through which goods derived from a wide array of sources moved. To what extent these items played significant roles in local political and economic processes is un-certain, as we cannot discern how the town's residents might have deployed such assets in support of their own projects. The few published accounts of Naco at the time of the Spanish conquest, therefore, hint at the operation of a dynamic political and economic system but do not allow us to address the basic questions of who was involved in interactions at multiple spatial scales, what resources were marshaled through these webs, and how they were employed in support of political projects enacted across local and interregional expanses. To begin to answer those queries, we must turn to the archaeological record.

HISTORY OF ARCHAEOLOGICAL RESEARCH IN SOUTHEAST MESOAMERICA AND THE NACO VALLEY

As noted earlier, there was little archaeological record to turn to before 1977. Naco valley prehistory, as was the case throughout most of Southeast Meso-america, was virtually unknown prior to the initiation of systematic fieldwork in the area in the late 1960s (Baudez and Becquelin 1973; Sharer ed. 1978). Pioneering programs of survey, sometimes accompanied by test excavations, have a long history in the zone, extending back to the late nineteenth century (Canby 1949, 1951; Gordon 1898; Longyear 1944, 1947, 1966; Lothrop 1925, 1927, 1939; Popenoe 1934; Stone 1940, 1941, 1942, 1957; Strong 1935; Strong, Kidder, and Paul 1938; Yde 1938; see Glass 1966 for a summary of work conducted in the area up through the mid-twentieth century and Healy 1984 and Sheets 1984 for more recent updates). Naco itself was the focus of one such initial study in 1936 when the Late Postclassic site core was mapped and five of its constructions were excavated to varying degrees (Strong, Kidder, and Paul 1938: 27–34). None of these early studies, however, gave rise to more detailed and extensive investigations on the scale of those conducted throughout the same period in the Maya area to the west.

The reasons for this neglect are numerous. Prominent among them is the theoretical framework within which much of the pioneering work was conducted. Based on the notion that behavioral variation across space and time could best be described in reference to territorially bounded "culture areas," early studies in the Southeast were centered on defining the limits of these supposedly distinctive zones. Not surprisingly, the areas that attracted the most attention were those that gave rise to what were taken to be major cultural fluorescences. Initial investigations throughout Southeast Mesoamerica were therefore designed primarily to define the limits of Maya culture, especially as that culture was manifest in the physically prominent symbols associated with elite behavioral spheres during the tellingly labeled Classic period (AD 200–900; Sharer and Traxler 2006). Any sites that fell outside this charmed circle were relegated to positions of secondary importance vis-à-vis Maya centers, the study of which promised to yield insights into the genesis and operation of this prominent culture. In Honduras, this meant that the lowland Maya capital of Copan was singled out for early and prolonged attention (e.g., Gordon 1896; Longyear 1952; Morley 1920) while other settlements were not. Naco was remembered as a potentially important Late Postclassic commercial center, but it did not pertain to the "right" time period or culture to warrant further study.

Attention gradually shifted to Southeast Mesoamerica as the conceptual frameworks within which archaeological research was conducted changed. Throughout the 1960s there was increasing recognition that cultural boundaries were porous (e.g., Caldwell 1964). At first, this permeability was imagined primarily in reference to trade. Members of no single spatially delimited culture secured all the resources they needed from within their borders (e.g., chapters in Earle and Ericson 1977; Renfrew 1975). Contacts must have been sustained with those living in other areas from which essential commodities could have been obtained. This was especially thought to be the case for large states, such as those found throughout the Classic period Maya lowlands, which were especially in need of foreign goods to sustain their complex and energy-expensive political and economic systems. As potential sources of such crucial items, polities in Southeast Mesoamerica might be of some relevance to comprehending developments in better-studied areas to the west.

It was also argued that understanding the origins of Classic era Maya civilization required searching outside the culture area's boundaries for important antecedents (see the review in Sharer and Grove 1989). Recently dated Early and Middle Preclassic (1500–400 BC) Olmec sites on the Mexican Gulf Coast seem to have been home to a "mother culture" from which all later Mesoamerican complex polities, including Maya states, arose. Identifying the territorial and spatial limits of this "Ur culture" became a major priority, pushing research into areas previously beyond the pale of serious investigations. It is no surprise, therefore, that the earliest systematic studies of sites in Southeast Mesoamerica focused on large centers, the long prehistoric occupation sequences of which stretched well back into the Preclassic (Baudez and Becquelin 1973; Canby 1949, 1951; Sharer ed. 1978). At least one of these settlements, Chalchuapa in western El Salvador, attracted attention because it possessed a prominent stone carving in the "Olmec" style (Anderson 1978).

Southeast Mesoamerican cultures may not have been of interest in their own right, but they were drawing researchers in unprecedented numbers for the first time. This is not to say that the area was flooded by eager investigators. The adjoining portions of Honduras, El Salvador, and Guatemala were generally seen as home to cultures that basked in the distant glow of their far better-known Maya neighbors (Schortman and Urban 1986, 1994). The central work of studying the rise and fall of ancient states still took place primarily at lowland Maya centers dating to the second century BC through the tenth century AD and not within the much smaller realms existing on their edges. The very designation of Southeast Mesoamerica as the "Southeast Maya Periphery" (e.g., Urban and Schortman 1986) reflects the marginal status attributed to the relevant cultures in ancient interaction networks and scholarly debates. Still, the times and research priorities were changing, and new information on Southeast Mesoamerica's diverse people has been growing considerably from the late 1960s onward.

RECENT RESEARCH IN THE NACO VALLEY

It is under the conditions sketched here that John Henderson initiated systematic investigations in the Naco valley in 1974 (1979; Henderson et al. 1979). The Naco valley encompasses roughly 96 km² and is watered by the Rio Chamelecon, which trends southwest-northeast across the basin. Overall, the Chamelecon drains an area of 4,350 km², running 256 km from its headwaters on the southwest to its junction with the Rio Ulua near the Caribbean coast (Kirshen and Sprang 2005). Within the Naco valley, the Chamelecon is fed by eight perennial and seven seasonal tributaries that issue from the surrounding slopes of the Sierra de Omoa, which delimit the basin on all sides. The valley bottom is 100–200 m above sea level and comprises a flat to gently rolling landscape made up of the Chamelecon's current and former terraces. Approximately 80 percent of this terrain consists of fertile Mollisols capable of supporting productive agriculture (Anderson 1994; Douglass 2002: 22–23). The remainder is divided between Entisols and Oxisols, the last of which is marginal at best for crop growth (Anderson 1994; Douglass 2002: 22–23). The sites of Naco and PVN 144 occupy Mollisols, whereas the soils on which Site PVN 306 was raised were not classified (Douglass 2002: 24). Assessments of land use during 1988 and 1990, coupled with local informant reports, suggest that the river terrace supporting the latter settlement was capable of sustained cropping in the past.

The primary restriction on ancient agriculture in the Naco valley and its environs was access to sufficient water (Anderson 1994; Douglass 2002: 22–25; Zuniga 1990). As of the late twentieth century, all of the rivers crossing the basin cut deep beds, making irrigation difficult without the use of mechanized pumps. There are no signs of channels by which water might have been redirected from these streams to agricultural fields dating to any period, and it is highly unlikely that they existed. Occupants of the Naco valley up until the twentieth century, therefore, depended on rain to water their crops. The most current figures indicate that the valley receives, on average, 1,300 mm of precipitation annually, most of it concentrated in May through December (Zuniga 1990). This is sufficient to support at least one harvest in November through December, although a second planting, the *postrera*, can yield crops in May during particularly wet years (informant reports). By the Late Postclassic, therefore, the Naco valley and its environs were capable of supporting sizable populations, as they had since at least the Middle Preclassic (1200–400 BC). There is no indication that climatic or edaphic conditions conspired to reduce the basin's carrying capacity during the fourteenth through sixteenth centuries.

The Naco valley is strategically situated athwart several potential communication routes that extend to the southwest and the northeast along the Chamelecon valley. To the northeast lies the Sula Plain, home to sizable Late Postclassic populations reported to have been engaged in long-distance trade—especially in cacao—with Yucatecan merchants at the time of the Spanish conquest (Chamberlain 1966: 53–57, 78; Henderson 1979; Roys 1972: 55; Strong 1935: 17; Wonderley 1981: 26–28). The nature of those societies located to the southwest is not well-known from archaeological or ethnohistoric accounts. The report of sizable indigenous settlements at "Quimistlan" and

"Zula" may refer to areas near the modern communities of Quimistlan and Sula, located 25 km and 40 km southwest of the Naco valley, respectively. As noted previously, early Spanish chroniclers indicated that residents of the Naco valley were in close contact with their neighbors in the Sula Plain and may have exercised political control over some populations in that area (Bancroft 1886(2): 161; Henderson 1979: 371). Leaving the question of suzerainty aside, it is highly likely that occupants of the basin were well situated to engage in commercial and other transactions with the denizens of neighboring zones and took advantage of these opportunities.

The research conducted in the valley proceeded in spurts. Henderson directed investigations there from 1974 through 1979, during which time Wonderley conducted his studies at Naco (1977, 1979) and Urban began her survey of the basin (1975, 1977–1979). We renewed the work from 1988 through 1996. Except for Wonderley's study, most of the research pursued throughout this period focused primarily on developments that pertained to the Late through Terminal Classic. As noted earlier, such a concentration was strongly facilitated by the physical prominence of the relevant remains. It was also encouraged by the traditional emphasis on developments dating to this period, which coincided with the fluorescence of major states in the Maya lowlands. The population growth and increasing evidence of political complexity seen in the Southeast during the Late and Terminal Classic were long tied to comparable events transpiring to the west (Schortman and Urban 1986). Although we increasingly questioned the causal primacy of "Maya influences" in these seemingly parallel developments (Schortman and Urban 1994), we remained fixated on this period and its fairly easy-to-recognize signs of occupation.

The relevance of these biases and predilections for the present study is that Late Postclassic remains were invariably found by accident. We were well aware of Wonderley's investigations at Naco and were happy to treat them as a record of Late Postclassic cultural patterns and processes applicable to the valley at large. Naco was the only indigenous center explicitly mentioned by the Spanish in the valley, and there was little incentive to search for more. Any late prehistoric occupation outside Naco was, we assumed, likely to be in the form of scattered farmsteads, the settlements most difficult to locate from surface remains. Fully ten Late Postclassic sites were eventually identified in the course of a total survey of the valley, most of them represented by surface scatters of artifacts found in plowed fields. Further, more intensive work at any of those sites did not promise to yield good returns on the effort involved. The exceptions were Sites PVN 306 and PVN 144.

The former was located during the 1988 survey along the north bank of the Rio Chamelecon (figure 1.2). Site PVN 306 is situated on the east edge of

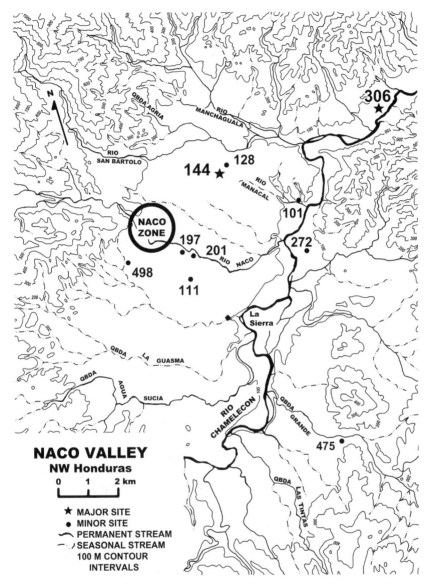

FIGURE 1.2 *Map of the Naco valley showing the distribution of known Roble phase (Late Postclassic) settlements. La Sierra on the Rio Chamelecon was the capital of the valley during the Late Classic and shows signs of scant use during the Roble phase.*

what was at that time the newly established small town of Brisas del Valle, 2 km northeast of the Naco valley. When first discovered, the settlement's 120 surface-visible buildings and 223 localized artifact scatters were relatively well

11

preserved, although commercial cultivation of oranges on its eastern margins and expansion of houses on the west were proceeding apace. Initial digging here in 1988 revealed that while the surviving buildings were raised during the Terminal Classic, Early Postclassic (AD 1100–1300), and Late Postclassic, most dated to the third interval. The latter include the sizable platforms that define Site PVN 306's two adjoining plazas in the site core.

The surprising discovery of a large center contemporary with Naco led us to reevaluate our earlier assumptions about valley prehistory. We especially questioned Naco's absolute dominance within the basin during the last prehistoric centuries. These new questions, coupled with the very likely prospect that the settlement would soon be overwhelmed by plowing and construction, led us to devote much of the 1990 field season to excavating Site PVN 306. In the end, thirty-four of the recorded buildings and nine of the artifact scatters were dug, along with a series of test pits sunk in areas lacking surface evidence of ancient activities (647 m² cleared in all).

Investigations at Site PVN 144, whose nineteen structures and twelve recorded artifact scatters lie between Naco itself and Site PVN 306, were also spurred by accidental discoveries. The settlement had been known since 1978, when it was recorded and mapped during the initial survey (Urban 1986). Our attention turned to Site PVN 144 when, in 1996, it was the focus of a land dispute. One set of claimants, seeking to substantiate their rights to the fields, built houses on the site and cut a road through part of it. These processes brought to light clear signs of a Late Postclassic occupation there, including evidence of relatively large-scale constructions roughly comparable to some of the sizable late prehistoric edifices seen at Naco and Site PVN 306. This date was not suggested by the surface remains, as no artifacts had ever been recovered from the settlement and the general building forms and arrangements were not temporally diagnostic. Given that Site PVN 144 represented yet another unexpected example of late prehistoric occupation in the valley and was threatened with imminent destruction, we excavated seven buildings and six surface-visible artifact scatters here during 1996 (553 m² cleared overall).

Several aspects of this research strategy need to be emphasized. First, there was little strategy involved. We began work in the Naco valley convinced that the eponymous site was the sole focal point of Late Postclassic occupation and hence did not seek any evidence that might contradict that view. What eventually challenged such notions came to light fortuitously, and then the work had to be carried out as quickly as possible in the face of rapidly advancing agents of destruction. These circumstances meant there was little chance of returning to either settlement to pursue issues raised in the initial work; nor did we have the opportunity to examine the sites in as systematic and controlled a manner as we would have liked. The emphasis was on uncovering as much of Late

Postclassic buildings and deposits as time and money allowed. Further, any hope we had of completing analyses of stored materials disappeared when the collection was lost in the wake of Hurricane Mitch in 1998.

This list of limiting circumstances should not be confused with an excuse. We bear full responsibility for the restrictions from which this study suffers. Late Postclassic sites and materials were not foci of our investigations, and their consideration was often rushed and deferred in comparison with the greater time and attention devoted to Late and Terminal Classic remains. We can still learn much from examining the Site PVN 144 and PVN 306 materials, if for no other reason than that they provide some of the brightest spots in the rather dull firmament of late prehistoric data points in Southeast Mesoamerica. What we can take away from such a disquisition is restricted, however, by the nature of the recovery and analysis process, and it would be misleading to ignore these limitations.

CHRONOLOGY

The assignment of major components at Sites PVN 306 and PVN 144 to the Late Postclassic is based on two principal lines of evidence: material similarities, especially as seen in ceramics and architecture, with late prehistoric remains recovered from other portions of southern Mesoamerica; and three C-14 dates obtained from samples closely associated with these materials.

Ceramics

Very little is known concerning Late Postclassic pottery styles throughout Southeast Mesoamerica. The best dated and published relevant collections for the Southeast outside the Naco valley are from the Sula Plain (Wonderley 1985) and the middle Ulua drainage in and around the Late Classic center of Gualjoquito (Schortman et al. 1986; Urban 1993a; Weeks, Black, and Speaker 1987), approximately 15 km northeast and 40 km south of the basin within Honduras, and Chalchuapa, roughly 220 km to the south in El Salvador (Sharer 1978). These materials are supplemented to some extent by reports from survey work conducted east of Naco in the Aguan drainage (Stone 1941, 1957; see figure 1.3 for the location of these and other areas mentioned here). The principal ceramic classes variably represented in these collections are characterized by several surface treatments: red slipping, red painting on natural surfaces, red-painted and incised designs on unslipped vessels, red painting on white slips, and polychrome designs applied over white backgrounds.

Red-slipped vessels are ubiquitous in known Late Postclassic collections, although they are rare along the middle Ulua (Visaina Fine Paste; Urban 1993a)

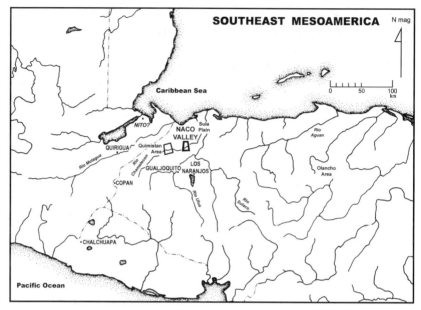

FIGURE 1.3 *Map of Southeast Mesoamerica showing sites and areas mentioned in the text*

and more prevalent in the Naco valley (Algo Red and Salto Red; Urban 1993b: 57–59) and the Sula Plain (Wonderley 1985). At Chalchuapa, Cozatal Hematite Red and Guajoyo Red-brown are comparably prevalent, although some of their number may date to the Early Postclassic (Sharer 1978: 62–63). Associated forms are generally open bowls in all these cases. Red-slipped mono-chromes are also reported in some numbers from the Agalteca valley, possibly in association with painted bichromes diagnostic of the Late Postclassic (Stone 1957: 67–69, 73).

Both the Naco and Sula valleys possess a distinctive class of ceramics characterized by open bowls, frequently supported by three legs in the form of stylized bird heads, feet, or both. The interiors and exteriors of these vessels are slipped white and decorated with red-painted designs (figures 1.4, 8.1, 8.2). Originally defined as Nolasco Bichrome (Wonderley 1981: 157–172, 1985: 261, 263), other representatives of this class made using a different paste recipe have been recognized at Sites PVN 144 and PVN 306 (glossed as La Victoria Bichrome in these cases; Urban 1993b: 60–61). Designs found in both taxa consist of "X's," guilloches, curvilinear and geometric elements, stylized feathers, and "serpent jaws" (Urban 1993b: 57–58; Wonderley 1981: 157–172). Nolasco and possibly La Victoria sherds were earlier classed as Naco Painted Ware (Strong, Kidder, and Paul 1938: 33–34) and Naco Style Ware (Strong 1957: 67–68). Red-on-white ceramics make up roughly 18 percent of the Naco

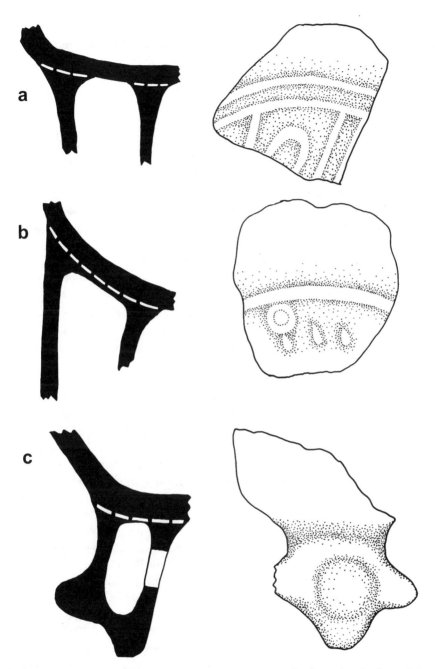

FIGURE 1.4 *Selection of diagnostic Naco Viejo Ceramic Complex forms. See also figures 8.1 and 8.2*

Late Postclassic assemblage, 5 percent of the combined collection from Sites PVN 306 and PVN 144, and 4 percent of the El Remolino and Despoloncal ceramics from the Sula Plain (Wonderley 1985). A single sherd from this taxon was found in a very late deposit at Gualjoquito in the middle Ulua drainage.

Similar bichromes are also reported east of the Sula Plain from the Olancho area and Aguan valley (Stone 1941: 89; Wonderley 1981: 165–172, 1985: 264). In the Aguan examples, however, the largely geometric designs are painted in black on a white slip, making them closer to Forastero Bichrome from the Naco valley (Stone 1957: 67–68; see also Urban 1993b: 59; Wonderley 1981: 182–186). The latter type is very rare in the basin at Naco and in the assemblages of Sites PVN 144 and PVN 306.

The greatest variety of late prehistoric polychromes is reported from the site of Naco. Here open bowls decorated with red-and-black painted designs on white-slipped backgrounds make up roughly 1 percent of the collection (classed as Vagando, Cortes, Hidaldo, and Posas Polychromes and Tormenta Trichrome; Urban 1993b: 58–60; Wonderley 1981: 172–176, 186–194; see also Naco Painted Ware, Strong, Kidder, and Paul 1938: 33–34; Wonderley included incense burner fragments in these taxa). Examples of these ceramics were recovered in very small amounts from Sites PVN 306 and PVN 144 (0.002% of the combined assemblages), as well as at Despoloncal (Wonderley 1985: 264).

No sherds of this type are known from the middle Ulua, although Doris Stone may have identified a few in the Aguan valley (1957: 67–68). The fifty-one sherds of Chinautla Polychrome reported from Chalchuapa constitute some of the only other vessels decorated in this fashion from Southeast Mesoamerica (Sharer 1978: 65–66). There is a general resemblance between Chinautla vessels and the polychromes found in the Late Postclassic Naco valley; in both instances geometric designs are painted in red and black on the cream-slipped surfaces of generally open bowls. Like Nolasco and La Victoria examples, Chinautla vessels are commonly supported by three modeled legs; it is unclear if the polychromes from the Naco valley were also elevated in this manner. These general resemblances in form and decoration most likely represent common participation in interaction nets through which broadly similar pottery vessels and their canons of decoration moved during the thirteenth through sixteenth centuries across the southeastern and eastern Maya highlands and western Honduras (Sharer 1978: 66; see also Wauchope's "Bright Paint Style," 1970: 108, 110–112). There is no clear evidence that the polychromes in question were made at any of the sites enumerated here.

Red-painted designs on unslipped vessel surfaces are recorded in the middle Ulua assemblage as well as at Chalchuapa. In the former case, sub-hemispherical and flaring-walled bowls, low plates, and jars are decorated with vertical and diagonal stripes, arcs, and possibly cross-hatching (Quezapaya Red-Painted; Urban 1993b: 168–169). The Chalchuapa examples (Marihua Red-on-Buff) consist of sub-hemispherical bowls the interiors and exteriors of which are adorned with such geometric figures as spirals, parallel curving lines, and "saw-tooth" designs (Sharer 1978: 63). There are no known counterparts to these vessels in the Naco valley and the Sula Plain, just as jars with simple incised geometric motifs on their low necks have been found to date primarily along the middle Ulua (Masica Incised, Maqueta var.; Urban 1993b: 168). Incising is also noted as a decorative treatment at Chalchuapa, sometimes applied on the red-slipped surfaces of bowls (Cuis Cuis Incised) or their unslipped interior bases (Tasajera Incised; Sharer 1978: 63–64). A very few containers from the Naco valley have evidence of simple incised designs on the interior bases of bowls (Wonderley 1981: 147).

Unslipped ceramics comprise the majority of the assemblages in all of the areas discussed here. Several commonalities in forms and, to a more limited extent, surface treatments link several of these zones, however. Comales are found throughout the collections, as are low-necked jars; the former is a new addition to, or is newly prevalent in, the form repertoire throughout most of Southeast Mesoamerica (Masson 2000a: 117; comales, however, are reported at Chalchuapa from Middle and Late Classic contexts, AD 400–900; Sharer 1978). At least some of the Naco valley and Sula Plain unslipped containers were burnished (Tal Burnished; Urban 1993b; Wonderley 1981: 152–157; 1985, 261). Strong and his colleagues, in fact, remarked that a great many of the sherds from Naco's Late Postclassic utilitarian ceramics (slipped or unslipped is unclear) were "fairly well polished" (1938: 33). Burnishing of untreated surfaces is not reported elsewhere in the Southeast (Wonderley 1981: 156–157).

Brushing of unslipped vessel surfaces is recorded in both the middle Ulua drainage (Yara Brushed) and the Naco valley (Carbano Brushed). In the former case, a multi-toothed instrument was used to create the desired effect, while Carbano Brushed vessels were apparently finished with something resembling a corn cob (Urban 1993a: 165–166, 1993b: 60). Bowls and jars were decorated in this fashion, and both taxa are relatively well represented in their respective collections. Recurved bowls may have been finished in this way at Chalchuapa (Kanil Unslipped), although it is not certain that brushing constitutes a decorative mode here (Sharer 1978: 64–65).

In general, therefore, Late Postclassic assemblages throughout Southeast Mesoamerica were characterized by certain very general similarities, the most obvious of which are red slipping and the prevalence of low-necked jars, usually unslipped, in various taxa and comales. Less widespread is the variable presence of white-slipped open bowls decorated with designs painted in red and, more rarely, red and black. The latter containers are found primarily in the Naco and Sula valleys, as is the burnishing of unslipped vessel surfaces. The use of simple brushing as a decorative technique is attested to in the Naco valley, the middle Ulua basin, and possibly at Chalchuapa. Red painting on unslipped surfaces distinguishes assemblages pertaining to the middle Ulua and Chalchuapa, as does the use of incision.

It may well be that there were different ceramic spheres within Southeast Mesoamerica, each set apart from its neighbors by certain distinctive decorative treatments that existed within a framework of broadly comparable formal and stylistic modes, such as red slipping (Rice 1986). The similarities emerging from studies of Naco valley and Sula Plain pottery point to this area as comprising one such sphere (Wonderley 1985: 261), a finding in line with the ethnohistoric reports of close political and economic ties between populations in the two basins (Bancroft 1886(2): 161; Diaz del Castillo 1916: 58; Henderson 1979: 371; Wonderley 1981). Very limited data recovered during early surveys in the Aguan valley and the Olancho area tentatively hint at the inclusion of these zones within the same ceramic sphere as the Naco valley and the Sula basin. The middle Ulua drainage, in contrast, largely stands apart from its near neighbors to the north, sharing relatively few ceramic modes with them. Chalchuapa's occupants, as would be expected given their great distance from the other areas considered here, also likely participated in a distinct ceramic sphere.

Taking a broader view, the stylistic choices made by the Naco valley's denizens resonate with those taken in the Maya highlands and lowlands during the fourteenth through sixteenth centuries. Specifically, red-slipped monochromes were found widely throughout the eastern and northern Yucatan peninsula at this time, marking a considerable shift from Classic period modes of vessel treatment (Masson 2001; Rice 1983; Smith 1971: 197–199, 220–228; Wonderley 1981). Similarly, white-slipped ceramics decorated with designs painted in red and red and black were recorded over large portions of highland Guatemala and along the base of the Yucatan peninsula during the Late Postclassic (Rice 1983; Wauchope 1970; Wonderley 1981). The motifs employed in these decorative programs are also generally similar, suggesting that Maya peoples were one source of inspiration for the bichromes found in the Naco valley (Wonderley 1981).

Although the situation is less clear, there are also a few hints that the forms of ceramic incense burners used in the late prehistoric Naco valley were derived from, or at least commensurate with, those employed in contemporary Yucatecan realms. In particular, censers decorated with small modeled spikes on their exteriors appear clearly for the first time in the basin now and resemble, in a general sense, those recorded from coeval settlements to the north and west, as well as from Chalchuapa (Mocal Modeled-appliqué, Sharer 1978: 61). These incensarios, however, are not common in the Naco valley; nor do they take the hourglass form frequently reported from Yucatan (Masson 2000a; Milbrath and Peraza Lope 2003; Smith 1971). Ladle censers, consisting of shallow bowls attached to long, hollow tube handles, are fairly common in the Naco valley collection, as well as throughout Yucatan and at Chalchuapa (Chequezate Unslipped, Sharer 1978: 61). Local antecedents for this form within the basin, where it extends back to at least the Late Classic, raise doubts concerning its foreign inspiration.

In general, therefore, the pottery containers that comprise the Naco Viejo Ceramic Complex broadly resemble their counterparts throughout Southeast and southern Mesoamerica. Such comparisons suggest that the former examples date to the same late period, as do their analogs in the Maya area and closer to home.

Architecture

Distinctive architectural forms found in Naco and at Site PVN 306 also point to participation by residents of these settlements in interaction networks dating to the Late Postclassic. The most notable of these constructions are the circular and cog-wheeled platforms found in the architectural cores of the afore-mentioned centers. These buildings (Structure 4F-1 at Naco and Structures 306-17, 306-19, and possibly 306-174; see figures 3.6, 3.10, 5.2) are similar to other round constructions reported from across much of the Maya high-lands and lowlands immediately prior to the Spanish conquest (Pollock 1936; Ringle, Gallareta Negron, and Bey 1998; Sidrys and Andersen 1978; see also Wonderley 1981). While round structures have a long history in the Maya lowlands especially, their relative prevalence in the Late Postclassic suggests that these examples served as models for the Naco valley constructions (a point considered in greater depth in chapter 8).

Carbon-14 Assays

The architectural and ceramic similarities outlined here point to a rough contemporaneity between the specified Naco valley materials and those tradi-tionally dated to the Late Postclassic in Southeast and southern Mesoamerica. The chronological placement of the former remains is further bolstered by the results of C-14 assays carried out on three samples recovered together with the aforementioned pottery and architecture (table 1.1).

Lot 144T/004 was retrieved from the top of charcoal-stained earth 0.06 m below the plaster mask that borders, on the south, the western staircase

19

ascending Structure 144-8 (see chapter 4). This mask was first raised during the second version of that platform (Structure 144-8-2nd) and was maintained throughout the rest of the edifice's use-life. The intercept of radiocarbon age with the calibration curve provided for lot 144T/004 is AD 1305, placing it near the beginning of the Late Postclassic; the calibrated results with 2-sigma variations are AD 1285–1405. These figures match very well expectations based on artifact samples and building sequences at Site PVN 144.

Lot 306AB/004 is from a shallow midden located north of that center's architectural core. This deposit contained large quantities of artifacts, all of which were assigned to the Late Postclassic on purely stylistic grounds. The calibrated intercept date for the sample is AD 1400, and the 2-sigma span is AD 1275–1450. Lot 306AJ/054, in turn, pertains to debris associated with the final use of Structure 306-128, an apparent elite residence in the eastern principal plaza of the site core (see chapter 3). The calibrated intercept date in this case is AD 1480, with a 2-sigma span of AD 1430–1645. Both results closely coincide with chronological expectations based on artifact analyses and construction histories. Overall, the consistency of the three radiocarbon assays from as many different deposits gives us increased confidence in dating the suite of ceramic and construction styles discussed earlier to the fourteenth through sixteenth centuries.

Summary

Chronological assessments of components at Sites PVN 306 and PVN 144 founded on artifact analyses, architectural sequences and styles, and radiocarbon assessments together indicate that late occupations at these settlements and Naco date to a single Late Postclassic phase within the valley. That interval is herein referred to as the Roble phase. The time range is so narrow, in fact, that it is highly likely that all three settlements were occupied at the same time, with their residents involved in many of the same political networks. This is a basic premise on which this book's discussion is founded.

PERIPHERIES OF PERIPHERIES

As noted earlier, the Late Postclassic Naco valley is doubly peripheral to modern scholarly concerns. This is true spatially, as the basin has traditionally been seen as existing on the margins of major cultural developments to the west and north. It is also the case temporally, in that the fourteenth through sixteenth centuries in southern Mesoamerica are often treated as peripheral to major sociopolitical and cultural transformations that occurred earlier, during the Classic period, and later with the establishment of the Spanish empire (Rice

TABLE 1.1 Carbon-14 assessments relevant to the Naco valley's Late Postclassic

Lot	Date	Provenience
144T/004	650 ± 40 BP	From immediately beneath a plaster mask on Structure 144-8
306AB/004	590 ± 80 BP	0.22–0.3 m below ground surface in a midden containing solely Late Postclassic materials
306AJ/054	380 ± 50 BP	0.2–0.4 m below ground surface, terminal debris, Structure 306-128

Note: All dates are given in uncalibrated forms as conventional radiocarbon ages followed by a 1-sigma spread (Beta Analytic Laboratory, laboratory numbers Beta-102687, Beta-40952, Beta-40953, respectively). "Lot" refers to the specific collection unit from which a sample was taken; the numeric prefix indicates the site where the material was excavated.

and Rice 2005: 140; see chapters in Kepecs and Alexander 2005 and Smith and Berdan 2003 for strong evidence of contradictory interpretive trends). It is no surprise, therefore, that work in the valley and on the time period has been so sporadic, a tradition to which we also contributed.

As is the case with all peripheries, however, the question immediately arises: peripheral in what ways and to whom (Kohl 1987; Kohl and Chernykh 2003; Schortman and Urban 1994)? Recent, exciting applications of modified versions of World Systems Theory (WST) to late prehistoric Mesoamerica provide some of the most thoughtful answers to that question (Alexander and Kepecs 2005; Kepecs and Kohl 2003; Smith and Berdan 2000, 2003). In this formulation, Naco is often seen as one of a series of entrepôts, on the margins of Mesoamerican cores, the residents of which facilitated trade within and across the boundaries of the multicentric Mesoamerican world (Gasco and Berdan 2003: 109; Smith and Berdan eds. 2003: 25). Cozumel, Wild Cane Cay, and El Tigre are among the other contemporary "international trade centers" that functioned in similar ways (Freidel and Sabloff 1984; Gasco and Berdan 2003: 109; McKillop 1996; Sabloff and Rathje 1975).

A viewpoint based on WST has the salutary effect of encouraging the investigation of all populations throughout Mesoamerica as simultaneously enmeshed in transactions going on at multiple spatial scales, with the results of one influencing the outcomes of all the others. This very strong advantage, however, is somewhat counterbalanced by the implication that Naco and its fellow entrepôts were important *because of* their positions within exchange and communication networks that extended well outside their immediate areas. We are dangerously close here to the argument that it was Naco and its compatriots' political marginality that enabled their economic and cultural importance, that it was their structural position within macro-regional webs that played a major role in determining the course of their late Precolumbian histories (Gasco and Berdan 2003: 112). "Marginality," no longer a pejorative term, still has causal power.

Our own research strategies have suffered from some of these biases. Nevertheless, we have approached the analyses outlined herein with the assumption that, from the perspective of those who lived in the Naco valley during the period AD 1300–1523, the basin was the core of their world. Different segments of that population were variably aware of events occurring in, and ideas derived from, distant locales and had differential access to goods obtained from foreign sources. They also likely made selective use of their own history, recalling some aspects while neglecting others. We very much doubt, however, that they were overwhelmed by either recollections of past greatness or the pretensions and proclaimed capacities of distant potentates. The valley's late prehistoric occupants showed no signs of acknowledging their peripherality to anyone past or present or of allowing that perception of marginality to determine their actions. Rather, we will argue that Roble phase Naquenos employed conceptual and tangible resources derived from the past and the present, from local and distant origins, to seek their own objectives in cooperation with some and competition with others. In pursuing these projects with varying degrees of success, they created their own version of the Late Postclassic Mesoamerican world in which foreign goods and concepts were implicated in local processes (Freidel 1985: 308; Lycett 2005: 101). That iteration was no less vibrant and dynamic for being constructed on the human scale of a 96 km² valley than were those renditions acted out elsewhere on grander stages within the isthmus. It is to the reconstruction of that vital world created and sustained by the interactions of variably well-connected and well-informed Naqueños that this book seeks to contribute.

ORGANIZATION OF THE BOOK

To gain an understanding of how the Naco valley's inhabitants reconstituted the Mesoamerican world in their daily lives, we must attend to the ways such broad processes were refracted through the experiences of specific social groups. We also need to focus on an aspect of their lives in which these general processes were arguably relevant. We have therefore developed a theoretical framework that centers attention on the manner in which the basin's late prehistoric occupants employed foreign as well as local, material, and conceptual resources in their contests for power. Our concern with politics is not meant to imply that this aspect of life is somehow more significant than any other. Nor are we arguing for a narrow focus on power. Rather, economic processes of production, distribution, and consumption will be considered along with religious practices and concepts of history. The point is that making sense of the material in hand requires concentrating attention on some themes that help us see connections among seemingly disparate pieces of information. Many such themes could undoubtedly be selected. We have chosen power relations, as they are particularly amenable to investigation using data pertaining to the Naco valley's Roble phase. When we discuss economics, ritual, and history, therefore, it will be to relate them to political competitions.

The central premise of this approach, considered in greater detail in chapter 2, is that basic elements of political structure—such as office, rank, status, and role—influence human behavior only to the extent that they and their relations are enacted in the numerous events through which power is wielded by goal-seeking individuals (Mauss 2007; Monaghan 1995; Schortman 2008). Such events unfold within fields of expectations, resource distributions, and patterned interpersonal connections that come down from previous generations. The extent to which these inherited structural components are explicitly codified within institutional arrangements can vary through time and across domains within a political field. No matter how fixed and enduring structural features may appear, however, their form, reproduction, and capacity to enable and constrain behavior rely on how and to what extent their premises are acted upon (Bourdieu 1977; Giddens 1984; Mauss 2007; Monaghan 1995; Schortman 2008). Structure and event, therefore, are inseparable aspects of the same social totality (Mauss 2007; Monaghan 1995; Schortman 2008). The former is forever vulnerable to the latter; structural principles can be, and are, modified in the course of their instantiation by self-interested agents pursuing their own goals.

Seeking power requires mobilizing allies within networks to marshal resources in support of political projects. Such efforts, in turn, are countered by opponents organized within their own nets to secure the assets needed to conduct their endeavors in support of their own ends. Political formations, therefore, are rarely the products solely of centrally imposed designs. Rather, they are the joint creations of those operating together, if rarely in unison and harmony, and are continuously subject to change as the fortunes of one faction are advanced at the expense of another's (Brumfiel 1992; Brumfiel and Fox 1994). To describe political structures, therefore, we must specify who was involved in which networks, what resources were mustered within the webs, which projects were fueled by these assets, and how and to what extent they contributed to the achievement of political aims. That is what we attempt to accomplish here.

Chapters 3 and 4 lay out the basic material and behavioral patterns identified during the investigations of Sites PVN 144 and PVN 306 in the Naco valley. We concentrate here on reconstructing the webs in which the residents of these settlements operated during the fourteenth–sixteenth centuries and the various projects through which the relevant nets were instantiated. Chapter 5 considers materials reported from Naco itself in the same light. We review what Wonderley (1981, 1985) and other researchers at the site (Strong, Kidder, and Paul 1938) uncovered and how these findings relate to the outcomes of more recent work at Roble phase Naco valley settlements. The nature of power relations at all three centers is outlined in chapter 6, while chapters 7–9 discuss the ways various agents championed and challenged hierarchy. Each of these last three chapters focuses on a specific set of resources that figured in late prehistoric power contests: craft products, religious symbols, and concepts of history. The general arguments advanced throughout the volume are summarized in chapter 10, as are implications of this study for understanding political relations generally.

Attention here centers on describing, not explaining, Roble phase political formations in the Naco valley. The main reason for this choice is ignorance. Very little is known about how Late Postclassic populations in Southeast Mesoamerica organized their political relations. In fact, outside of the Naco valley, only a handful of sites found in this broad area and dating to the last Precolumbian centuries have been investigated and reported (Sharer ed. 1978; Weeks, Black, and Speaker 1987; Wonderley 1985). Providing detailed descriptions of the political structures that took shape throughout the zone is therefore an essential first step to understand the varied ways power contests were waged, what their outcomes were, and how they might have been interrelated. As it stands, it is difficult at this juncture to know what it is that we wish to explain, let alone how causation might be specified.

The paucity of information on how political developments played out in different areas is especially problematic in that power is contested through networks operating on multiple spatial scales that extend from the immediate domestic group to webs that link participants scattered over great distances (see chapter 8). It is never possible to describe all of the relevant connections by which resources were mobilized in support of some objectives and in opposition to the agendas of others. Still, the paucity of data pertaining to developments occurring over vast expanses of Southeast Mesoamerica at this time renders explanations that incorporate interconnections among populations speculative at best. In the absence of such information, any effort to account for why power relations took the forms they did in the Roble phase Naco valley must remain partial. This restriction will not stop us from offering suggestions as to how and why power was secured by some and not by others and what factors limited the expression of hierarchy in the late prehistoric Naco valley. Such explanatory forays are offered as hypotheses that may suggest fruitful areas of further inquiry, not as definitive accounts of past realities.

The book is also an experiment in using a "network perspective" on interpersonal relations to describe political structures within purely prehistoric contexts. As argued in chapter 2, we are convinced that this vantage point offers a productive foundation from which to evoke the contingent, fluid interactions that shape, and emerge from, human behavior. Considerable effort is therefore devoted to outlining the ways such an approach might be applied with the hope that it will inspire others to think along similar lines and refine its premises. We do not contend that there is one right or best way to approach studying the past in general and political formations in particular. Instead, we argue that concentrating on the ways people actually wage political contests close to the ground provide a different perspective on these struggles and their results than does one that privileges the operation of broad structural variables in determining human action. The two viewpoints are complementary, although the potential utility of the former has yet to be evaluated fully. This volume contributes to that effort.

A final caveat is that every effort is made to understand political events and formations in the Late Postclassic Naco valley in their own terms. There is a strong temptation when working in Southeast Mesoamerica to apply behavioral models drawn from the much richer ethnographic, ethnohistoric, and archaeological datasets available for the neighboring Maya area to our more poorly understood materials. Attending to this siren song is encouraged by the reasonable argument that there were considerable cultural continuities across these lands throughout prehistory. Maya cultural practices and sociopolitical formations were therefore probably generally analogous to those seen in Southeast Mesoamerica. The problem lies in identifying when drawing inspiration from Maya patterns ceases being a source of useful insights and starts predetermining results. Imposing models derived from outside the research zone runs the real risk of submerging behavioral and cultural variations within a homogenizing view based on investigations conducted in the better-known area. This is especially the case in late prehistoric Southeast Mesoamerica, where the available data are not usually robust enough to challenge such "Maya imperialism" (Euraque 2004).

We are not arguing that information pertaining to Late Postclassic developments in the Maya lowlands, or in any portion of Mesoamerica, is irrelevant to understand power contests in the Naco valley; far from it. As many have effectively argued (e.g., Kepecs 2005; Kepecs and Alexander 2005; Smith and Berdan 2003), the fourteenth through sixteenth centuries encompass a period throughout the isthmus when interregional contacts were particularly intense. No one area's developments can be fully understood in isolation from events initiated elsewhere within this extensive web. Nonetheless, these cross-border transactions occurred, and had their impacts, through the agency of people operating simultaneously within parochial as well as more expansive nets. It is critical, therefore, to model local processes as products of human actions taken within distinctive historical streams that were affected, but not determined, by long-distance interactions, such as trade and inter-elite alliances. There may well be similarities in the ways residents of different portions of southern Mesoamerica drew foreign assets into local power contests, but such commonalities are best recognized after investigations in a number of areas have been completed rather than being imposed from the start. We will therefore draw on findings from other segments of southern Mesoamerica, especially the Maya lowlands and highlands, in reconstructing the course of political history in the Naco valley from the fourteenth through early sixteenth centuries. Every effort is made, however, to see the valley's denizens for who they were: participants with diverse viewpoints who actively construed their relations with other peoples, including the Maya, in ways that made sense to them.

TWO

The Interpretive Structure

(Written with Hayden Schortman)

This volume focuses on the ways universal processes of political centralization and hierarchy construction played out within the specific culture-historical context of the Roble phase Naco valley. Our general contention is that the valley's late prehistoric political structure was, at any one time, a dynamic configuration shaped by the actions of diverse people engaged in ongoing, unresolved efforts to claim preeminence or to undermine the pretensions of those staking such claims. In the process, people organized themselves into networks, the members of which contested for material and conceptual assets crucial to their political projects. These schemes were variably successful, resulting in a political structure forever vulnerable to change as the abilities of one faction or another to secure essential resources shifted.

To use this model in illuminating late prehistoric developments in the Naco valley, we must specify the crucial variables of which it is composed. In particular, we will outline the key nexus among resources, networks, and political projects.

MOBILIZING RESOURCES IN SEARCH OF POWER

A basic premise underlying the approach followed here is that people are neither slaves to custom nor constantly innovating cultural patterns free of structural constraints. Rather, following Marcel Mauss (e.g., 2007; see also Goffman 1997: 36; Schortman 2008), we see them as managers who manipulate the economic, political, ideological, and social resources available to them by virtue of the structural positions they occupy in search of goals deemed significant and achievable within specific historical circumstances (Earle 1997; Mann 1986; Runciman 1982). Individuals thus selectively deploy assets in combinations that may be innovative. Such creativity, however, is always exercised within limits imposed by the resources bequeathed to people as occupants of specific social positions at particular moments in time (Beck et al. 2007; Giddens 1984; Goffman 1997: 144; Monaghan 1995: 360; Sewell 1992).

Resources and Power

Among the objectives individuals seek is power *over* the actions of others and power *to* attain their own ends by their own means (Foucault 1995; Wolf 1990). Achievement of these goals requires the manipulation of resources that may be material or ideological in form, of local or foreign origin, derived from the past or the present. Material resources are those variables that are in some senses crucial to physical survival. Ideological factors, in turn, play central roles in defining and conveying an authoritative understanding of the world and the relations among the people and supernaturals who inhabit it (this parallels Giddens's distinction between allocative and authoritative resources, 1984: 38, 258–261). Would-be leaders seek privileged rights to determine how and by whom significant material and ideological variables are acquired, fabricated, distributed, and used. Their subordinates, in turn, try to frustrate such monopolies by challenging these prerogatives (Bloch 1977a, 1977b; Brumfiel 1992; de Certeau 1984; Douglas and Isherwood 1979; Gailey 1987; chapters in McGuire and Paynter 1991).

Such contests result in power competitions that are perpetually unresolved. No individual or faction ever secures absolute dominion, as no one person or group can completely monopolize all of the assets on which power is based. Consequently, some power to articulate, accomplish, and legitimize goals remains in the hands of subordinates based on their abilities to secure at least a subset of the resources needed for their own survival and to define, to some extent, their relations with other people as well as with sacred beings (Foucault 1995; Wolf 1990). Such control over their own actions, no matter how limited, is an important basis from which elite privileges can be challenged and overthrown (Abercrombie, Hill, and Turner 1980; Adams 1992; Bloch 1977b; Bourdieu 1979: 82, 1989: 20–23; de Certeau 1984; Gailey 1987; Giddens 1984: 16; Ortner 1995; Paynter and McGuire 1991; Roscoe 1993: 115).

One result of these competitions is that the processes by which goods and ideas are acquired, produced, consumed, and distributed are linked into coherent, if unstable, political economies. Each move and countermove by groups and individuals involved in power contests leads to changes in extant political relations, these shifts resulting from purposeful actions that may have unintended consequences (Bourdieu 1977; Giddens 1984; Ortner 1995; Roscoe 1993).

The unstable, negotiated outcomes of these competitions are often described with reference to political centralization, dealing with the extent to which power is concentrated in a few hands, in part as a result of the aforementioned monopolies over goods and ideas, and hierarchy, a measure of how clearly defined and institutionalized were social rankings based on differential access to material and ideological assets (Bourdieu 1977; Giddens 1984; McGuire 1983; Paynter 1990; Paynter and McGuire 1991; Roscoe 1993).

Power and Networks

Individuals rarely gain or lose advantage on their own (chapters in Brumfiel and Fox 1994; Preucel 2000: 59). Instead, crucial assets are secured and put to work through participation in networks composed of people engaged in similar political and economic projects (Campbell 2009; Earle 1997; Galaskiewicz and Wasserman 1994: xiii; Knox, Savage, and Harvey 2006; Mann 1986; Marcus 2000: 239; Ortner 1995: 187, 191; Preucel 2000: 59–61; Trigger 1984: 286). Cooperation within such webs is founded on their members sharing a social identity, or a sense of themselves as possessors of a distinct persona hedged round with identifying symbols (Barth 1969; Cohen 1969; Curtin 1984; Ferguson and Mansbach 1996; Jones 1997; Rapoport 1982; Royce 1982; Schortman 1989; Spence 2005: 175–176; Vincent 1974, 1978; Wobst 1977, 1999). Networks are therefore means for coordinating the actions of a group of people who deploy resources in support of common political endeavors and who reflexively set themselves apart from others similarly organized in the pursuit of complementary or conflicting goals (Giddens 1984; Knoke 1994: 290; Knox, Savage, and Harvey 2006; Preucel 2000: 59–61; Spence 2005). It is through such webs that political struggles are waged.

People can belong to multiple networks simultaneously or change memberships through time, employing the associated identities in different contexts, to access different resources, and for different purposes (Alcock 2005; Goffman 1997: 23; Horning 2000: 225; Knox, Savage, and Harvey 2006: 129–130; Lightfoot and Martinez 1995: 479–480; Preucel 2000: 61, 73; Schortman, Urban, and Ausec 2001; Stein 1999). Any particular society, therefore, is composed of a dense concentration of social networks that variably unite and divide its members along shifting lines of cooperation and competition. These webs also extend, to differing degrees, beyond a society's spatial boundaries, tying at least some members to their compatriots in other realms who seek similar resources to support comparable political projects (Barth 1969: 10; Cohen 1978: 387; Jones 1997; Lightfoot and Martinez 1995: 472, 474; Royce 1982; Vincent 1974: 376). Together, these networks of networks comprise a political structure in which people living at different places participate to varying degrees (Campbell 2009: 824).

Political webs are created and reproduced within structural constraints that, like the nets themselves, play out over multiple, overlapping spatial scales (Bourdieu 1977; Campbell 2009: 825; Giddens 1984; Knoke 1994; Wolf 1990). These structural features, which combine physical aspects of the environment with extant sociopolitical and economic relations and variably shared worldviews, define the ways material and conceptual resources are distributed among all participants and, hence, what political projects are possible. They do not, however, determine how those potentialities are translated into action. Rather, the manner in which individuals take advantage of the opportunities offered by extant arrangements of structural features to secure assets by allying with some in opposition to others is what shapes power relations on local to interregional scales (Giddens 1984).

Political structures in this formulation are therefore inseparable from the events in which power relations are enacted (Goffman 1997: 101; Mauss 2007; Monaghan 1995: 13–14). Structural principles are implicated in every choice people make. For this reason, structure is always vulnerable to change through the deeds of people seeking their own goals in concert with some and opposition to others (Bourdieu 1977; Giddens 1984; Goffman 1997: 106; Monaghan 1995: 15; Ortner 1995). Networks are simultaneously parts of and the means for transforming political structures as these structures operate over multiple territorial extents. Distinctions between structure and agency, local and foreign, are thereby collapsed in that decisions made and actions taken by agents working within webs at any one place both shape and are constrained by extant distributions of material and conceptual resources found both at that locale and over broader spatial expanses (Giddens 1984; Knox, Savage, and Harvey 2006: 125; Wolf 1982, 1990).

The sorts of networks described here clearly do not describe the full range of interpersonal interactions in which people engage. Nor is it the case that all social identities are linked in equal degrees, if at all, to particular webs in the manner outlined here. Interpersonal interactions may always be structured around the mutually understood social personas people adopt in different contexts. This does not mean, however, that such affiliations are invariably related to enduring and distinctive webs, the personnel of which clearly set themselves off from all others.

We argue, however, that the subset of regularly recurring interpersonal contacts concerned with acquiring and challenging claims to power is often conducted in terms of these reflexively constituted webs because such efforts require forging enduring alliances that link collaborators in explicit opposition to those who organize along similar lines in pursuit of comparable political goals (Hodder 1979; Knox, Savage, and Harvey 2006: 125; Lightfoot and Martinez 1995: 483–484). Repeated mobilization of material and ideological resources during oft-repeated confrontations in which all parties have significant stakes reinforces a pronounced sense of self among web members who see each other as essential allies in important, life-defining transactions. Shoring up and conveying such feelings of distinctiveness often involve the mobilization of physically prominent symbols of network affiliation (Goffman 1997: 57–58; Hodder 1979; Lightfoot and Martinez 1995: 485; Lightfoot, Martinez, and Schiff 1998: 202; Schortman 1989; Spence 2005: 175–176; Wiessner 1983; Wobst 1977, 1999). It is through identities so defined and expressed that claims to various forms of preeminence are established and legitimized.

Patterned relations among the physical signifiers of network identities, therefore, provide a basis for inferring the duration, spatial extent, and political significance of ancient networks. It may not be possible to reconstruct from archaeological remains all the social webs in which a person could have participated. Those that were particularly salient in power competitions, however, are the most likely to be recognized from the physical distribution of their material markers (Lightfoot and Martinez 1995: 485; Schortman 1989; Schortman and Nakamura 1991).

Network Forms

Salient political nets can take many forms. They may grow out of those routinized dealings in which prosaic items and material styles are regularly, repetitively, and perhaps implicitly used in daily interactions to secure essential resources and convey identity. At the other end of the continuum are linkages explicitly proclaimed and demarcated by prominent material symbols that may be actualized only infrequently.

This distinction points to two general strategies by which people who occupy different structural positions organize their lives and, in the process, create and reproduce political structures. For example, those seeking power frequently make these claims based on their participation in networks that link them to potent allies located at significant physical or conceptual distances (Curtin 1984; Donley 1982; Stein 1999; Wells 1984). Elite control over the dissemination of valuables secured from such allies can form the basis of unequal intra-societal exchange relations in which subordinates render labor and loyalty to paramount lords in return for receipt of locally rare but generally esteemed items (e.g., Cohen 1981: 2–4; Ekholm 1972; Friedman 1982; Friedman and Rowlands 1977; Peregrine 1991; Spencer 1982; Wells 1980, 1984). Participation in these interaction webs commonly involves manipulating symbols that clearly and overwhelmingly express their members' identities and distinguish them from near neighbors (Helms 1988, 1992; Wheatley 1975: 239). Drawing such explicit symbolic boundaries ensures that the advantaged few enjoy local monopolies over the use of ideological and material resources whose exhibition and deployment are instrumental in securing power and building hierarchies at home (Arnold 1995; Ekholm 1972; Hayden 1995; Paynter 1990: 370, 381; Peregrine 1991; Wells 1984).

Routinized, quotidian interactions, on the other hand, are often the ones by which people of all backgrounds seek to gain—through their own efforts—the means to survive physically, reproduce extant social relations, and define themselves in reference to other humans as well as to supernatural figures. These contacts, which occupy much of everyone's day, tend to operate on local scales, if only because it is difficult to maintain close, regular ties with people or sacred forces at great distances (Bowser 2000; Smith 2007). Such logistical problems, however, do not rule out the possibility that at least some individuals of non-elite status may enjoy significant, ongoing relations with those they only interact with periodically (e.g., at trade fairs or on pilgrimages; Freidel and Sabloff 1984; Hammond and Bobo 1994: 19; Wells and Nelson 2007). Regardless of a network's spatial extent, however, webs that regularly and predictably unite a group in search of essential ideological, social, or economic resources at least implicitly challenge efforts by would-be rulers to claim preeminence based on monopolies secured through participation in their symbolically prominent, physically far-flung nets (Bowser 2000; Gailey 1987; Lightfoot and Martinez 1995: 488; Schortman, Urban, and Ausec 2001; Yaeger 2000). Such often-repeated interactions also encourage development of a group's sense of self as distinguished from others who pursue life's course in different ways, according to different principles (analogous to Bourdieu's notion of "habitus" [1977] and Yaeger's "practices of affiliation" [2000: 125, 129–131]).

This discussion simplifies a complex reality. It conveys a neat distinction between two major types of interaction networks, one linking its members in assertions of dominance and the other rallying participants to resist such claims. Nothing could be further from the truth. The dense networks that converge within any one society join varied sets of people in ways that defy easy categorization (e.g., Alcock 2005: 326). For example, elites who engage in occasional, if politically significant, distant transactions are also tied to their immediate neighbors through contacts repeated on a daily basis (Ferguson and Mansbach 1996: 26). These leaders must therefore both distinguish themselves from their followers and assert connections to them, being of and above "their people." Otherwise, these magnates risk being perceived as irrelevant to, or no different from, everyone else, with no special claims on power in either case. Achieving these seemingly disparate goals depends on the magnates' ability to manage several different identities tied to distinct networks that vary in their inclusiveness (Ferguson and Mansbach 1996: 26; Goffman 1997; Schortman, Urban, and Ausec 2001; Yaeger 2000).

Non-elites, in turn, likely comprise a heterogeneous group whose members are variably willing and able to resist elite pretensions or to ally themselves with ascendant lords (Yaeger 2000). Some may see advantages in novel hierarchical relations; others likely detest and reject them; while still more remain uncertain about, or indifferent to, the changes. In all of these cases, networks are restructured over varying spatial scales to take advantage of perceived opportunities offered by shifting power relations to advance within the new system, undermine its operation, or reestablish some version of the status quo (Ferguson and Mansbach 1996: 36; Schortman, Urban, and Ausec 2001; Yaeger 2000; Yoffee 1991: 287). These efforts may well form the bases for variably successful strategies—involving a diverse array of cross-cutting networks through which an equally wide range of assets is mobilized—to resist or accommodate elite demands, or both. These strategies have at least implicit political significance.

Individuals of all persuasions thus are constantly engaged in creating political structures as they enact their principles through patterned interactions conducted in a host of different settings (Brumfiel 1994, 1996; Paynter and McGuire 1991). The result is a diverse set of relations through which people are increasingly distinguished by, among other factors, their power, social affiliations, and positions within single or multiple hierarchies operating at varied temporal and spatial scales (Crumley 1979). These ties and their material symbols are variably stable. All are susceptible to change through time as a result of shifts in a complex array of local and foreign variables and the ways those factors are perceived by actors and those perceptions acted upon.

The approach outlined here offers a very instrumental perspective on social interactions. In this view, people establish and maintain contacts to achieve specific objectives, the goals of primary interest here being those related to securing power. There are other rewards for maintaining interpersonal ties, but they are largely put to one side here. This decision is determined by our focus on ancient power relations, an interest that, in turn, is dictated in part by the nature of the data available from our investigations. In the present volume, therefore, we concentrate on describing and understanding the strategies Roble phase Naqueños employed to contest for power. Such an admittedly limited view of interaction yields insights into the structured distribution of resources with which ancient people contended, although it hardly captures the full richness of their experiences.

NETWORKS IN THE ARCHAEOLOGICAL RECORD

To apply a network perspective to the study of prehistoric political structures, we must infer the dynamics of past interactions from static archaeological remains. We propose to address this challenge by identifying what nets were in operation in the Roble phase Naco valley; who belonged to them; what resources were accessed through such connections; how, if at all, these assets and alliances were employed in political struggles; and what the outcomes of those contests were.

Identifying Networks

Reconstructing which networks were available to a population at any moment in time relies on using two sets of criteria: spatial proximity and material styles. These features are variably useful in recognizing ancient webs, depending on where the nets fall on the scale of spatially rooted to rootless. For those webs near the former pole, physical proximity can be an important indicator of shared network membership. Propinquity is equated with web participation based on the argument that those living close to each other likely interacted on a regular basis. They at least had the chance to forge a common identity around engagement in a range of projects, some of which were political in nature. Opportunity is not destiny, however. Proximity cannot by itself be accepted as a measure of network ties. At the very least, the manner in which daily tasks are conducted within localized social groups must be addressed. Such studies may provide insights into how much and in what ways those living near each other cooperated in common projects. More indirectly, an analysis of how daily activities were structured within neighboring social units can reveal the extent to which different people incorporated similar understandings of themselves and their relations to others within routine performances (Goffman 1974, 1997; Isbell 2000; Jackson 2001: 12). This last point speaks directly to the existence of those shared values and premises that underlie all social identities and cooperative endeavors.

Regardless of a web's relation to space, membership in a net is signaled by symbols intelligible to participants and outsiders alike (Goffman 1997: 57–59, 97–98; Jackson 2001). Recognition of the former existence of such networks, therefore, relies on identifying patterned spatial and temporal relations among surviving markers of network affiliation. Because of their relative freedom from technological and functional constraints, material styles are the most likely signifiers of web membership (Carr 1995; Wiessner 1983; Wobst 1977, 1999). These culturally conditioned choices of fabrication, decoration, embellishment, and arrangement have significant potential for conveying social information (Carr 1995; Wiessner 1983; Wobst 1977, 1999). Some of that information has to do with the networks, and their associated identities, to which a person subscribed.

As discussed earlier, the means by and contexts in which network participation is conveyed vary. In some instances, the relevant material symbols are evident in the choices people make in a wide array of daily activities and the implements used to complete those chores. The organization of space within a house, patterns of trash disposal, and selections made among widely available materials in fashioning commonly used tools may therefore signal network participation as loudly as the ways those implements and domiciles are decorated (e.g., Blanton 1994; Bourdieu 1977). Alternatively, the symbols used to convey network affiliations may overtly and self-consciously specify membership in a web. The form, organization, and dimensions of monumental edifices employed in elite ritual and administration may fall within this category, as would elaborately decorated jewelry, serving vessels, and other accoutrements all deployed to signal the segregation of some activities and people from the world of the mundane (LeCount 2001).

It may be that physical aggregation reduces the need for communicating membership through explicit material symbols (Yaeger 2000). Those who live in each other's midst probably do not require frequent manipulation of prominent markers in various media to identify their compatriots and distinguish them from non-members. Participants in these nets may rely on their own intimate knowledge of each other's histories in coordinating their actions and cooperating on projects. This information, in turn, can be reinforced by the display of subtle material cues to network affiliations, cues embedded in the daily round of quotidian tasks.

Similarly, people who interact relatively infrequently might depend on just those sorts of prominent symbols that are irrelevant at the local scale to separate allies from others (Wobst 1977, 1999). Here, web affiliations may be conveyed by the use of particularly ostentatious diagnostics to ensure that they are easily legible to all participants (Wobst 1977, 1999). While such a correlation between distance and symbolic marking may hold generally, there are a variety of reasons why those who see each other daily would want to employ explicit symbolic makers to distinguish themselves from their neighbors. The often-repeated case of elites seeking to define themselves as a group apart from those they rule is just one example of this phenomenon.

These two broad forms of web signification define extreme points on a continuum in which the prosaic and the exceptional often interpenetrate. Thus members of non-elite domestic units may express overtly their participation in some networks through the sparing use of richly decorated items, such as ceramic serving vessels, that convey crucial social information appropriate to certain infrequently enacted contexts. Their high-born counterparts, in turn, likely also employ locally fashioned items in activities structured according to principles that link them and their subordinates within webs rooted in parochial affiliations. Symbols of different origins can also be combined to varying extents within the same object or related set of items as parts of efforts to forge new identities and networks that link previously disparate social groups (see chapter 8). In all cases, attention is devoted to the ways the distribution of material styles in diverse media might have been affected by the decisions of people seeking to express participation in one or more political networks. The more important certain webs are to the accomplishment of a person's crucial objectives, the more prominent and diverse the markers that distinguish membership in those affiliations (Hodder 1979). As noted, it is through the patterned distribution of such symbols that the existence, duration, and extent of salient nets can be reconstructed.

Networks in the Roble Phase Naco Valley

The four localized networks we consistently identified in the Naco valley investigations are houses, households, sites, and the settlement cluster that includes Sites PVN 144, PVN 306, and Naco (see also Canuto and Yaeger 2000: 10; Smith 1994: 146–148). The nature and relevance of each of these entities to understanding political developments in the Naco valley varied over time. During the Roble phase, the basin's residents employed all four webs in structuring their lives and their participation in political formations.

Houses consist of individuals who occupy the same residence and use its associated outbuildings over a protracted span (Blanton 1994; Gillespie 2000; Joyce 2000; Sheets 1992, 2002). These entities are therefore composed of people who regularly and repeatedly cooperate in basic economic and social chores as parts of networks firmly rooted in specific places and reinforced by intense daily interactions born, in part, of their proximity (Freidel and Sabloff 1984: 111–112; Gillespie 2000; Joyce 2000). Houses may vary considerably in size and are recognized in the Roble phase Naco valley by anything from a single residence raised atop a platform to distinct, shallow trash deposits likely generated by people who lived in perishable constructions in the immediate vicinity.

Households are composed of multiple residences and their outbuildings clustered together, usually around a plaza (e.g., Flannery 1976). They incorporate members of distinct houses who cooperate regularly in basic economic, social, political, and ritual tasks (Ashmore and Wilk 1988; Blanton 1994; Sheets

1992, 2002; Wilk and Ashmore 1988). Households are widely recognized as basic units of production and reproduction across ancient Mesoamerica (Ashmore and Wilk 1988; Blanton 1994; Wilk and Rathje 1982; see chapters in Santley and Hirth 1993; Tourtellot 1988; Wilk and Ashmore 1988). Close interpersonal collaborations are inferred, therefore, from both the near spacing of domestic constructions and their mutually adjusted organization surrounding a patio. Such concentration and coherence in building arrangements physically manifested, and provided venues for the repeated re-creation of, those values, premises, and understandings that underwrote intra-network cooperation (Hendon 1996).

Roble phase Naco valley sites are defined as locales composed of numerous houses, households in which a wide range of activities was pursued, or both (Urban 1986). These entities are usually separated from comparable units by 100 m or more of seemingly open, unoccupied space. They are tentatively treated, therefore, as physically discrete settlements, the occupants of which likely interacted more intensely with each other than with the denizens of other such units. As we will see in chapters 6 and 10, however, there is reason to think that Sites PVN 144, PVN 306, and Naco were subsumed within a more inclusive interaction network represented by the settlement cluster. The latter extends for 5 km southwest-northeast and is anchored on the former end by Naco and by Site PVN 306 on the northeast. Site PVN 144 is situated between these two centers, in the midst of what was likely continuous Roble phase occupation—the signs of which are difficult to identify from surface remains. Like houses, households, and sites, spatial proximity within and between these three settlements bespeaks regular, coordinated contacts founded on the understandings and identities of shared networks. Membership in these webs, from house to settlement cluster, was expressed and reinforced through a variety of symbols, material dependencies, and behavioral similarities that figured in diverse aspects of Roble phase life operating within sites (described in chapters 3–5) and across them (reviewed in chapters 6–9).

During the last Precolumbian centuries, therefore, the Naco valley was home to a dense concentration of networks created by their members as they cooperated in the pursuit of common goals, not all of which were directly concerned with power and wealth. At least some of these webs were linked to particular locales organized on a graduated scale, from the house to site to settlement cluster. Chapters 6 and 10 consider where the concept of "society" fits within this network of networks.

The territorially rooted nets outlined here are not the only ones in which ancient Naqueños participated. Cross-cutting these entities were webs that linked their members, directly and indirectly and to differing degrees, to each other and with those residing at variably great distances beyond the Naco valley.

Spatial contiguity provides little guidance in reconstructing these ties. Instead, we must rely on tracing patterns of similarities in material styles across Naco valley houses, households, sites, and settlement cluster with those found among their counterparts in other areas. As we move from territorially specific to more spatially diffuse connections, we, like the actors themselves, rely on the patterned distribution of styles in a number of media to identify ancient, spatially extensive interaction networks and their participants.

Power and Webs

The possible relevance of different webs to political contests is approached here by evaluating the degree to which variations in measures of power correlate with distinct nets. This set of variables speaks to how successful different population segments were in controlling their compatriots' actions.

Power is measured here by the differential ability of some to command the labor of others. Such productive efforts can be harnessed to many tasks, most of which are not enshrined in the Naco valley archaeological record. One set of projects that did leave tangible remains was the construction of buildings associated with specific population segments (Abrams 1994; DeMarrais, Castillo, and Earle 1996; Masson 2003b: 280; Smith 1994: 151–153). The Roble phase architectural corpus in the Naco valley spans a continuum stretching from perishable edifices raised directly on ground surface to sizable platforms. Differences in the dimensions of, and the engineering skills needed to raise, such constructions imply comparable distinctions in the sizes of the networks mobilized by those who commissioned these edifices (Abrams 1994; Trigger 1990).

A second rough measure of power is people's differing ability to attract and hold the loyalty of others, assessed here based on variations in the nucleation of settlement between sites. This correlation is based on the assumption that controlling the actions of subordinates relies in part on keeping those associates close so they are readily available for conscription into tasks that require their efforts (de Montmollin 1989; Roscoe 1993). Such concentration also helps ensure that labor pledged to a central individual or group is not siphoned off by competitors (de Montmollin 1989; Roscoe 1993).

Variations in building sizes and settlement aggregation, therefore, materially express the sizes of political networks focused on certain nodal people or groups and indicate how effectively the latter could channel web members' actions to their benefit. The more densely concentrated residences are within a site, the larger the constructions raised in the house, household, or site. In addition, the more numerous these sizable edifices are, the more power we infer was vested in those who occupied the centers of these nets (Trigger 1990).

These measures are, to be sure, crude approximations of power. There are many ways in which people's labor can be directed in production, war, ritual, and the like. This approach tacitly assumes that building sizes and settlement nucleation are valid proxies for all forms of control, that those who could commission large edifices and attract considerable followings also had privileged claims on their subordinates' food surpluses, as well as on their prowess in combat and participation in religious observances. Such connections may well have pertained, and we will point out some instances where we believe they did operate in the Roble phase Naco valley. Still, it is wise to bear in mind that different forms of cooperative action occurring at distinct scales may have been coordinated by diverse people who exercised control through varied networks (Crumley 1979). Labor mobilized to raise large constructions, therefore, could have been marshaled by different means, drawing on different participants than those involved in organizing for rite, combat, and production.

Networks and Resources

People operating within networks might have employed numerous potential resources as they sought to advance and challenge claims to power. For the purposes of this study we distinguish between those material assets deemed essential to a people's physical survival and those that defined the basic premises of existence (see Giddens 1984: 33, 258–262). The former include raw materials, the technologies by which those materials are transformed for human use, and the products of those transformations (Giddens 1984: 258). The latter are the conceptual structures, as well as the symbols by which they are expressed, through which people understand, organize, and relate to each other and to the world around them (Giddens 1984: 258). These two sets of resources are closely interconnected; political preeminence may be founded on effective exploitation of physical assets, those processes imagined, understood, rationalized, and conveyed through ideological frameworks and their symbols. In political contests, therefore, success goes to those who can stake privileged claims to essential resources, their acquisition, production, distribution, and consumption, and also ensconce those demands within conceptual structures in such a way as to make them seem reasonable and beyond question (Earle 1997; Giddens 1984: 258–262). People who wish to challenge such assertions must work through their networks to subvert both elite control over aspects of the material realm and the frameworks by which such command is presented and rationalized (Gailey 1987).

This distinction between material and conceptual assets is therefore an arbitrary one adopted here to facilitate discussion of political processes in the Roble phase Naco valley. Convenient as this division may be, it must be acknowledged that the importance of any resource in political struggles was informed simultaneously by its physical properties as well as its cultural meanings. We are variably able to address these two broad aspects of ancient resources with the data in hand. There are times, therefore, when we will stress the material or the conceptual pole of an asset's significance. Such bows to the nature of our information should not obscure the complex reality of a world where, in the past no less than in the present, ideological and physical features intersected to determine the significance of resources within political competitions.

As noted at the start of this chapter, we are pursuing the notion that power flows to those who can redirect resource streams to their benefit by reconfiguring social networks and the ideological underpinnings of those connections. How, then, are such material and ideological transformations to be recognized archaeologically? One of the prime indicators of these changes available in the Naco valley data involves the extent to which the production of materially and symbolically significant objects was centrally controlled or diffused throughout the population of houses, households, and sites. In part, therefore, attention focuses on the scale, intensity, and contexts of the production of prosaic implements as well as items that symbolized conceptual structures (Costin 1991, 2001; Schortman and Urban 2004a). Elite control over these manufacturing locales could effectively convert the mass of the population into clients dependent on the monopolists' largesse for goods needed to survive and to fashion satisfying relations with other people and supernatural entities. Alternatively, dispersal of production loci might signify efforts to retain some level of household autonomy as people fabricated their own goods to meet their own needs, as well as for exchange with others engaged in complementary economic pursuits (Costin 1991, 2001; Schortman and Urban 2004a). We address these issues in chapter 7.

Another set of resources that might have been significant in political contests are those finished goods and ideas acquired from afar. The parochial importance of these foreign concepts and objects is in part a factor of their local rarity, as well as of attributions of sacred potency derived from their associations with distant, high-prestige realms and figures (Helms 1979, 1988, 1992, 1993). Those who effectively insinuated themselves within the networks by which such imports were acquired would have enjoyed a decided advantage in intra-valley political contests. They would have been in an excellent position to use prized items as markers of elevated status and as gifts recipients would have been hard-pressed to reciprocate (Ekholm 1972; Friedman 1982; Friedman and Rowlands 1977). In either case, privileged access to foreign goods and concepts could have been a foundation for creating invidious distinctions based on power.

However symbols were acquired and whatever their inspirations may have been, central control over their use and definition can be crucial to establishing political hierarchies because symbols both express an understanding of the world and motivate action within a world thus construed (DeMarrais, Castillo, and Earle 1996; Geertz 1973; Turner 1964). The power of symbols to control behavior is based on varied sources (e.g., Geertz 1973; Turner 1964). From the network perspective, such conceptual assets are particularly significant in that they are crucial to defining web membership. As we will see in chapter 8, Roble phase Naco valley notables devoted considerable effort to restructuring social relations to their liking through the strategic use of symbols expressed on ceramics and also through architecture.

It is difficult to infer the presence and extent of resource monopolies from archaeological data alone. Essentially, we adopt the position that concentration of specific goods, symbols, and the means of fabricating them within specific houses or households reflects centralized control over local access to, and use of, these assets. Still, the degree to which members of some nets could effectively deny resources to others may not be readily apparent from archaeology's mute remains. Further, the mechanisms by which goods and symbols were deployed in political struggles are not always or easily apparent from the distribution of materials recorded in excavations. These issues are revisited throughout the volume but especially in chapters 7 and 10.

Power might also be secured through monopolies over the provision of certain key administrative, social, economic, or ritual services to the population-at-large. Attention once again focuses on how, if at all, would-be scions forged networks of clients willing to surrender labor, loyalty, and some measure of autonomy in return for inclusion in activities of import to all but enacted by only an advantaged few. Archaeological signatures of this process might include close associations between venues for the performance of behaviors that had polity-wide significance and the domiciles of the elites who officiated at such performances (e.g., Conlee 2003).

The material patterns used to discern variations in power, resources, and network membership overlap to a considerable extent. For example, the same large-scale constructions might have expressed centralized control over labor, symbolized membership in a particular network, and served as venues for the performance of rites through which elites exercised control over their subordinates. This interdigitation reflects a reality in which materials have multiple connotations and serve several purposes. From a practical standpoint, such complex associations mean that any one item may at the same time be a means to and an expression of power. Arguments concerning network membership, power, and resource control that are based on one line of evidence therefore tend to be circular, with monumental edifices in the earlier example signifying all three processes simultaneously. It is far better to infer aspects of political structures using independent lines of evidence, and we will do this where we can (Wylie 2002). Nevertheless, limitations in our dataset often leave us little choice but to reconstruct multiple features of political structures and processes from a restricted array of material remains. In these cases our descriptions are particularly susceptible to revision and remain hypotheses that need further examination to evaluate fully.

SUMMARY

The acquisition and defense of power require mobilizing support from people of varying backgrounds living at different locales to secure material and conceptual resources that, in turn, come from diverse sources. Distant peers may provide goods and ideas useful in projects such as expressing status differences, establishing unequal intra-societal exchange relations, and rationalizing both. Resident artisans might be co-opted within domination strategies as the fabricators of political valuables used to ensnare clients in dependency relations. Aspiring magnates then employ these and other assets to convert people with diffuse and conflicting loyalties into a network of supporters who owe allegiance and tribute solely or at least primarily to their leaders (Cohen 1979; Curet 1996; Ferguson and Mansbach 1996: 36; Schortman, Urban, and Ausec 2001; Yoffee 1991: 287). By mobilizing resource flows and reconfiguring social relations at varying scales, enterprising elites create hierarchically structured, spatially demarcated realms. That, at least, is the goal.

While leaders may push to secure the absolute, unquestioned allegiance of supporters within clearly demarcated polities, those they would rule push back. Just as magnates forge webs to serve their purposes, those resisting such pretensions also marshal assets of varying sorts to meet their own agendas, including preserving some degree of autonomy. This may take various forms, from engaging in craft production, to establishing independent means of acquiring distant goods, to meeting their own needs for administrative, social, and ritual services by their own efforts. In short, any way of undermining elite monopolies over crucial assets is at least an implicit challenge to paramount power. Nonelites, like their high-born compatriots, do not act alone in politico-economic contests. Instead, they participate in networks of varying spatial, temporal, and demographic scales. Given that different people will have access to diverse nets and that this access will change over time, the resulting political configurations will be heterogeneous, as measured in part by the power various participants achieve at any one moment.

It is very difficult to reconstruct this dynamic interplay of shifting forces based solely on archaeological data. Not only are the networks themselves difficult to make out from material remains, but the full array of resources their participants manipulated in their struggles is impossible to grasp. We will therefore offer an incomplete account of who was involved in Roble phase competitions for power in the Naco valley, what resources they employed in their struggles, and the implications of these unresolved contests for the area's late prehistoric political structure. Many aspects of these interchanges are forever lost to us. We hope that what can still be discerned of political structures and processes conveys an accurate sense of the general nature of these developments, even though many of the details are missing.

Throughout this volume, therefore, we will seek to identify the networks through which the Naco valley's Roble phase residents organized to secure and manipulate resources in their search for power, the assets deployed in this process, how successful these efforts were, and the factors that might help account for the political configurations that emerged from such struggles. As noted earlier, the webs and resources integral to power contests were not restricted to the Naco valley but encompassed people, alliances, and goods distributed across potentially great distances. These features are also not restricted to the two final Precolumbian centuries. Instead, assets and networks have histories that contribute to appreciations of their shifting relevance in political competitions (chapter 9). Temporal spans and territorial distances may therefore be collapsed in the political strategies of people maneuvering, with variable success, for advantage within variably stable political networks.

THREE

Activity Structures and Networks at Site PVN 306

Site PVN 306 is located 2 km northeast of, and outside, the Naco valley on the north bank of the Rio Chamelecon (see figure 1.2). The narrow passage the Chamelecon cuts here is bounded by steep slopes on the north and south. Site PVN 306 is bordered by the river on the south and occupies a relatively broad terrace of that watercourse, which slopes up gradually from south to north. When first investigated in 1988, Site PVN 306 was divided between cattle pasture and cultivated fields on the eastern margin of the town of Brisas del Valle. Since that time settlement has been steadily encroaching on the center.

Site PVN 306 contains 120 structures and 223 artifact scatters covering roughly 350,000 m² (35 ha; figure 3.1). The site's center consists of two contiguous plazas running almost due east-west and measuring approximately 33 × 50 m (the western principal plaza, WPP) and 67 × 70 m (the eastern principal plaza, EPP). These spaces are delimited by some of the settlement's largest buildings. A dense concentration of 26 surface-visible constructions extends 100 m east of the site center, while more dispersed remains spread 300 m to the north, 275 m west, and 210 m south of the principal plazas. Distinct patio groups are difficult to discern outside the site core. Plowing around Site PVN 306's margins is partly responsible for the large number of artifact

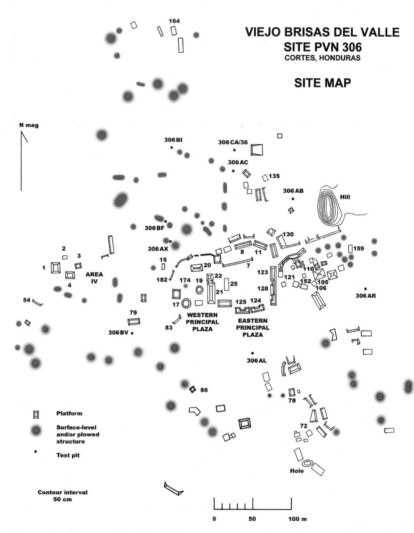

VIEJO BRISAS DEL VALLE
SITE PVN 306
CORTES, HONDURAS

SITE MAP

FIGURE **3.1** *Map of Site PVN 306. Artifact scatters are shown in gray and retain, where relevant, their original structure numbers.*

concentrations recorded here. These scatters are generally shallow middens that were likely associated with perishable buildings raised directly on ground surface. Mechanized cultivation, therefore, has both revealed and disturbed these ancient remains.

Thirty-four surface-visible structures were dug here during 1988 and 1990. In addition, nine of the artifact scatters situated away from the principal plazas and identified by dense concentrations of surface debris were probed in 1990 and reported by the excavator, L. Theodore Neff, in his MA thesis (1993). Much of what we have to say here about those middens is based on Neff's work. Test pits measuring from 1 m to 0.5 m on a side were sunk in transects across the EPP and southwest of the WPP to determine the nature of activities pursued away from physically salient remains. An additional thirty-six probes measuring 0.5×0.5 m were dug in the northeast corner of the center in an area of 12,000 m² north of Suboperation 306AB and east of Str. 306-135 ("Suboperation," a distinct unit of excavation, is hereafter abbreviated as Subop.; "Structure" is hereafter abbreviated as Str.). These tests were designed to evaluate the extent of Roble phase occupation where surface-visible evidence of settlement is lacking. During the latter work one midden (designated on figure 3.1 as 306CA/36) was recorded. A total of 647 m² was dug at Site PVN 306 during 1988 and 1990.

One outcome of these investigations was the identification of a lengthy occupation history at the center. From the Late Preclassic through Late Classic periods, settlement was concentrated in the 7,300 m² area east of the EPP. The only architecture associated with any of these early periods is limited to a few traces dating to the Late Classic. It appears, therefore, that buildings were generally modest in size throughout this lengthy span. During the Terminal Classic, far more substantial constructions were raised at the center. These stone-faced platforms and surface-level edifices remain concentrated on the eastern margin of Site PVN 306, where 21 extant buildings are crammed within the aforementioned 7,300 m². A second node of construction was new established, roughly 260 m to the west, and is composed of four stone-faced platforms (Strs. 306-1/4) clustered around a patio with a low stone terrace (Str. 306-54) situated 36 m downslope to the southwest. The extensive area intervening between these two focal points lacks any signs of Terminal Classic architecture, although trash deposits dating to the ninth to tenth centuries have been identified under portions of the EPP and the WPP. Continued renovation of existing Terminal Classic buildings continued into the Early Postclassic, with Str. 306-105 in the eastern cluster reaching its maximum height of 1.9 m either at the end of the Terminal Classic or early in the Early Postclassic (figure 3.2). By the Terminal Classic/Early Postclassic transition, therefore, Site PVN 306 consisted of two distinct centers of occupation: a densely settled eastern focus clustered around Str. 306-105 and a much smaller western patio group.

During the Roble phase, earlier constructions were largely abandoned but not dismantled, and a large site core encompassing 67×130 m was established in the area between the earlier architectural foci. Twenty-four buildings, among them the largest and most elaborately decorated edifices known from the center at this time, define the two adjoining plazas that comprise the architectural core. An additional 70 Roble phase structures are scattered to the north, west,

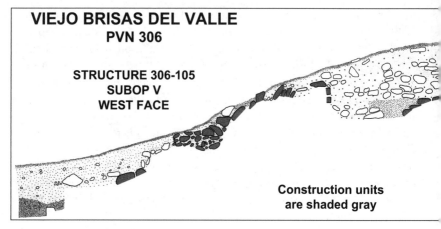

FIGURE 3.2 *Section through Structure 306-105*

east, and south of these plazas, along with 223 artifact scatters that likely mark the locations of shallow middens associated with perishable constructions. By the last Precolumbian centuries, therefore, Site PVN 306 was home to a dense agglomeration of people loosely spread out around two principal plazas. This chapter focuses on the organization of activities within that Roble phase community.

In making those inferences, we rely on evidence provided by architecture as well as patterning among recovered cultural materials. Unlike Site PVN 144, where all of the investigated buildings were cleared laterally, excavations at Site PVN 306 tended to be limited to 1-m-wide trenches dug against surface-visible constructions. The primary goal of these probes was to recover datable remains needed to reconstruct the center's complex history and to relate the visible edifices to that sequence. As time allowed, digging was expanded to reveal as much of a building as possible. Overall, however, information on construction forms and dimensions is much less detailed than is the case for Site PVN 144.

There are also differences in the ways cultural materials recovered from Site PVN 306 were handled vis-à-vis the procedures employed in dealing with objects retrieved from Site PVN 144. First, the processing of large quantities of items from a diverse array of investigations in 1990 precluded collecting and counting all of the numerous shells, primarily those of *Pachychilus* sp. (*jute*), recovered from middens excavated at Site PVN 306. To compensate for this loss, probes measuring 0.5 m on a side were dug in the centers of most investigated trash deposits immediately adjacent to the main trench that cut across the deposit. The matrices from the 0.5 m × 0.5 m pits were screened through ¼-inch

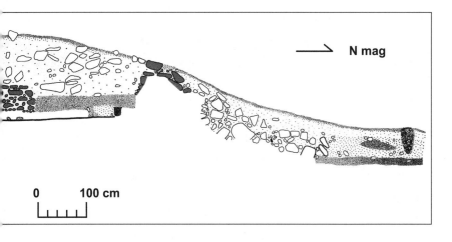

mesh, with all of the recovered items counted and recorded. This provides the basis from which densities of shell are extrapolated in this chapter.

Second, the procedures used in analyzing chipped stone tools and debris (primarily obsidian and chert) changed somewhat during these years. The primary differences relate to assessments of use wear, obsidian sources, and the distinction between perlite and obsidian. The original analysts did not feel confident making inferences concerning the first two issues for the Site PVN 306 materials. Consequently, use-wear studies were not carried out, and sourcing was limited to a sample of twenty-two items from Site PVN 306 (twenty-one from Roble phase contexts) submitted to X-ray refraction analyses by P. Bouey at the Department of Geology, University of California, Davis (see table 7.1). As to the last point, prior to 1992 we did not differentiate between perlite, which invariably appears in Naco valley collections as small flakes and nodules, and obsidian, the latter primarily taking the form of blades and the polyhedral cores from which they were struck. Technological analyses of chipped stone tools in all years adhered to the same procedures, employing nearly identical categories and distinctions. Information relating to implement forms and manufacture is hence directly comparable across the collections. Something of the nature of the obsidian sources used can be inferred by extrapolating from the X-ray diffraction results from Site PVN 306 and comparing them to the outcomes of visual assessments made at Site PVN 144. The ratio of obsidian to perlite at the former center can be roughly approximated by equating blades with obsidian and perlite with flakes and nodules (table 3.1), a correlation that holds true at every investigated Naco valley site of all periods, including Site PVN 144. There is no way at this point to reconstruct patterns of use for

TABLE 3.1 Observed distribution of lithic materials by excavated terminal debris and midden contexts

Structure/Subop.	Obsidian Blades	Obsidian Flakes	Obsidian Nodules	Obsidian Blade Cores	Chert Flakes	Chert Cores
306-8	3	6	—	—	4	—
306-11	1	—	—	—	—	—
306-17	1	—	—	—	—	—
306-20	13	14	—	1	—	—
306-21	3	1	—	—	5	2
306-72	—	4	—	—	1	—
306-78	—	1	—	—	—	—
306-79	16	17	—	—	2	—
306-83	60	63	2	1	5	—
306-86	—	1	—	—	—	—
306-123	3	—	—	—	—	—
306-124	1	3	—	—	—	—
306-125	4	7	—	—	4	—
306-128	11	9	—	—	1	—
306-130	1	11	—	—	—	—
306-164	12	—	—	1	—	—
306-174	—	1	—	—	—	—
Subop. 306AB/AD	49	23	—	1	4	—
Subop. 306AC/AE	77	28	—	—	12	—
Subop. 306AL/BQ	6	23	—	—	5	—
Subop. 306AR/BL	254	39	2	7	13	1
Subop. 306AX/BK	26	37	—	3	4	2
Subop. 306BF/BS	30	14	—	—	—	—
Subop. 306BI	47	—	—	2	3	1
Subop. 306BV	17	21	—	—	3	—

Notes: Projectile points made on blades were identified in material recovered from Str. 306-20 (1), Str. 306-79 (1), Subop. 306AC/AE (3), Subop. 306AR/BL (3), and Subop. 306BF/BS (1). They are included with the blade totals given above.

These figures are based on analyzed items, not extrapolations from processed materials.

lithics from the Site PVN 306 Roble phase assemblage, and this variable is not discussed further here.

Finally, available funds were not sufficient in 1988 and 1990 to hire enough trained laboratory assistants to process (count by material category) all of the items recovered during excavations at Site PVN 306. Consequently, only a sample of the collection units (lots) associated with particular middens and structures was processed during the 1988 and 1990 field seasons. We have therefore used a formula (summarized in table 3.2) to estimate the numbers of artifacts from different categories originally present in the sample. Although the accuracy of the specific numbers resulting from these computations is questionable, the general orders of magnitude they convey can be used with confidence in comparing overall patterns of material distribution.

ACTIVITY PATTERNING WITHIN AND AROUND THE EASTERN PRINCIPAL PLAZA

The EPP covers 67×70 m and is defined by thirteen structures ranging in height from those flush with modern ground surface to platforms rising to 1.33 m high. The area thus enclosed is largely devoid of visible construction save for an apparent surface-level building set west of the EPP's center (Str. 306-25) and what we originally supposed was a low terrace (Str. 306-7) fronting the northern line of edifices. Structure 306-25 was not investigated, and Str. 306-7 turned out, on excavation, to be part of a natural south-to-north ascent unmodified by construction. Fully eight of the structures delimiting the plaza were excavated: three along the plaza's northern line (Strs. 306-8, 306-11, and 306-22), one on the west (Str. 306-21), both of the buildings that define the patio's southern margin (Strs. 306-124 and 306-125), and two on the east (Strs. 306-123 and 128). Digging in each case was largely restricted to narrow (1-m-wide) trenches that intersected architecture. Consequently, activity inferences are based primarily on artifact distributions supplemented by what can be discerned of construction features (table 3.2).

North Side of the EPP

Structure 306-8 is a low, stone-faced platform situated in the approximate center of a line of three comparably modest edifices that define the north side of the eastern principal plaza. The edifice, built over a natural south-to-north ascent, covers 5.97 m north-south, is oriented 80 degrees, and stands 0.24 m high on the north and 0.5 m tall on the south. Structure 306-8 is fronted by one stone-faced terrace each on the north and the south measuring 1.38 m and 0.88 m across, respectively. These terraces give way to a 0.12-m-high rock-faced ascent that demarcates the stone-paved summit. The latter area measures 3.71 m north-south and bears no signs of additional architecture.

A 1×2 m trench was sunk off the back (north) side of Str. 306-8 in search of materials associated with the use of that edifice. The slightly denser concentration

Table 3.2 Density of recovered materials per excavated square meters

Structure/Subop.	Pottery Sherds	Incensarios	Chipped Stone	Shell/Bone	Ground Stone	Bajareque	Other Items
306-8	46.4	0.1	1.6	0/0.1	—	0.1	—
306-11	30.0	0.4	1.0	0/0.2	—	3.7	—
306-15	20.6	0.8	1.5	0/6.1	—	—	0.8 fig
306-17	3.0	0.07	0.6	0/0.5	—	—	—
306-19	5.1	—	0.07	—	—	—	—
306-20	25.6	0.2	4.0	0.3/2.8	—	—	—
306-21	24.3	—	1.7	0/0.08	—	0.3	0.08 sw
306-22	32.7	—	2.3	—	—	—	0.7 ws
306-72	5.0	—	1.3	—	—	—	0.3 sw
306-78	1.2	0.6	0.2	—	—	—	—
306-79	22.0	0.1	2.3	3.4/0.1	0.03	0.3	—
306-83	219.6	1.7	10.5	35.4/10.6	—	0.06	—
306-86	36.6	7.9	2.0	0.1/3.9	—	—	0.1 ss
306-123	148.4	0.3	1.0	—	—	0.8	0.6 cu
306-124	13.5	—	0.8	0.5/0	—	—	—
306-125	63.0	0.6	1.1	—	—	0.5	—
306-128	169.9	0.4	2.3	—	—	1.0	—
306-130	96.6	0.2	4.4	—	—	0.2	—
306-164	487.3	2.4	8.4	26.9/15.9	—	0.4	—

306-174	6.9	—	1.1	—	—	—	—
306-182	116.3	4.4	1.6	—	—	0.4	—
East Plaza Tests	11.5	—	3.4	—	—	—	—
306AB/AD	1,114.2	3.1	86.2	5,696/100	3.1	0.4	0.4 sd, 2.7 sw, 0.9 fig
306AC/AE	818.7	1.3	70.2	6,448/160	0.4	—	2.7 gs; 1.3 fig
306AL/BQ	521.8	3.1	18.7	772/8	5.3	—	0.4 fig
306AR/BL	692.0	1.9	16.1	7,524/204	—	1.3	0.1 bead, 0.6 gs, 0.3 fig, 0.1 pot. mold
306AX/BK	1,113.3	1.3	299.1	5,696/168	—	1.8	0.4 gs, 0.4 sw
306BF/BS	274.7	3.1	30.2	1,780/44	—	—	—
306BI	205.5	1	26.5	495.5/11.0	—	—	1 fig
306BV	346.0	2.5	21.5	0/0.5	—	0.5	—
306CA/36	416.8	1.6	12.0	0.8/1.6	—	1.6	—

Key:

cu.: copper; fig: ceramic figurine; gs: grooved ceramic sphere; pot. mold: pottery mold; sd: sherd disk; ss: stone sphere; sw: spindle whorl; ws: worked sherd

Estimates for shell and bone in those middens where a 0.5 × 0.5 m control probe was dug are based on the results of that sample.

These figures are estimated using the following calculation:

Processed T = T (processed lots/all terminal debris lots)

In other words, the total recorded for an artifact class from the processed lots is equal to the estimated total (T) of all artifacts of that category times the number of processed lots divided by the total number of terminal debris lots defined for an excavation. For example:

300 sherds = T (10 processed lots / 20 total lots)

300 (20/10) = T

600 = T

This assumes that artifacts are fairly evenly distributed across all excavated terminal debris lots. Such an assumption may be valid for relatively common artifacts (especially pottery sherds, shell, and chipped stone) but is more problematic for rarer items (such as incensarios and ground stone).

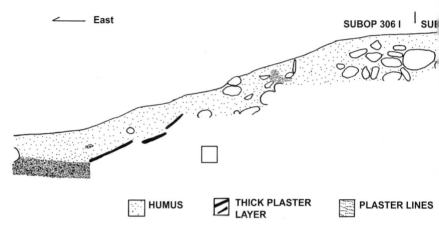

FIGURE 3.3 *Structure 306-21, section*

of artifacts found here implies that debris associated with Str. 306-8 likely accumulated on the platform's non–plaza-facing side. The figures given for Str. 306-8 in table 3.2 include items retrieved from the northern probe.

Structure 306-11, an approximately 1.2-m-high platform, is 3 m east of Str. 306-8 and closes off the northeast corner of the EPP. The limited portion of this edifice's southern (patio-facing) flank revealed in our excavations consists of a 0.57-m-high stone-faced terrace oriented 270 degrees and backed by a dense packing of cobble fill. This surface was likely covered with earth. Based on surface indications, the aforementioned terrace was probably succeeded on the south by at least one more riser leading up to the summit.

Structure 306-22 occupies the northwest corner of the EPP. It is built into low south-to-north and west-to-east natural ascents. Only a 1-m-wide segment of Str. 306-22's eastern basal facing was exposed, revealing a 0.2-m-high wall fashioned of river cobbles set on end and aligned 138 degrees. Based on surface indications, it is very probable that the platform never stood much higher than 0.2 m on this, its upslope eastern side.

West Side of the EPP

Structure 306-21 separates the eastern and western principal plazas. A trench dug across the platform running east-west revealed three construction stages, all dating to the Roble phase (figure 3.3). The earliest version (Str. 306-21-2nd) was, minimally, 0.5 m tall and capped by a white plaster surface that was refurbished at least three times. Only 0.9 m² of the summit was exposed,

VIEJO BRISAS DEL VALLE
PVN 306

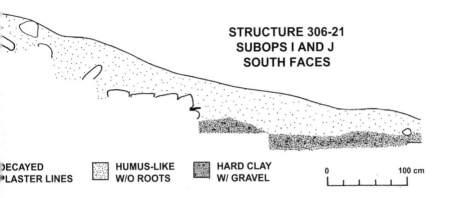

**STRUCTURE 306-21
SUBOPS I AND J
SOUTH FACES**

| | DECAYED PLASTER LINES | | HUMUS-LIKE W/O ROOTS | | HARD CLAY W/ GRAVEL | 0 | | 100 cm |

and the building's basal dimensions were not revealed. Construction of Str. 306-21-1st covered its predecessor, raising the platform's height to 0.88 m. The building now measured 8.15 m east-west, was oriented 178 degrees, and may have been as much as 23 m long north-south (the latter estimate is based solely on surface evidence). Two stone-faced terraces, 0.6 m and 1.2 m wide, respectively, ascend the building on the east and the west, giving way to the summit. The 1-m-wide swath of Str. 306-21-1st's superstructure that was exposed revealed a room surfaced with white plaster, open on the east overlooking the EPP, and backed on the west by a 0.2-m-high by 1-m-wide stone wall. The latter construction is sufficiently broad to have served as a support for a perishable upper wall and as a bench. The western basal terrace, facing Str. 306-19, 7 m to the west, is 1.2 m wide and surfaced with the only stone pavement known from the building. Its eastern counterpart is fronted by an earthen sloping zone capped with a 0.02-m-thick layer of white plaster. This construction rises 0.58 m over 1.16 m east to west, ascending at an angle of about 35 degrees. The final building episode attested to at Str. 306-21-1st involved raising the summit an additional 0.45 m. The new summit floor seems to have been surfaced with white plaster, although no additional signs of superstructure architecture were recognized.

East Side of the EPP

Structure 306-123 is the northern member of a pair of linked buildings that together close off the east side of the EPP (Str. 306-128 is its southern

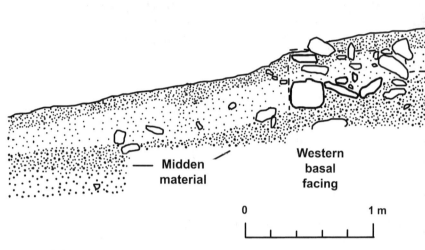

W mag

Midden material

Western basal facing

0   1 m

FIGURE 3.4 *Structure 306-128, section*

counterpart). On the surface, this edifice measures 20 m long north-south by 8 m across. Excavations here revealed a 0.64-m-high building fronted on the east and west by low (0.08- to 0.1-m-high) basal facings, made of unmodified stones, that are aligned 352 degrees. The western facing may be part of an out-set construction, possibly a staircase, that projects an undetermined distance west of the main body of the platform. The eastern terrace is 0.97 m wide and is surfaced with stone. A 0.58-m-high ascent to the summit rises above this pavement and was apparently fashioned of earth capped with a single course of unmodified rocks. Excavation across the summit for 2.02 m revealed a stone floor that apparently did not continue north beyond the limits of our trench. No other summit architecture was recorded in our restricted exposure of the summit.

Structure 306-128, Str. 306-123's southern neighbor, is built over a west-to-east rise, thus standing 0.46 m high on the west and 0.23 m tall on the east (figure 3.4). This platform measures 3.97 m east-west, is oriented 350 degrees, and—based on surface evidence—is approximately 31 m long. The summit was reached by a single ascent on the east and west. Remnants of three rooms that comprised part of Structure 306-128's superstructure were partially exposed. These compartments are defined by stone foundations 0.14–0.26 m wide by 0.5 m high. The northernmost enclosure revealed in our excavations

VIEJO BRISAS DEL VALLE
PVN 306
STRUCTURE 306-128
SUBOP AJ SOUTH FACE

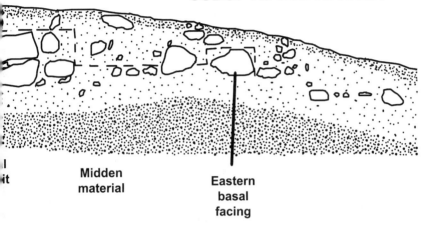

Midden material

Eastern basal facing

covers at least 2.75×3.02 m and is surfaced with stone. Immediately south of this room are two earthen-floored compartments set in an east-west line. The western example is 0.5 m wide east-west, while its eastern neighbor measures 1.67 m across. No built-in furniture was recorded in any of these enclosures.

South Side of the EPP

Neighboring Strs. 306-124 and 306-125 are 1 m apart and bound the EPP's southern flank. Moving from east to west, Str. 306-124 is a 0.36-m-high platform ascended from the north, patio-facing side by two low risers oriented 270 degrees. This dyad's basal element is 0.13 m high and consists of earth capped by a single line of stones. This element gives way after 0.2 m to a 0.23-m-tall stone facing backed on the south by a rock pavement that runs for at least 1.59 m (the summit's southern edge was not exposed). There are no signs of superstructure construction in the small portion of the summit we uncovered; nor were any pieces of *bajareque* (burned fragments of clay walls) found on or near the building. Fronting the edifice on the north is a stone floor that projects 1.7 m into the EPP. Overall, Str. 306-124 was a low platform, the stone-surfaced summit of which was left open at least on the side overlooking the plaza.

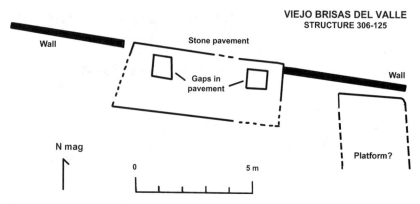

FIGURE 3.5 *Structure 306-125, plan*

More extensive clearing of Str. 306-125 (37 m² exposed) revealed a sur-face-level building covering 17 m east-west by 2.6 m north-south (figure 3.5). Most of the edifice was taken up by a stone floor, encompassing 2.6 × 6.5 m, into which two square features open to the underlying earth are set. These entities are 3.2 m apart east and west of Str. 306-125's center line and measure 0.8 × 0.9 m and 0.86 × 0.9 m, respectively. Excavation into the eastern square revealed that it was 0.08 m deep and had no formal floor. Flanking the central pavement on the east and west, and more or less even with the northern line of that floor, are two 0.19-m-high stone walls that average 0.2 m wide. These constructions extend 5.2 m east and 4.9 m west of the pavement and may have been footings for perishable upper constructions; there is no evidence that they are parts of platform facings. Whereas the western wall stops 0.35 m shy of the stone floor, its eastern analog intersects that surface 0.35 m south of its north-east corner. Located at the eastern end of the east wall and 0.42 m south of it is a 0.48-m-high stone wall. This entity seemingly defines the northern limit of a small platform 2.85 m wide east-west by at least 3.22 m long north-south (the southern facing was not encountered). Excavations were not carried far enough to see if a comparable platform was located in an analogous position south of the western wall.

In general, Str. 306-125 is a complex of at least one low platform and several surface-level constructions centered on an extensive stone surface and aligned 275 degrees. If the walls flanking the pavement on the east and west supported upper constructions, then this grouping of architectural units may have combined both spaces open to public view (i.e., the central paved area) and those to which access was blocked, at least from the plaza (i.e., east and west of the stone surface behind the aforementioned footings).

Testing in the EPP

Eight test pits were dug in three east-west lines, spaced 15 m apart, within the EPP in areas devoid of surface-visible architecture. These probes were designed to search for the existence of a plaza floor, as well as remnants from any activities performed away from physically salient constructions. No formalized surface was recorded, and no cultural remains of any sort were much in evidence. Densities of ceramics were very low, although the figures for chipped lithics were relatively high. The latter finding may point to the conduct of activities involving these tools within the plaza or, just as likely, could reflect the vagaries of sampling error. At the very least, it appears that the EPP was kept largely free of debris during its use-life.

Summary

The EPP was apparently home to several networks: those localized within specific houses erected on its north, east, and west margins and a household that incorporated these residents within a larger web focused on the central plaza. The house-based nets were created on a daily basis by members' regular interaction in the course of their coordinated pursuit of domestic tasks involving moderate to large quantities of ceramics and chipped lithics (table 3.2). The preponderance of ceramics at Structures 306-123 and 306-128 (148.4 and 169.9 pieces/excavated m^2 [p/em^2], respectively) hints at a focus here on behaviors in which pottery serving and storage vessels played significant parts. It is possible that differences in the frequencies of jars and bowls in the small analyzed samples signal a greater emphasis on storing comestibles among the northern buildings and on serving food and liquid along the plaza's eastern flank (table 3.3). Ritual activity, signaled by the distribution of incense burners, was seemingly conducted at low levels of intensity in most of these residences save Str. 306-21, where no such objects were identified. Food processing, especially of meat, as well as consumption apparently occurred on and around Strs. 306-8, 306-11, and 306-21 but not at Strs. 306-123 and 306-128.

The fact that residents of these houses were incorporated into a household is indicated by the mutual arrangement of their domiciles around a central plaza. Proximity ensured daily interactions among participants in the oft-repeated enactment of the same round of activities that employed identical elements of material culture. These connections among household members may have been reinforced through activities conducted in special-purpose buildings. Structures 306-22 (on the north) and 306-124 and 306-125 (on the south) share two features: they lack clear signs of domestic activity and were open to view from the plaza. The actions that transpired within these settings are unclear. Still, whatever they were was meant to be viewed primarily, perhaps

TABLE 3.3 Bowl/jar percentage distributions from Roble phase contexts at Site PVN 306

Structure/Subop.	Bowls	Jars	Total Rim Sample
Str. 306-8	33	67	9
Str. 306-11	0	100	3
Str. 306-15	100	0	1
Str. 306-17	100	0	2
Str. 306-20	100	0	8
Str. 306-79	23	77	13
Str. 306-83	85	15	128
Str. 306-86	43	57	14
Str. 306-123	52	58	23
Str. 306-124	100	0	3
Str. 306-125	67	33	6
Str. 306-128	100	0	2
Str. 306-130	25	75	4
Str. 306-164	79	21	207
Str. 306-182	50	50	4
Subop. 306AB/AD	78	22	253
Subop. 306AC/AE	75	25	48
Subop. 306AL/BQ	83	17	117
Subop. 306AR/BL	85	15	281
Subop. 306AX/BK	57	43	70
Subop. 306BF/BS	90	10	62
Subop. 306BI	71	29	75
Subop. 306BV	69	31	62
Subop. 306CA/36	90	10	48

exclusively, by those living within the EPP. This emphasis on household engagement in the actions staged in Strs. 306-22, 306-124, and 306-125 suggests that they constituted common projects, participation in which enhanced feelings of unity among those occupying the plaza and their sense of distinction from others residing elsewhere in the settlement.

ACTIVITIES WITHIN AND AROUND THE WESTERN PRINCIPAL PLAZA

The WPP is much smaller than its eastern analog, covering approximately 33 × 50 m. The ten buildings that delimit this space are generally modest in size, ranging from terraces around 0.2 m high on the north to Str. 306-21, which stands 1.33 m tall, on the plaza's east flank. Six areas identified as structures from surface remains were excavated here: Strs. 306-19, 306-20, and 306-174 within the plaza; Str. 306-17 on the WPP's south margin; Str. 306-182 on the plaza's west edge; and Str. 306-83, 10 m southwest of Str. 306-17 off the WPP's southwest corner. Structures 306-83 and 306-182 turned out, when cleared, to be trash deposits produced by activities conducted within the WPP and not on and around any specific building. The descriptions in this section are organized by structure, followed by a synopsis of the material derived from the two trash deposits.

Structure 306-17, together with Str. 306-18, 4 m to the east, defines the southern limit of the WPP. This round platform was ascended by three stone-faced and stone-surfaced terraces rising 1.03 m to the stone-paved summit (figure 3.6). An earthen sloping zone, capped by a 0.01-m-thick layer of white plaster, blankets the basal riser (figure 3.7). It is canted up at an angle of roughly 45 degrees, extends 0.45 m beyond the basal terrace, and runs up to and abuts the second ascending terrace. A staircase set flush with the building's basal line occupies most of Str. 306-17's northeast quadrant facing toward Str. 306-19, 12 m distant within the plaza (figure 3.8). The staircase consists of three stone-faced and stone-surfaced steps and narrows from 2.58 m across at the base to 1.52 m at the point where it intersects the summit. The latter surface, together with most of the building's south side, was heavily disturbed by looting prior to investigation in 1988. Based on the surviving evidence, we infer that Str. 306-17 had a diameter of 8 m and an open summit unencumbered by foundation walls and built-in furniture. The one item that might have originally stood here was a carved stone monument found lying facedown on the aforementioned floor (figure 3.9).

Near the end of its use-life, the basal sloping zone was covered by an apron composed of schist slabs blanketed by a thin coating of white plaster. This addition slopes up at an angle of 30 degrees, covering the first basal terrace and abutting the second ascending terrace. Passage over the renovated sloping zone was then negotiated by stepping on a 0.2-m-high unmodified stone set in line with the northeast stairs and projecting 0.47 m north of the apron.

Structure 306-19 occupies a position slightly south and east of the WPP's center, about 20 m south of Str. 306-20. Excavations here revealed at least three construction phases, each of which yielded a distinctive building form unmatched in the known architectural corpus for Site PVN 306 (figure 3.10). The initial version consists of a small central platform measuring 1.65 m on a side and standing 0.62 m high. The diminutive earthen-floored summit is bounded by a 0.1-m-high cobble wall but is otherwise featureless. Eight stone-faced, white-plastered arms project in pairs 1.1–1.2 m from each side of the

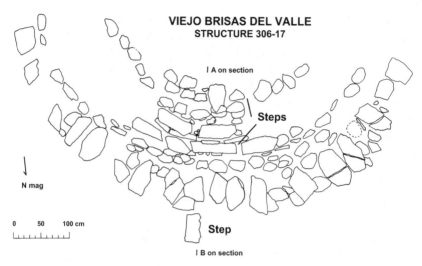

FIGURE 3.6 *Structure 306-17, plan*

core (figure 3.11). These arms are 0.6–0.76 m high by 0.47–0.64 m wide and are separated by 0.85–0.95 m. The resulting structure is roughly circular and has a diameter of 3.5 m.

During the next phase, the core platform was raised to 0.8 m high and somewhat enlarged, now measuring 1.65 m × 1.88 m. The summit was still delimited by a low stone wall, although that wall now stood 0.3 m tall. Located in the center of this space is a pit measuring 0.2 × 0.51 m and at least 0.46 m deep. This declivity is bounded on the south and the east by three large rocks and may have been a socket designed to hold the base of a monument, although no sign of one was found on Str. 306-19. The pairs of adjoining arms on each side of the core were now linked, thus transforming eight narrow spokes into four broader ones. The construction joining each pair stood 0.4 m high, thus leaving the original arms protruding about 0.2 m above the additions. The enlarged spokes were blanketed with white plaster, some sections of which were refurbished at least five times. Structure 306-19 retained its original diameter of 3.5 m.

The core platform was apparently not modified during the final building episode, and the spokes projecting from it were little altered. The principal change involved the addition of an earthen construction that extended 1.7–2.7 m out and away from the edifice's perimeter. This new element was capped by plaster and sloped up toward the projecting spokes (figure 3.12). At first, those spokes probably continued to rise as much as 0.5 m above the surrounding apron. As more plaster levels were added during subsequent resurfacings (36

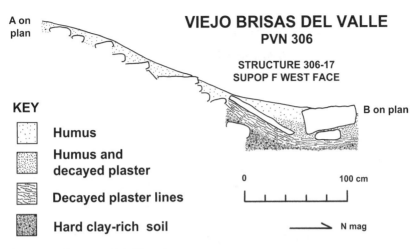

FIGURE 3.7 *Structure 306-17, section*

FIGURE 3.8 *Structure 306-17, photograph of the northern steps and bordering terraces*

separate layers were counted in one well-preserved location), only 0.34 m of the original eastern arm could still be seen, and the southern spoke no longer protruded above the addition. Two stone steps were built atop the plaster-coated apron against Str. 306-19's southeast face, apparently providing a way to access the summit over the addition. These steps narrow from their base as

63

VIEJO BRISAS DEL VALLE
MONUMENT 306-1

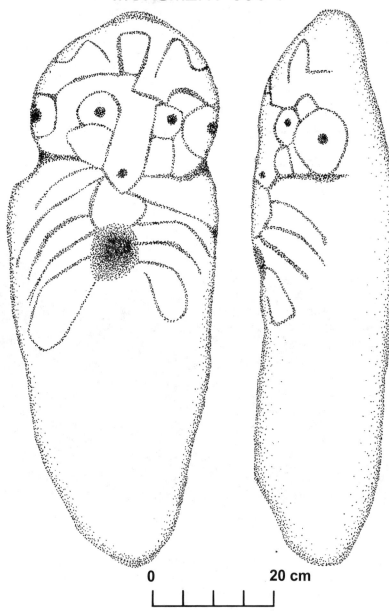

0   20 cm

FIGURE 3.9 *Monument 1; found atop Structure 306-17*

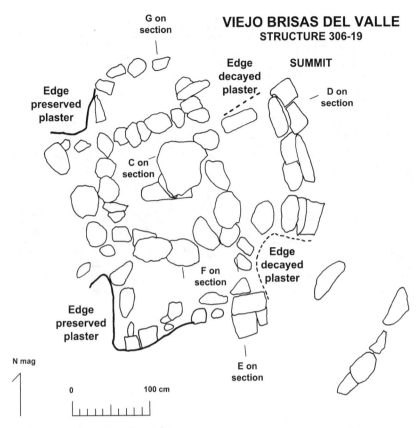

FIGURE 3.10 *Structure 306-19, plan*

they ascend the building; the lowest course is 1.5 m long, while the second ascending riser covers 0.57 m. One consequence of the transformations visited on Str. 306-19 was to convert it into a roughly oval construction, the perimeter of which defines a space measuring 6.9 m × 9.9 m.

The forms assumed by Strs. 306-17 and 306-19 in their various iterations stand out from the corpus of known Roble phase architecture in the Naco valley. Both are circular to oval in shape and lack clear signs of substantial superstructure architecture. Structures 306-17 and 306-19 also share a marked paucity of associated remains. The frequency of artifacts in each case is among the lowest recorded at Site PVN 306, suggesting that both buildings were kept fairly clean during their use-lives. It is very likely, in fact, that much of the debris encountered in Strs. 306-182 and 306-83 initially resulted from behaviors conducted on and around Strs. 306-17 and 306-19. This is especially the case for Str. 306-83, which lies immediately south of Str. 306-17.

FIGURE 3.11 *Structure 306-19, photograph showing the exposed terminus of one of the building's projecting spokes*

Structure 306-20 sits within the WPP. Unlike its southern neighbor, however, Str. 306-20 is a stone-faced, rectangular platform standing 0.6–0.91 m high, oriented 260 degrees, and covering 4.14 m (north-south) by 15.2 m (east-west; figure 3.13). The summit is demarcated on the north by a single steep ascent from the plaza, while on the south it is fronted by a 0.4-m-high stone-surfaced terrace. The latter construction measures 1.4 m across and was covered by a white plaster floor, the preserved remnants of which are 0.08 m thick. A 0.51-m-high stone-faced ascent rises above the southern terrace and leads to the earthen summit, which measures 1.76 m north-south. There was no evidence of stone foundations or other superstructure architecture within the 1-m-wide swath we cut across the summit's approximate center. Although portions of the east and west basal facings were exposed, we did not pursue excavations far enough in these areas to determine how these walls related to the summit.

Structure 306-174 lies 12 m north of Str. 306-17 and about the same distance west of Str. 306-19 within the WPP. It appeared on the surface to be a roughly circular rock concentration set flush with the plaza and measuring 2 m in diameter. Limited excavations here revealed a loose concentration of stones covering 2.9 m east-west and extending no more than 0.35 m below modern ground level. Structure 306-174's behavioral significance is unclear;

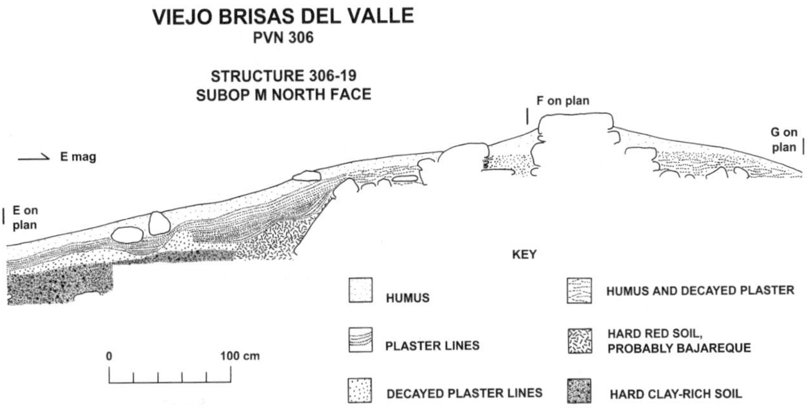

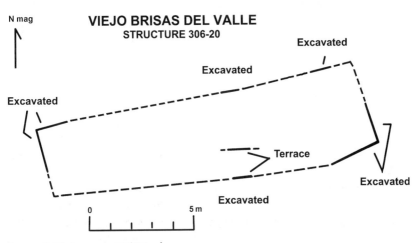

VIEJO BRISAS DEL VALLE
PVN 306

STRUCTURE 306-19
SUBOP M NORTH FACE

F on plan

G on plan

E mag

E on plan

KEY

☐ HUMUS

▦ HUMUS AND DECAYED PLASTER

▤ PLASTER LINES

▦ HARD RED SOIL, PROBABLY BAJAREQUE

▦ DECAYED PLASTER LINES

▦ HARD CLAY-RICH SOIL

0   100 cm

FIGURE 3.12 *Structure 306-19, section showing details of multiple plastering*

N mag

VIEJO BRISAS DEL VALLE
STRUCTURE 306-20

Excavated

Excavated

Excavated

Terrace

Excavated

Excavated

0   5 m

FIGURE 3.13 *Structure 306-20, plan*

it seems highly unlikely that its constituent rocks fell from other architecture (the closest of which is roughly 6 m distant) or arrived at their final resting place by natural means. Instead, Str. 306-174 was apparently a very casually built circular stone surface embedded within the ancient earthen plaza. Like Structures 306-17 and 306-19, this construction appears to have been regularly swept clean.

The Str. 306-182 midden is a 0.04- to 0.1-m-thick deposit of densely packed cultural material (figure 3.14). This lens extends for 2.52 m west, from near the edge of the plaza up onto the natural ascent that delimits the WPP on this side. The debris is unassociated with any known construction; it likely

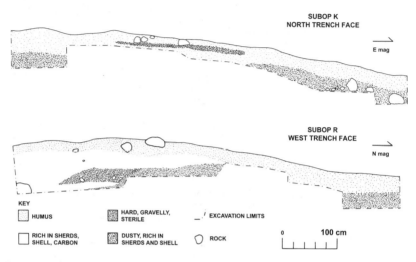

VIEJO BRISAS DEL VALLE
PVN 306

DOMESTIC DEBRIS
NOT ASSOCIATED
WITH PLATFORM CONSTRUCTION

SUBOP K
NORTH TRENCH FACE

E mag

SUBOP R
WEST TRENCH FACE

N mag

KEY

☐ HUMUS

▦ HARD, GRAVELLY, STERILE

_ _ ' EXCAVATION LIMITS

☐ RICH IN SHERDS, SHELL, CARBON

▨ DUSTY, RICH IN SHERDS AND SHELL

○ ROCK

0   100 cm

FIGURE 3.14 *Sections of the middens originally designated Structure 306-182 (Subop. 306K) and Structure 306-164 (Subop. 306R)*

contains material generated during the course of activities conducted in the WPP.

The density of pottery sherds in the Str. 306-182 trash deposit is particularly high (116.3 p/em²; table 3.2), exceeding the limits recorded at all other investigated locations in both principal plazas except Strs. 306-123 and 306-128 in the EPP. Unfortunately, the small sample size of form-classified rims does not provide a strong basis for inferring the activities in which these pottery containers were employed (table 3.3). The inferred frequency of incensario fragments (4.4 p/em²) is remarkably elevated and is unmatched in any of the other Roble phase analyzed collections at the center save that from Str. 306-86 (but see later discussion). The figures for chipped lithics fall toward the middle of the distribution for this artifact class as seen at other Site PVN 306 structures (1.6 p/em²). Interestingly, the complete absence of faunal remains bespeaks the relative unimportance of these food sources, or at least their processing, in the events from which this detritus was derived. The few fragments of *bajareque* included in the sample may point to the presence of perishable constructions within the plaza; alternatively, some elements of collapsed superstructures from the surrounding buildings may have inadvertently been swept up in the trash.

Structure 306-83 is another trash deposit, this one situated off the southwest corner of the WPP approximately 10 m southwest of Structure 306-17. The Structure 306-83 trash covers 22.57 m east-west by at least 16.1 m north-south and is 0.09–0.5 m thick, thinning out to the south and east from its approximate center. As discussed earlier, given that "Str. 306-83" is not associated with any known building and adjoins the WPP's southwest corner, the detritus recorded here likely resulted from activities conducted within that plaza.

The Str. 306-83 trash is distinguished by high concentrations of ceramics and chipped lithics (219.6 p/em^2 and 10.5 p/em^2, respectively; table 3.3), both of which exceed even the densest concentrations of these materials recorded in either of the principal plazas. In fact, the figures for ceramic fragments coincide with the low end of density measures for middens located outside the architectural core. Incensario pieces are relatively common here (1.7 p/em^2), exceeding concentrations everywhere in the EPP and WPP except those attested to at Str. 306-182. Unlike the latter trash deposit, however, excavations at Str. 306-83 yielded relatively large quantities of faunal bones and shell (10.6 p/em^2 and 35.4 p/em^2, in turn). These latter measures are the highest obtained within principal plaza contexts. The few *bajareque* pieces identified in the Str. 306-83 materials may have been derived from perishable buildings within the plaza or from superstructures originally perched atop platforms that define the WPP.

The contents of the Str. 306-83 trash deposit point to the processing and consumption of fairly large quantities of comestibles within the WPP. The vast majority of the form-classified pottery rims were derived from bowls (85%, N=128), implying that serving food and drink was a major component of the behaviors pursued in the adjacent plaza (table 3.3). The retrieval of substantial quantities of shell and animal bones amplifies this picture somewhat, suggesting that some extraction of meat from these sources also took place in or near the WPP. The absence of grinding implements within the assemblage, however, indicates that the preparation of grain for consumption almost certainly occurred elsewhere. The analyzed segment of the lithic assemblage is about evenly divided between obsidian blades and flakes, the latter probably of perlite (60 blades, 63 flakes; table 3.1). Some of these tools may have been fashioned in the plaza; identified in the assemblage were one polyhedral core and two nodules, probably of perlite, the latter likely used in fabricating casual flake implements using the direct percussion method. It appears, based on the information gleaned from these analyses, that the WPP served as a focus for gatherings in which sizable quantities of food were processed and consumed. During these events stone tools were also fashioned, possibly in support of the food-processing tasks noted earlier. Religious paraphernalia, in the form of incense burners, was well represented, suggesting that the aforementioned prosaic activities occurred in association with those devoted to propitiating and celebrating sacred forces.

Summary

The WPP is distinguished from its eastern neighbor by the relative absence of residential constructions and a proliferation of special-purpose architecture. Structures 306-17, 306-19, and 306-174 all exhibit unusual circular to oval forms and yielded very few artifacts of any sort. This combination of features implies that these edifices were not domiciles but were kept especially clean and reserved for activities that fell outside the norm of daily prosaic chores. The nature of these behaviors is indicated by the trash deposits associated with the WPP (Strs. 306-83 and 306-182). Both of these debris collections are characterized by relatively high concentrations of incensario fragments, suggesting that religious observances were an important element in the activities pursued within the WPP. More prosaic tasks, involving the use of large quantities of chipped stone and ceramic containers, were also pursued here. The preponderance of bowls within the relatively large collection of form-coded rims from Str. 306-83 points to the significance of food serving in this round of behaviors. The Str. 306-83 trash also indicates that meat was processed to some degree within the plaza, possibly using stone implements knapped in that same area. Structures 306-17, 306-19, and 306-174, therefore, as well as their immediate environs, were seemingly foci for large-scale feasts and religious observances. Unlike the EPP, which was primarily devoted to residential tasks, the WPP was a place of gatherings in which most of Site PVN 306's population took part. The relative ease with which the WPP could be entered along its north, west, and south flanks supports this view.

The array and frequency of cultural materials found in the course of excavating Str. 306-20 differ significantly from the patterns recorded for Strs. 306-17, 306-19, and 306-174. Here, the density of ceramic fragments is far higher (25.6 p/em^2), falling easily within the range identified for the putative residences that define the EPP. All of the eight form-classified rims are from bowls, providing tentative evidence that most of the vessels used here were employed in serving comestibles. Similarly, pieces of incense burners (0.2 p/em^2) are comparable in frequency to those identified for the EPP's domiciles. The retrieval of shell and faunal remains also points to the processing and consumption of at least some food here, although the absence of grinding implements does not support the preparation of grain at the edifice. Chipped lithics are unusually well represented at Str. 306-20 (4 p/em^2), registering some of the highest densities outside midden contexts at Site PVN 306. Examples of the obsidian blade core industry are well represented here (13 blades and 1 polyhedral core fragment; table 3.1). The remaining fourteen items are flakes, probably of perlite. At the very least, it is clear that Str. 306-20 was not kept nearly as clean as were Strs. 306-17 and 306-19.

Structure 306-20 might have been a residence in which domestic activities involving pottery containers, incensarios, and meat derived from animals and snails were pursued at moderately low levels of intensity. The building's location within the WPP is at odds with such a view, however. In fact, much of the debris found around Str. 306-20 might have resulted from activities conducted in the surrounding plaza and not specifically on the edifice itself. The materials recovered while clearing the platform generally match those found in the Str. 306-83 debris, including one polyhedral obsidian core and an elevated density of chipped stone tools for a main plaza context. It is possible, therefore, that the Str. 306-20 materials constitute detritus from behaviors enacted in the WPP that was never swept up and jettisoned off the plaza's southwest corner.

Taking these factors into account, we do not believe Str. 306-20 was a residence. Instead, it may have been a community building analogous to Strs. 144-8 and 144-18, which were also associated with a locale that hosted large gatherings (see chapter 4). Whatever might have transpired in Str. 306-20, its location within the WPP strongly implicates it and the behaviors it housed with the activities enacted in that extensive open space.

Contrasts in the contents of the Str. 306-83 and Str. 306-182 deposits deserve further attention. Whereas both contain large quantities of ceramic and incensario pieces, the latter has much higher densities of incense burner fragments, whereas the former yielded shell and animal bones completely absent in the Str. 306-182 materials. It would appear that trash generated by activities conducted in the WPP was segregated; that is, material deposited on the plaza's west margin was largely free of organics but high in ritual paraphernalia, whereas detritus jettisoned beyond the plaza was much richer in faunal remains but somewhat poorer in objects used in religious devotions. The significance of this discrepancy is unclear. The western edge of the plaza may have been associated with the sacred and thus been seen as a place where items linked to that realm could be disposed of appropriately. The contents of the Str. 144-19 deposit on the western edge of that site's main plaza (see chapter 4) follow the same pattern, as does the location of ritual venues west of the EPP at Site PVN 306. Debris more closely tied to the prosaic realm, such as shell and animal bones, might have been viewed as potentially contaminating the sacred domain if included with ritual items. Whatever the fate of these interpretations, the distinctions between the Strs. 306-83 and 306-182 deposits may suggest that "trash" continued to have cultural significance even after its deposition.

ACTIVITY PATTERNING SOUTH OF THE PRINCIPAL PLAZAS

This area is characterized by a fairly dense concentration of irregularly arranged buildings that lack clear patio foci or any signs of mutual orientation. Three constructions were investigated here, Strs. 306-72, 306-78, and 306-86, none of which was sufficiently well preserved to warrant horizontal clearing. One midden was also investigated (Subop. 306AL/BQ).

Architectural Excavations

Structure 306-72, approximately 160 m south/southeast of the EPP, is located in the midst of four neighboring buildings that average 3.5 m apart. The platform measures 1.64 m north-south, stands 0.37 m tall, and consists of a stone hearting bounded by casually fashioned rock facings. The earthen-floored summit shows no evidence of superstructure construction.

Structure 306-78 is approximately 46 m north of Str. 306-72. As with its southern counterpart, Str. 306-78 sits near the center of a concentration of buildings that lack any apparent formal organization. The nearest constructions are 5 m and 3 m to the west and the east, respectively. Structure 306-78 rises 0.54–0.61 m, covers 2.76 m east-west, and has an apparently featureless earthen summit. The stone hearting is retained by casually fashioned rock facings that rise directly to the summit. No clear orientation could be discerned from the poorly preserved remains of either Str. 306-72 or 306-78.

Structures 306-72 and 306-78 share generally similar, if indistinct, architectural forms and yielded comparably small numbers of cultural materials (table 3.2). They each, for example, are characterized by some of the lowest densities of ceramics recorded anywhere at Site PVN 306 (5 p/em^2 and 1.2 p/em^2, respectively). Organic remains, specifically shell and animal bones, were also not recorded here, nor were fragments of wattle-and-daub. Excavations at Str. 306-78 did encounter some pieces of incense burners (0.6 p/em^2), although their density did not exceed measures noted at most other constructions within the settlement; no such objects were found at Str. 306-72. Chipped lithics are relatively rare at the two buildings, comprising 1.3 p/em^2 at Str. 306-72 and 0.2 p/em^2 at Str. 306-78. Overall, the paucity of material remains noted for these buildings matches most closely the pattern recorded for Strs. 306-17, 306-19, and 306-174 in the WPP. What little can be discerned concerning the forms of these edifices does not, however, replicate the distinctive appearances of the last three edifices. Structures 306-72 and 306-78, therefore, stand out in their form and artifact patterning from all other recorded Roble phase constructions at the center, but whatever purposes they served are maddeningly vague. They may represent ritual foci analogous to their equally clean WPP counterparts. The apparent open nature of their summits (tentatively supported by the absence of *bajareque* in the collections), taken together with the substantial appearance of both buildings (as measured by local standards), weakly supports such a view.

Structure 306-86 is about 120 m west of Str. 306-78 and 98 m south of Str. 306-17 in the WPP. This building is near the middle of a set of constructions that form a rough northwest-southeast–trending line extending over approximately 130 m. Excavations here revealed a poorly preserved platform that stood 0.3–0.43 m high and covered 3.72 m east-west; surviving constructions were not sufficiently preserved to infer their orientations. Single basal facings fashioned of unmodified stones rise directly to the earthen-floored summit, which lacks any signs of superstructure architecture in the 1-m-wide area exposed that runs across the summit's full east-west extent. A complete incensario, lying facedown, and a stone sphere measuring 0.1 m in diameter were found within 0.1 m of each other—3.22 m east of, and 0.54 m downslope from, Str. 306-86 (figure 3.15). These items were apparently recovered where they were originally left sitting on ancient ground surface and are not parts of a trash deposit.

What we can discern of Str. 306-86's architecture is not diagnostic of the uses to which it was put. Materials associated with the edifice, however, generally resemble in range and density those found at residences elsewhere throughout the settlement. This is especially the case for pottery sherds and chipped stone (36.6 p/em^2 and 2 p/em^2, in turn), with concentrations of both falling within the range identified at Strs. 306-8, 306-11, and 306-21. The distribution of form-codified rims within the small analyzed sample (N=14) suggests that these ceramic fragments were derived in roughly equal numbers from bowls and jars. Recovery of some shell and animal bones from Str. 306-86's environs also points to meat processing, albeit on a fairly small scale, in the immediate area. Structure 306-86's assemblage, however, is distinguished by its unusually high concentration of incensario fragments (7.9 p/em^2), which are nearly twice as common as in the next largest collection, Str. 306-182 in the WPP. Most of these pieces are from the one incense burner found lying east of the building. If this vessel is treated as one unit of measurement, then the density of incensario fragments is reduced to 0.7 p/em^2. Although this no longer represents the highest concentration of incense burner remains, the figure is still fairly substantial by the standards of Site PVN 306. The small stone sphere found near the aforementioned incensario also sets Structure 306-86's assemblage apart from others at the center. The behavioral significance of this locally unique artifact is unclear, although its close association with an incense burner in a seemingly undisturbed context points to its use as ritual paraphernalia.

Structure 306-86 may well have served as a residence, based on its general form and associated ceramics, lithics, and faunal remains. The unusually high

FIGURE 3.15 *Structure 306-86, photograph of the in situ deposit containing a nearly complete spiked incensario and stone sphere*

concentration of incense burner pieces near the building, especially the largely intact spiked incensario and stone ball, points to its occupants' conduct of religious observances at levels of intensity greater than those recorded elsewhere outside the WPP. These rites were possibly concentrated east of Str. 306-86.

Midden Excavations

Suboperation 306AL/BQ was dug across the approximate center of an artifact scatter situated approximately 65 m south of Str. 306-125, on the southern border of the EPP. This concentration occupies an area largely devoid of even the hint of surface-visible architecture, with the closest known building roughly 28 m to the south. Digging here revealed a pit, measuring 2.94 m across by 0.59 m deep at its center, filled with a dense concentration of cultural material set in a fine-grained, dark gray soil (figure 3.16). The declivity's base is uneven, but the two exposed sides slope up smoothly and continuously.

The Subop. 306AL/BQ deposit yielded densities of ceramics that fall toward the lower end of the range defined for excavated middens beyond the site core (521.8 p/em²); recorded concentrations of chipped lithics here are also near the bottom of that continuum (18.7 p/em²; table 3.2). Concentrations of shell and animal bones, although high by the standards of principal plaza constructions and trash collections (780 p/em^2 altogether), are again near the tail end of the distribution for middens situated outside the WPP and the EPP. Incensarios (3.1 p/em^2) and ground stone implements (5.3 p/em^2), on the other hand, are more common in the Subop. 306AL/BQ assemblage than is the case in all but the Subop. 306AB/AD trash deposit north of the site core.

The materials retrieved from the Subop. 306AL/BQ trash pit reflect the practice of a wide array of activities in the immediate area at moderately high levels of intensity. The preponderance of bowls among the form-classified rims in the collection suggests that most of the pottery vessels represented in the assemblage were used in food serving rather than storage (table 3.3). The grinding stones found here, along with fairly high concentrations of shell and bone, point to the processing nearby of at least some of the comestibles these bowls contained. Obsidian blades as well as more casually fashioned flakes of chert and, most likely, perlite were employed in some of these tasks (table 3.1). Percussion flakes dominate the chipped stone assemblage (82% of the analyzed collection, N=34), implying that these implements were better suited to the chores pursued in the area, that those conducting such tasks did not have easy access to blades, or both. The relatively high concentration of incense burner pieces in the assemblage hints at the importance of religious observances in the activities pursued nearby. This view is supported by the recovery in Subop. 306AL/BQ of one of the few, and among the largest, ceramic figurines recovered from the settlement. Insofar as these distinctive human effigies were used in rituals, the item found here points to the conduct of religious observances that employed a relatively diverse array of ritual items.

Summary

Excavations conducted south of the principal plazas indicate the presence of at least one residence (Str. 306-86) and three possible ritual foci (Strs. 306-72, 306-78, and, more certainly, an area immediately east of Str. 306-86). The one trash deposit excavated here (Subop. 306AL/BQ) also yielded a locally high concentration of ritual paraphernalia in the form of incense burners and a fired clay figurine. The evidence pointing to religious activity in southern Site PVN 306 is less clear than it was in the WPP. Taken together, however, data in hand suggest that at least some areas south of the site core served as venues for the conduct of rites at variable scales. The contents of the Subop. 306AL/BQ trash pit may even point to the enactment of some of these observances within the context of feasts. The high proportion of bowls, likely used in food serving, among the form-coded pottery rims from the Subop. 306AL/BQ assemblage tentatively suggests such an interpretation, as does the presence of

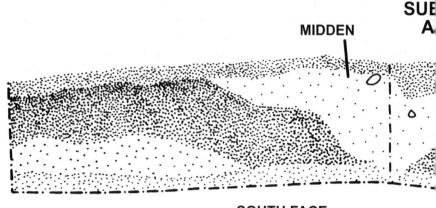

MIDDEN

SUE
A

SOUTH FACE

VIEJO BRISAS DEL VALLE
PVN 306

FIGURE **3.16** *Section through the Subop. 306AL/BQ midden*

food-processing equipment and faunal remains in this collection. There may have been several centers for celebrations of the sacred at Roble phase Site PVN 306, intermingled among which were houses of various sizes.

ACTIVITY PATTERNING WEST OF THE PRINCIPAL PLAZAS

Construction here is widely and fairly evenly dispersed, with no obvious patio groups. The two Roble phase edifices investigated in this zone are Strs. 306-15 and 306-79, while one midden was excavated as part of Subop. 306BV.

Architectural Excavation

Structure 306-15 is approximately 10 m northwest of Str. 306-182 and an equivalent distance off the northwest corner of the WPP. Excavation here revealed a 1-m-wide swath of the building's south facing. This stone wall, oriented 84 degrees, is 0.21 m high by 0.97 m wide and either retains the hearting of a low platform or is the foundation delimiting the perimeter of a surface-level building; surface indications tend to favor the latter interpretation.

Not enough of Str. 306-15 was exposed to permit inferences of activity patterning based on its architecture. Similarly, the paltry numbers of artifacts

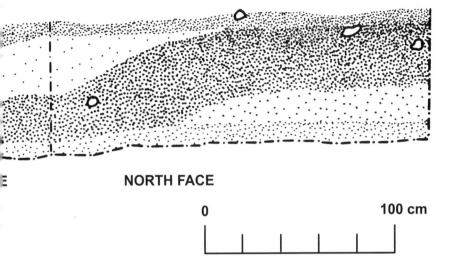

NORTH FACE

0   100 cm

analyzed from this building do not provide a strong basis for advancing arguments concerning the construction's use (table 3.2). The extrapolations of artifact diversity and density presented in table 3.2 are founded on a very small sample, the representativeness of which is uncertain. Bearing that caveat in mind, it is interesting that Str. 306-15 yielded significant quantities of ritual gear in the form of at least two incensario fragments and one figurine. The densities of these objects presented in table 3.2 must be treated with a good deal of caution. Still, given the relative rarity of such items in most Site PVN 306 assemblages, their presence in the small studied collection associated with Str. 306-15 very tentatively suggests that the building served as a venue for religious devotions possibly conducted at levels of intensity that exceeded those observed in most other parts of the settlement. This edifice, and its associated activities, may represent a westward extension of the rites conducted within the WPP.

Structure 306-79 lies roughly 50 m west/southwest of the WPP in an area largely devoid of contemporary architecture; the closest recognized constructions are 20 m to the north and 40 m to the east. Structure 306-79 is a stone-faced platform standing 0.27–0.34 m high, oriented 265 degrees, and measuring 4.8 m × 14.75 m (figure 3.17). The summit covers an estimated 70.8 m², was seemingly paved with a layer of small stones, but lacked clear evidence of a superstructure. The retrieval of wattle-and-daub fragments from the building's

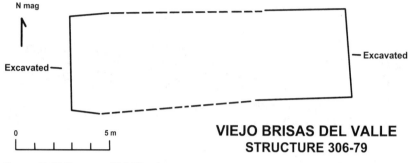

VIEJO BRISAS DEL VALLE
STRUCTURE 306-79

FIGURE 3.17 *Structure 306-79, plan*

environs may point to the former existence of a perishable building set atop the platform, albeit one without clear stone foundations.

The array and density of cultural materials retrieved during the investigation of Str. 306-79 suggest that it served as a fairly substantial residence. The density of ceramics is on the low end for domiciles at Site PVN 306 (22 p/em^2), although far greater than the systematically cleaned surfaces and environs of what were arguably ritual constructions (such as Strs. 306-17, 306-19, and 306-174 in the WPP; table 3.2). Jars dominate the small sample of pottery rims identified as to form (table 3.3). If this pattern is representative of vessel categories in the overall collection, it would suggest that storage, rather than serving, of food and drink dominated the uses to which vessels were put at this edifice. The recovery of one grinding implement along with moderately dense concentrations of faunal remains (mostly *Pachychilus* sp. shells, 3.4 p/em^2) implies that a diverse array of food was processed at this building. The density of chipped stone falls toward the upper end of the observed range for residences at the center (2.3 p/em^2) and is composed in nearly equal parts of obsidian blades (16, of which one was converted into a projectile point) and flakes (19, two of chert and the rest probably derived from perlite; table 3.1). The low density of incensario pieces in the Str. 306-79 assemblage (0.1 p/em^2) closely parallels measures from other domiciles.

Structure 306-79, therefore, seems to have been a sizable residence at which a variety of domestic tasks (food processing, storage, some food serving) and ritual observances (represented by the few fragments of incense burners) were conducted. The latter rites were pursued at low levels of intensity.

Midden Excavations

Suboperation BV is a 1 m × 2 m trench dug into the estimated center of an artifact concentration located 10 m south of Str. 306-79 and about 75 m southwest of Str. 306-17 on the south edge of the WPP. Digging here confirmed the existence of a midden that, in this case, included a dense concentration of cultural debris set in sandy silt that grades from gray to tan with increasing depth. The deposit is 0.11–0.18 m thick and slopes up over the natural ascent of the land from west to east. A series of four test pits (each measuring 0.5 m on a side) was dug in a line extending 90 m southwest of Subop. 306BV to determine the extent of the midden (the latter tests are designated Subop. 306BZ). No signs of the trash deposit were encountered in these probes.

The range of cultural materials retrieved during the course of digging Subop. 306BV generally matches that found in other middens (table 3.2). The density of ceramic sherds (346 p/em^2), for example, falls toward the lower end of the continuum noted at excavated trash deposits outside the site core. As was the case in most Site PVN 306 Roble phase middens, the greater prevalence of bowls vis-à-vis jars in Subop. 306BV suggests that serving comestibles loomed larger than their storage in the activities pursued here (table 3.3). The chipped stone density is also near the bottom of the range for middens at the settlement (21.5 p/em^2), and, as was the case at Subop. 306AL/BQ, obsidian blades (17) are outnumbered by percussion flakes of chert (3) and what is likely perlite (21; table 3.1). The frequency of incense burners is somewhat elevated (2.5 p/em^2) but does not exceed the figures recorded for the Subop. 306AL/BQ and 306AB/AD middens. What is striking about the 306BV collection is the near-total absence of shell and animal remains. Processing of these meat sources was seemingly not a major part of the behavioral round pursued here.

Overall, it appears that the material recovered from Subop. 306BV was used in tasks that included food serving, some storage, and the possible processing of comestibles (represented by the chipped lithics) that did not include, to any great extent, faunal sources. Rituals were pursued somewhere in the vicinity of this deposit, apparently at a relatively high level of intensity. The few fragments of wattle-and-daub found in Subop. 306BV might have derived from surface-level structures undetected on ground surface.

Summary

The area west of the principal plazas seemingly provided venues for the conduct of both residential and ritual activities. Structure 306-79 is the clearest example of the first set of behaviors, although it, too, yielded evidence for the conduct of at least some religious devotions on a small scale. Structure 306-15, as noted earlier, weakly suggests that rituals conducted in the WPP might have continued westward beyond that space. The debris retrieved from Subop. 306BV reflects a mix of domestic and ritual behaviors in which serving and, to a limited degree, processing comestibles occurred in association with rites that employed fairly large numbers of incense burners.

ACTIVITY PATTERNING EAST OF THE PRINCIPAL PLAZAS

This area is characterized by an extremely dense packing of architecture that extends for roughly 100 m east of the EPP. Most of the buildings investigated here (Strs. 306-105, 306-106, 306-110, 306-121, 306-152, and 306-159) were erected and used during the Terminal Classic and Early Postclassic, having fallen into disuse by the Roble phase. Our attention at this point focuses on excavated remains that clearly pertain to the last of these intervals.

Architectural Excavations

Structure 306-130 was mapped as a low terrace facing west toward the northeast corner of the EPP. Structure 306-120, which closes off the northeast corner of that plaza, is 5 m west of Str. 306-130. Excavations here revealed a 0.48 m high by 1.7 m wide stone wall raised atop the crest of a gradual west-to-east natural ascent. Backing this construction to the east is the unmodified earth of the original ground surface. Structure 306-130, therefore, seems to have been a terrace designed to slow erosion down the east-to-west slope; the locally unusual thickness of the one exposed wall likely reflects the need to maintain the construction's stability in the face of that erosion. A *bajareque* fragment retrieved from Str. 306-130 very tentatively points to the erection of a perishable building atop the rise fronted by this stone-faced terrace.

The range and density of artifacts found on and around Str. 306-130 match those measures recorded for other Roble phase residences at the center (table 3.2). The inferred concentration of pottery sherds is at the high end of the distribution for this variable among domiciles (96.6 p/em^2), whereas the figures for chipped lithics and incensarios are toward the middle of that range (4.4 p/em^2 and 0.2 p/em^2, respectively). Too few rims were categorized as to their forms to advance an interpretation of activity patterning based on this data class. The analyzed stone tools and debris primarily appear as flakes (11), probably perlite, with only one obsidian blade in the study collection (table 3.1). The complete absence of faunal remains and ground stone implements suggests that food processing was not a significant part of the residents' daily round.

Midden Excavations

Suboperation 306AR/BL was dug to investigate a low earthen rise situated on the eastern margin of Site PVN 306, approximately 100 m east of the

EPP. This eminence, sitting on the edge of an east-to-west ascent, itself rises about 0.8 m on the east and 0.42 m on the west and is shaped in the form of a crescent open on the southwest, where roughly 30 m separates the ends of the arc. Excavations within Subop. 306AR did not clearly determine whether the C-shaped rise was the product of cultural or natural processes. By the Roble phase, however, the summit and slopes of the eminence supported a sustained human occupation. An extensive but shallow (0.28-m-thick) midden, characterized by a high density of cultural materials set in a fine-textured, gray-brown soil, was found extending over an estimated 5.1 × 6.2 m of the summit and adjoining slopes (figure 3.18). There is no evidence that this trash was ever contained within a pit; instead, it seems to have been spread in a fairly continuous sheet. Located 0.2 m west of the exposed limits of the trash deposit is a concentration of *bajareque* measuring 1.1 m east-west by at least 1 m north-south (the northern and southern limits of the deposit were not uncovered). Although no clear architectural features were noted here, this concentration of burned daub may pertain to a surface-level structure fashioned of perishable materials and located in the immediate area. The equivalent stratigraphic positions of the trash and *bajareque* concentration, coupled with their propinquity, strongly suggest that those using the putative wattle-and-daub building contributed to the debris found in the adjoining midden.

The variety and density of cultural material found in the course of excavating Subop. 306AR/BL generally match those noted at other trash deposits south and west of the principal plazas (Subops. 306AL/BQ and 306BV; table 3.2). Ceramic densities are high (692 p/em^2) but do not match the very elevated figures noted in the northern middens (Subop. 306AB/AD, AC/AE, AX/BK, and BF/BS). The overwhelming preponderance of bowls among the form-coded rims of pottery vessels points to the importance of serving comestibles in the immediate area (table 3.3). Storage in ceramic jars seems to have been of less significance in the suite of behaviors conducted here. Pieces of incense burners are well represented in the assemblage (1.9 p/em^2), although their frequency falls out toward the middle of the range noted for Site PVN 306 Roble phase middens. Members of another artifact category with potential ritual connotations, figurines, are also found here in low numbers (0.3 p/em^2).

As was the case for pottery fragments, the density of chipped stone tools and debris in the Subop. 306AR/BL trash (16.1 p/em^2) parallels that seen at the two excavated debris concentrations south and west of the principal plazas and is lower than the very high figures recorded for this data class in the northern middens (save for Str. 306-164). What truly distinguishes the Subop. 306AR/BL assemblage is the very high numbers of obsidian blades (254) vis-à-vis flakes of both chert (13) and possibly perlite (39; table 3.1). This ratio of 4.9:1 dwarfs that seen among all other analyzed collections from the site. One

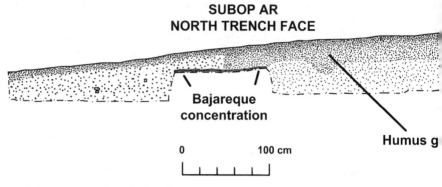

FIGURE 3.18 *Section through the Subop. 306AR/BL midden*

reason for this discrepancy may be the relatively large number of polyhedral blade cores (7) recovered from the Subop. 306AR/BL debris (table 3.1). Blade knapping may well have been one specialty of those who jettisoned their trash in the investigated area. Identification of two small perlite (?) nodules and one nucleus of chert in the collection also suggests that tools were made here using these materials, employing a relatively simple, direct percussion technology. In addition to the manufacture of stone implements, the recovery of two ceramic molds for shaping bowls points to the fashioning, in low volumes, of pottery vessels somewhere nearby.

The density of shell and animal remains within the Subop. 306AR/BL midden, as extrapolated from the findings in the 306BL probe (7,728 p/em² in all), is remarkably elevated. These figures exceed the top limits of the northern middens, where faunal remains tend to be very common, and dwarf the levels of this data class reconstructed for the investigated southern and western trash deposits. Clearly, processing meat was a central activity pursued by those living and working in the immediate vicinity of the Subop. 306AR/BL deposit. Just as obviously, the processing of food using grinding stones is not well represented here.

Debris jettisoned in the 306AR/BL area seems to have resulted from a variety of tasks, including the manufacture in significant numbers of stone tools within several different traditions, employing distinct sets of raw materials; small-scale fabrication of pottery vessels; serving and, to a lesser extent, storing comestibles; processing meat from shellfish, snails, and other animals at a high level of intensity; and the consistent, if not intense, conduct of religious rituals employing incensarios and figurines. The processing of grains on grinding stones, if it occurred at all, was not a major part of the activities that generated this trash.

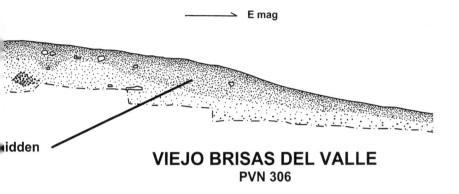

E mag

idden

VIEJO BRISAS DEL VALLE
PVN 306

Summary

It appears that by the Roble phase, residents of Site PVN 306 were using the area east of the principal plazas as both residences and work areas. Structure 306-130 fits fairly well within the first category based on analyses of its associated cultural material and what little we can discern of the building's architecture. Material recovered from the extensive Subop. 306AR/BL deposit points to the performance of a wide array of behaviors in this area, ranging from specialized production of stone tools and pottery to the conduct of ritual, meat processing, and food serving. Recovery of the remains of a perishable structure off the west edge of the aforementioned trash deposit implies that the people responsible for these activities lived nearby.

The behaviors outlined here occurred in areas immediately surrounding the densely settled nucleus of the center's Terminal Classic settlement. The buildings that comprise the latter zone were largely left untouched throughout this late period. Exceptions include the interment of seven individuals along the margins of Strs. 306-106 (1 burial), 306-110 (3 burials), and 306-121 (3 burials). Dating the latter burials is made difficult by the total absence of included grave goods. Their stratigraphic positions, well above the bases of Terminal Classic construction, strongly imply that the interments long postdated the original use of these edifices. It appears, therefore, that the core of the Terminal Classic site was converted in part into a necropolis by the Roble phase.

ACTIVITY PATTERNING NORTH OF THE PRINCIPAL PLAZAS

Excavations north of the site core that pertain to the Roble phase investigated trash deposits unassociated with surviving architecture. All told, six of these

TABLE 3.4 Frequency of polyhedral obsidian, percussion chert, and "perlite" cores recovered per excavated square meters

Structure/Subop.	Polyhedral Cores	Chert Cores	"Perlite" Cores
306-20	0.03	—	—
306-21	—	0.2	—
306-83	0.06	—	0.1
306-164	0.1	—	—
Subop. 306AB/AD	0.4	—	—
Subop. 306AR/BL	0.3	0.04	0.08
Subop. 306AX/BK	1.3	0.9	—
Subop. 306BI	1.0	0.5	—

middens were studied in an area stretching for 200 m east-west, beginning at "Structure 306-164" on the west, and for 280 m north of the principal plazas.

Midden Excavations

Five of these deposits appeared on ground surface as distinct artifact concentrations that generally measure 6 m in diameter. Each such deposit was investigated by digging a 1 m × 2 m trench across its approximate center, coupled in four cases with a 0.5 m × 0.5 m probe sunk next to the original excavation to obtain a controlled sample of the midden's contents. These investigations (Subop. 306AB/AD, 306AC/AE, 306AX/BK, 306BF/BS, and 306BI) each revealed trash deposits composed of dense concentrations of cultural materials packed within 0.19–0.5 m of gray to dark brown soils. No clear pits were identified. The sixth midden identified during survey was originally thought to have been a low platform (Str. 306-164), although digging here proved otherwise.

Structure 306-164 lies approximately 280 m north of the site core in the midst of a widely scattered collection of what we initially took to be low platforms with ill-defined boundaries. Typical of this loose aggregation, Str. 306-164 measures 6 × 10 m and rises about 0.1 m above the surrounding ground surface. Excavations here in 1988 revealed that the slight eminence that distinguished this locale from its environs was the result of trash accumulation. A 1-m-wide trench cut into the east side of the diminutive rise revealed a midden at least 0.85 m thick that ran, minimally, for 3.84 m east-west (time did not permit identifying the deposit's full depth or western limit; figure 3.14). This debris was contained by a pit dug into the underlying soil. The trash eventually overtopped the boundary of the declivity on the east. Densities of cultural material declined consistently over the exposed 3.16 m east of, and away from, the pit.

The last excavation discussed here is Subop. 306CA/36. This test pit, covering 1.25 m², was sunk in the center's northeast quadrant where there was no clear surface evidence of occupation. Although the 35 other probes dug as part of this effort yielded only scattered Roble phase materials, Subop. 306CA/36 revealed a dense concentration of cultural remains indicating the presence of a previously unrecognized midden. The deposit extended to 0.2 m below modern ground surface and was found throughout the trench.

There is little doubt that these excavations encountered the remains of purposefully created trash deposits. These debris concentrations vary in several significant ways, however. Suboperations 306AB/AD, 306AC/AE, and 306AX/BK are all characterized by very high densities of ceramics, chipped lithics, and faunal remains (table 3.2). Suboperations 306BF/BS, 306BI, 306CA/36, and Str. 306-164 yielded much lower concentrations of these materials. Such discrepancies may hint at variations in the numbers of people depositing trash within these middens, the use intensities of ceramics, lithics, and faunal remains being equal among the diverse locales. Alternatively, there may have been differences in the extent to which pottery containers, stone tools, shells, and bone were employed in the actions pursued by equivalent numbers of individuals scattered across Site PVN 306's northern reaches. At present, both possibilities are equally likely.

The proportions of bowls among the form-classified rims in each instance range from 57 to 90 percent, with all but Subop. 306AX/BK having figures for bowls above 70 percent (table 3.3). The serving of comestibles seems to have loomed larger than storage of food and liquids in the activities in which these ceramic vessels were employed.

The chipped lithic assemblages of Subops. 306AB/AD, 306AC/AE, 306BF/BS, 306BI, and Str. 306-164 were dominated by obsidian blades, with ratios ranging from 1.8:1 to 15.7:1 of blades to chert and perlite (?) flakes; excavations at Str. 306-164 retrieved 12 blades and no flakes of any material (table 3.1). This pattern is reversed in the Subop. 306AX/BK collection, where flakes outnumber blades by a ratio of 1.6:1. Polyhedral obsidian cores are found in Subop. 306AB/AD and Str. 306-164 (1 each), Subop. 306BI (2 examples), and Subop. 306AX/BK (3 specimens; table 3.4). This pattern implies that blades were knapped in numerous places throughout northern Site PVN 306. Interestingly, the presence and frequency of blade cores do not necessarily correlate with locales where blades were concentrated; Subop. 306AX/BK yielded the largest quantity of cores from a northern midden but is the only known instance from this area where flakes outnumber obsidian blades. The 2 chert cores found at Subop. 306AX/BK and the 1 retrieved from Subop. 306BI indicate that percussion flaking of this material was pursued, in some cases within the same general areas where blades were fashioned.

The very large numbers of shell and animal remains recovered from Subops. 306AB/AD, 306AC/AE, and 306AX/BK point to the processing of meat in sizable quantities in each case. Excavations in Subops. 306 BF/BS and 306BI and Str. 306-164 yielded significant but much smaller concentrations of these materials. The Subop. 306CA/36 deposit, on the other hand, contained very few faunal remains. Nonetheless, it appears that throughout most known portions of northern Site PVN 306, meat was extracted from shellfish, snails, and other animals in significant quantities. Variations in the densities of these materials may reflect differences in the numbers of people involved in such chores, the levels of intensity at which these tasks were conducted, or both.

The frequencies of incense burners vary somewhat among the investigated assemblages, ranging from 1 to 3.1 p/em^2. These distinctions do not correlate with density measures for other artifact classes. For example, Subop. 306BF/BS evinces relatively low concentrations of pottery sherds, chipped lithics, and faunal remains and yet has one of the highest densities of incense burner fragments. Structure 306-164 exhibits a similar divergence in density measures. It seems unlikely, therefore, that differences in incensario frequencies are merely products of the quantities of artifacts found in various middens. More likely, the observed distinctions reflect variations in the intensities at which religious rites employing incense burners were conducted. Figurines are found in three of the seven excavated northern middens, their frequencies not correlating in any clear way with those of incensarios.

Grinding stones are spottily represented in the investigated middens; they appear in two of the analyzed assemblages, where their densities range from 0.4 p/em^2 (Subop. 306AC/AE) to 3.1 p/em^2 (Subop. 306AB/AD). As was the case with incensarios, the appearance and density of grinding implements do not co-vary with the frequency of other, more common material classes such as ceramic sherds, chipped lithics, and faunal remains. Preparing grains using grinding stones was therefore apparently a task pursued at varying levels of intensity across northern Site PVN 306.

The recovery of wattle-and-daub fragments in four of the investigated northern middens likely points to the presence of buildings fashioned of this perishable material somewhere in the vicinities of Subops. 306AB/AD, 306AX/BK, 306CA/36, and Str. 306-164. We cannot rule out the possibility that similar constructions were also originally found near the other studied trash deposits, with remains of the buildings simply never having been preserved by burning. The extant evidence therefore implies that at least some, probably all, of the northern middens were initially associated with constructions.

The spinning of thread, as indicated by the presence of spindle whorls, was recorded at Subops. 306AB/AD and 306AX/BK, with by far the greatest concentration recognized at the former location (2.7 p/em^2). Admittedly, spindle whorls are rare components of Roble phase Site PVN 306 assemblages. Further excavation at places where they were not identified might therefore have turned up at least a few examples. Based on the data in hand, however, it appears that thread preparation and probably weaving were variably practiced across northern Site PVN 306; in those spots where they were conducted, spinning and weaving were not pursued at equal levels of intensity.

Other uncommon artifact categories are variably attested to in the excavated collections, including net weights (found in Subops. 306AC/AE [2.7 p/em^2] and 306AX/BK [0.4 p/em^2]) and sherd disks (identified only in Subop. 306AB/AD [0.4 p/em^2]). The behavioral significance of these items is unclear, although sherd disks may also have been used as spindle whorls.

Summary

The behavioral significance of material derived from the excavated middens depends on how these deposits were originally implicated in the rounds of activities pursued in northern portions of the settlement. The discontinuous nature of the artifact scatters, of which the investigated trash deposits are just seven examples, suggests that the excavated middens were not parts of a continuous sheet of debris. Rather, each seems to have been a relatively discrete unit of trash disposal. The relatively shallow nature of these debris levels (0.19–0.85 m thick, with all but Str. 306-164 falling within the 0.19–0.5 m range) hints at their formation over relatively short periods of time. It may well be that whatever happened at these distinct locales did not long endure.

A major question that arises is whether the studied deposits were linked to specific residences or represented debris generated by specialized activities conducted away from domiciles. No in situ remains of domestic architecture were identified on the surface or in excavations. As noted earlier, the few wattle-and-daub pieces retrieved from four of the middens point only to the presence of perishable constructions in their immediate vicinities; they do not indicate the dimensions and functions of these putative buildings. Similarities in the materials recovered from the excavated deposits do imply that much the same general range of activities was pursued in each known case. The nature of these items, mostly utilitarian ceramics and stone tools as well as the remains of meat processing, tentatively suggest that they were employed in domestic chores associated with individual houses. At present, the most likely interpretation is that each of the investigated trash collections was the product of behaviors conducted in discrete residential units, the architectural manifestations of which did not survive.

All concentrations of cultural material identified on the surface of northern Site PVN 306 could therefore represent the locations of specific houses. Not all of them need have been contemporary; the shallowness of the studied middens suggests that house groups did not remain in one spot throughout the entirety of the center's Roble phase. Hence, the northern part of the settlement may have been characterized by a shifting landscape of domestic groups residing in perishable structures and engaging in much the same array of tasks.

There was some variation in how intensely these shared behaviors were pursued and even in the nature of the activities conducted. This interpretation is implied by variations across trash deposits in the frequencies of the most commonly found materials (pottery sherds, chipped lithics, and faunal remains). These distinctions imply that the intensity of settlement and actions involving ceramic vessels, chipped stone implements, and meat differed significantly over the investigated area.

Throughout northern Site PVN 306, however, the serving of comestibles in pottery bowls seems to have been a very significant activity. Only in the area of Subop. 306AX/BK was the proportion of jars and bowls nearly equal (comprising 43% and 57% of the form-classified rims, respectively). Samples of rims coded by vessel shape are large enough in each case to warrant confidence in the results. Similarly, in the analyzed chipped lithic collections, blades are almost invariably the most prevalent tool form; Subop. 306AX/BK once again is the sole contradictory case. In the absence of use-wear studies, we cannot discern in what tasks the blades, as well as flakes, were employed. What we *can* say is that obsidian blades were generally available to all those living in this area, and, insofar as blades and flakes were used for different purposes, those tasks associated with the former tools predominated throughout northern Site PVN 306.

Variations in the observed concentrations of incense burner pieces among the investigated deposits hint at some possible differences in the performance of religious rituals in this portion of the settlement. There is no clear correlation between the prevalence of incense burners and the locations where they are found; high densities are not identified, for example, close to the principal plazas or to each other. Incensario frequencies also vary independently of density measures for other artifact classes. It therefore seems unlikely that figures for these ritual objects are solely a function of the number of people who used them. Consequently, it appears that religious devotions were not conducted at the same levels of intensity throughout northern Site PVN 306.

Evidence for manufacturing tasks is also variably expressed across the excavated middens. Signs of obsidian blade knapping were noted at Subops.

306AB/AD, 306AX/BK, 306BI, and Str. 306-164, where fragments of poly-hedral cores were recovered. Suboperations 306AX/BK and 306BI also yielded evidence, in the form of chert cores, for fashioning flake tools by the direct percussion method. The identification of ceramic spindle whorls in the Subop. 306AB/AD and 306AX/BK assemblages indicates that at least some steps in the weaving process were pursued in the environs of these deposits. Specialized production tasks were therefore widespread, if not quite ubiquitous, through-out northern portions of the center during the Roble phase, and there were differences in the intensity and array of these tasks pursued by those who tossed debris in specific middens.

GENERAL SUMMARY

The basic social networks identified at Roble phase Site PVN 306 encompass numerous houses, at least one household composed of large residential plat-forms, and a community that includes the site and its immediate environs. The house is the most widespread and smallest of these webs. Members in each such net lived in discrete constructions and cooperated in comparable activities using the same forms of material culture. To be sure, the architectural foci of these interactions varied considerably, from buildings raised atop platforms to constructions set directly on ground surface. Nevertheless, an equivalent array of behaviors using similar items of material culture was performed in each of these settings, although there were some differences in the scales and intensities of these activities. For example, the processing of meat and grain was seemingly less significant in houses bordering the EPP than it was in other domestic webs at Site PVN 306. Such variations in site-wide patterns of activity distribution may point to some level of behavioral segregation with, in this case, the messier aspects of food preparation relegated largely to areas outside the one known household.

Evidence for specialized manufacture was even more spatially restricted. Diagnostics of obsidian blade production, the fashioning of flake tools from chert and perlite cores, and, to some extent, spinning/weaving and pottery production are unevenly distributed among excavated residences. This pattern implies that houses were differentiated to some extent by their varied participa-tion in craft manufacture. An implication of this finding is that these small-scale domestic units were dependent on each other for goods their members did not produce. Webs of economic exchange therefore cross-cut domestic net-works centered on specific houses. We return to these issues in chapter 7.

The one recorded household centers on the EPP, where several residences bound a formally defined plaza. This entity incorporates the largest, most im-pressively decorated domiciles known from the center. The network linking occupants of the EPP was encouraged by their proximity to each other and was enacted through common engagement in tasks conducted within the plaza. A sense of unity was likely enhanced by cooperation in daily chores using identical materials, along with participation in activities pursued in special-purpose structures at least witnessed by those with access to the plaza. The paucity of incensarios associated with the latter edifices suggests that the behaviors they hosted were not overtly couched in a sacred context.

Houses and households, in turn, were linked into broader networks. One such web involved the exchange of specialized products among artisans resident in some houses with consumers living in others. Participation in rituals was another means of forging ties that cross-cut physically localized nets. The widespread distribution of incense burner fragments among houses of all sizes and locations within Site PVN 306 points to the performance of religious devotions in most, probably all, houses and households. In fact, general participation in these observances was probably one of the common projects through which intra-house and intra-household unity was enacted. Variations in incensario frequencies might point to distinctions in the intensity and frequency with which religious observances were carried out among domestic groups. Whereas members of all these entities used much the same ritual paraphernalia in, presumably, much the same ways, a few houses might have served as foci for more intense or frequent enactments of religious performances. The houses associated with Subops. 306AB/AD, 306AL/BQ, and 306BF/BS, therefore, may have been centers for religious activities to a much greater extent than were their compatriots. These data suggest that some houses were foci of ritual activity in which members of other social units participated periodically.

Operating at a larger scale, specialized ritual constructions that define the WPP apparently served as a nexus that unified all residents of Site PVN 306 and possibly those living in the center's immediate vicinity. Here, Strs. 306-17, 306-19, and 306-174 are distinguished from all other constructions at the Roble phase center by their circular to oval forms and lack of clear domestic debris. The first two edifices are also the most elaborately decorated buildings at Site PVN 306; their surfaces are covered with, in some cases, multiple coats of plaster, and their tops are capped with stone monuments. The kinds of activities conducted around these buildings are suggested by the nature of the trash deposits found off the WPP's west and southwest sides. This mix of ritual paraphernalia, production debris from making stone tools, and materials associated with food serving (ceramic bowls and faunal remains) points to the WPP as a venue where manufacturing, feasting, and celebrations of the sacred were synthesized. The easily accessible WPP, therefore, apparently served as a locale in which large segments of the settlement's population periodically congregated to reinforce commitment to each other and to the community-wide network of which they were a part through common participation in rites of worship, consumption, and production. Structure 306-20 may have hosted gatherings of community leaders who coordinated such events.

In essence, the same basic sets of activities were instrumental in forging networks at Roble phase Site PVN 306 at all scales. Members of specific houses and households ate and worshipped with other members of their domestic webs. These processes of consumption and communing with the sacred were among the projects through which each network's existence was enacted. Similarly, residents of the center gathered in the WPP to instantiate the interpersonal ties that comprised a site-wide web by engaging in these same tasks, involving much the same array of goods but on a larger scale. This is not to say that Site PVN 306 was a homogeneous community during the Roble phase. Rather, the center's inhabitants of all ranks used similar behaviors as tropes by which to create, reproduce, and emotionally strengthen the unity of social webs that operated at multiple spatial scales. These efforts did unite members in distinct networks despite the differences that separated them in other contexts. We consider these differences in chapters 6–9.

FOUR

Activity Structures and Networks at Site PVN 144

Most of the nineteen surface-visible structures, 2.5 m and less in height, that comprise Site PVN 144 are organized into two distinct sectors, each characterized by very different organizing principles (figure 4.1). The largest buildings, Strs. 144-1/3, 5, 8/12, and 18, are arranged in a roughly circular pattern around a large patio (57 m × 71 m). Building orientations vary from 296 degrees 30 minutes to 11 degrees. Structure 144-19 was mapped as a low, amorphous construction situated within the plaza on its west side. The much smaller Strs. 144-13/15 sit atop the summit of a 0.7-m-high platform (Str. 144-16) about 95 m northeast of the aforementioned group. The remaining buildings are scattered within 50 m south (Str. 144-17) and west (Strs. 144-4, 6, and 7) of the main patio.

Roble phase materials unassociated with clear buildings were found scattered over roughly 4.1 ha around the main plaza. Twelve distinct and dense concentrations of artifacts and *Pachychilus* sp. (freshwater snail) shells were recorded within this area. Each of these clusters, 3–6 m in diameter, probably represents a relatively discrete trash deposit associated with Roble phase constructions erected directly on ancient ground surface. High, dense grasses covering Site PVN 144 during both the 1978 and 1996 field seasons, when the

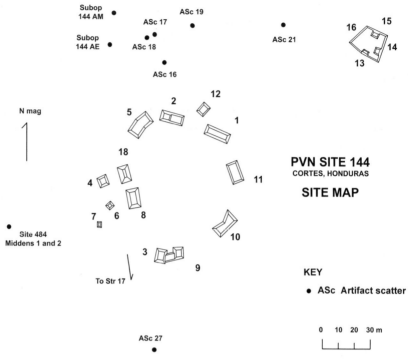

FIGURE 4.1 *Map of Site PVN 144*

settlement was initially recorded and excavated, respectively, almost certainly hid other such concentrations from view.

Seven of the buildings that define the main patio (Strs. 144-1, 2, 5, 8, 11, 18, and 19) were excavated, as were fifty-six test pits, ten of which were dug in as many artifact concentrations located beyond that plaza. Fully 527 m² of Roble phase deposits were cleared in and around these edifices, with an additional 26 m² dug as part of the test-pitting program. Structures 144-13/16 were not investigated and are not included further in this discussion; their distinctive arrangement and isolation from the rest of the site raise the real possibility that they were not built and used during the Roble phase.

BUILDING FUNCTIONS AROUND AND WITHIN THE MAIN PLAZA

Residential Architecture

Structures 144-1 and 2 (figures 4.2 and 4.3), located along the northern arc of the patio, are comparably extensive surface-level buildings that encompass 60.4 m² (minimally) and 87.36 m², respectively. Their perimeters are

PVN 144
STRUCTURE 144-1

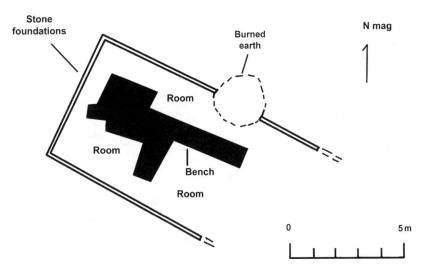

FIGURE 4.2 *Structure 144-1, plan*

in each case defined by stone foundations that measure 0.1–0.35 m high by 0.18–0.35 m wide. These walls enclose sizable spaces divided by substantial, east-west–running medial stone walls.

Structure 144-1's earthen-floored interior was entered through a 2.2-m-wide doorway in the approximate center of its northern foundation. An area of intensely burned soil measuring approximately 2.2 m in diameter completely fills this entrance and extends 1.3 m outside the edifice and 0.9 m into it. The restricted distribution of this heating implies that the charring resulted from a controlled fire and was not part of an accidental conflagration. Whether that burning was integral to regularly repeated actions conducted on the threshold or was part of a onetime event, possibly associated with Str. 144-1's abandonment, is uncertain.

The northern enclosure covers 11.9 m², while south of the medial wall are two compartments separated by a southern projection of the central wall. The southwest enclosure measures 7.6 m², with its southeastern analog covering 12.4 m². A fourth possible room seems to lie immediately east of these compartments, although it was not uncovered. Passage among these rooms was fairly straightforward: the northern example was entered through the ample doorway described earlier, and the southern enclosures were reached by passing around the east and west sides of the medial wall (these entrances are 0.65

95

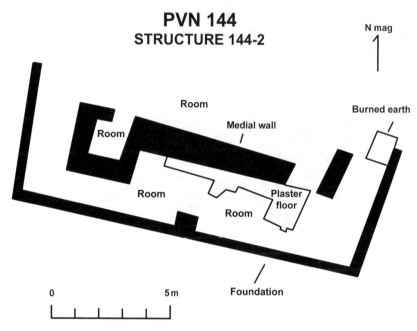

FIGURE 4.3 *Structure 144-2, plan*

m wide at their narrowest points). The westernmost 2.5 m of the medial wall is sufficiently broad (1.45 m across) and high (0.43 m tall) to have doubled as a wall support and bench, possibly facing into both the northern and south-western rooms.

Structure 144-2, 10.4 m west of Str. 144-1, also apparently faced north and away from the patio, like its eastern neighbor. Here, however, there is no foundation to impede access to the extensive northern enclosure, which covers 19.9 m². A diminutive compartment, encompassing 2.1 m², borders this room on the west, where it is built against the west flank of Str. 144-2's medial wall. This cubicle was accessed through a 0.7-m-wide doorway in its northeast corner facing directly into the north room. The southern compartment covers 31.4 m² and was reached by moving through ample passageways on the east and the west (1.4–1.7 m across). Unlike Str. 144-1, Str. 144-2's interior was apparently surfaced with burned earth, parts of which were covered with a 0.02-m-thick limestone plaster. As with Str. 144-1, Str. 144-2's medial wall is sufficiently wide (0.95–1.25 m across) and tall (0.4–0.7 m high) to have served as both a bench and wall support; it certainly seems wider than necessary to sustain a perishable central dividing wall. A 0.46-m-high stone block, measuring 0.8 m across, projects 0.6 m north into the approximate center of

TABLE 4.1 Density of major material classes by structure and artifact scatter as measured per excavated square meters

Structure/Artifact Scatter (AS)	Pottery Sherds	Incen-sarios	Chipped Lithics	Shell/Bone	Ground Stone	Bajareque
144-1	25	0.3	0.9	0.4/0.2	0.1	0.7
144-2	15	0.1	0.6	0.09/0.3	0.04	0.7
144-5-1st	14	0.4	0.4	0.9/0.1	—	2.3
144-8-1st	2	0.05	0.2	0.06/0.04	0.02	3
144-11	30	0.3	0.9	43.7/2.3	—	1.3
144-18	2	0.02	0.2	0.07/0.02	0.01	0.3
144-19, Unit 1	61	6	4	0/0.4	—	1.5
AS 16	295	—	73	6/82	—	—
AS 17	834	1	29	1,013/1,250	1	2
AS 18	799	2	17	210/305	—	2
AS 19	936	1	27	52/68	—	3
AS 21	560	—	27	133/162	—	118
AS 27	311	—	14	44/90	—	2
Subop. 144AE	564	—	24	32/36	—	—
Subop. 144AM	604	—	—	60/15	—	—
Subop. 484, Midden 1	—	—	40	1,964/2,007	1	8
Subop. 484, Midden 2	392	1	11	755/769	—	—

Suboperations 144AE and 144AM are tests measuring 0.5 × 0.5 m that were dug into areas lacking surface-visible signs of ancient occupation.

the southern room from Str. 144-2's southern foundation. This construction may have been used as a shelf.

The recovery of *bajareque* fragments in some numbers from both Strs. 144-1 and 144-2 (table 4.1) strongly suggests that the upper walls of these edifices were fashioned of clay applied over a woven stick framework. The footings supporting these perishable walls consist primarily of river-rounded cobbles set horizontally and held in place with a mud mortar.

The features and arrangement of space within Strs. 144-1 and 144-2 point to the use of both buildings as domiciles. Each contains sizable rooms that could easily have accommodated the pursuit of daily routines, and each also has a centrally located bench. A potential storage receptacle is located off the west side of Str. 144-2's bench; this function is suggested by the room's small size (2.1 m²) and lack of interior features. No analogous facility was recorded

TABLE 4.2 Proportions of jar and bowl rims per structure at Site PVN 144

Structure/Artifact Scatter (AS)	Bowls	Jars	Total Rim Sample
144-1	52	48	60
144-2	51	49	37
144-5-1st	74	26	39
144-8-1st	71	29	21
144-11	77	23	22
144-18	66	34	9
144-19, Unit 1	86	14	14
AS 16	68	32	19
AS 18	56	44	90
AS 19	47	53	15
AS 21	78	12	83
Subop. 144AE	39	61	13

in Str. 144-1. The range of artifacts associated with these two edifices supports the attribution of domestic functions to them (table 4.1).

The near-total clearing of Strs. 144-1 and 144-2 yielded substantial quantities of ceramics, 25 and 15 pieces per excavated m² (p/em²), respectively. These figures are high for Roble phase contexts at Site PVN 144, suggesting that the activities pursued in and around these constructions involved what was by local standards the regular and intense use of pottery containers. The nearly even representation of bowls and jars in the collection of rims classified by form further implies that the serving and storage of food and liquid played roughly equivalent roles in these behaviors (table 4.2).

Ground and chipped stone artifacts, probably used in food preparation, are well represented in both cases, as are fragments of bone and shell (primarily *Pachychilus* sp.) likely derived from ancient meals. The ground stone items are fragments of *manos* and *metates* almost certainly used in processing grains, such as corn, into flour.

The vast majority of chipped stone tools found in both buildings consist of imported obsidian (97% and 72% of the analyzed stone tool assemblages from Strs. 144-1 and 144-2, respectively). This foreign material is supplemented in both cases by a few fragments of perlite likely secured from sources in the valley (3% and 25% of the respective assemblages) and, in the case of Str. 144-2, some chert (3% of the studied collection) (table 4.3). The obsidian occurs almost exclusively as blades (98% of all obsidian analyzed from both edifices has this form). The perlite and chert consist of flakes produced through

TABLE 4.3 Distribution of analyzed lithic materials by material, form, and excavated context

Structure/Artifact Scatter (AS)	Obsidian Blades	Obsidian Flakes	Perlite Flakes	Perlite Nodules	Reused Polyhedral Cores	Chert Flakes	Chert Nodules
144-1	57	1	2	—	—	—	—
144-2	47	1	17	—	—	2	—
144-5-1st	18	—	6	1	—	—	—
144-8-1st	11	—	3	3	—	2	—
144-11	19	1	12	3	—	2	—
144-18	6	5	13	1	—	0	1
144-19, Unit 1	32	—	4	—	—	2	—
AS 16	47	2	—	—	—	5	—
AS 17	14	2	—	—	1	—	—
AS 18	11	—	—	—	—	—	—
AS 19	13	2	—	—	—	—	—
AS 21	16	—	—	—	—	1	—
AS 27	8	—	1	—	1	2	—
Subop. 484, Midden 1	26	3	1	—	1	1	—

Subop. 484, Midden 2 was not analyzed by material and form.

hard-hammer percussion. There is no evidence in either case that these blades or flakes were fashioned in or near Strs. 144-1 and 144-2. Use-wear analyses of the tools revealed a mix of scraping, cutting, and whittling, with cutting the most common (table 4.4). Structures 144-1 and 144-2 also yielded examples of small projectile points made on obsidian blades; one was retrieved from Str. 144-1, while seven were found in and around Str. 144-2. In general, much the same round of behaviors, involving the same types of chipped lithics, conducted at similar levels of intensity are attested to at Strs. 144-1 and 144-2, suggesting that both edifices served similar functions. This range of activities matches what would be expected of domestic chores.

The recovery of incensario pieces, mostly from ladle burners, at Strs. 144-1 and 144-2 points to the conduct of similar rituals at both locales. Their greater concentration at Str. 144-1 implies that the occupants of this edifice pursued such observances more intensively than did those at its western neighbor. All in all, architectural forms and artifact distributions point to Strs. 144-1 and

TABLE 4.4 Functional assessments of obsidian blades from Site PVN 144

Structure/Artifact Scatter (AS)	Scraping	Cutting	Whittling	Points
144-1	2	32	7	1
144-2	5	24	5	7
144-5-1st	4	9	2	—
144-8-1st	—	1	—	4
144-11	5	10	4	1
144-18	—	—	—	1
144-19, Unit 1	10	17	4	3
AS 16	2	13	3	4
AS 17	—	—	—	1
AS 18	6	1	—	—
AS 19	—	—	—	1
AS 21	1	5	1	2
AS 27	—	2	—	1
Subop. 484, Midden 1	3	2	1	1

144-2 as distinct houses, the members of which pursued a wide range of comparable activities, including domestic chores as well as religious rites.

Special-Purpose Architecture

Structure 144-11, on the south side of the patio, has a very different form from that of its two northwestern neighbors (figure 4.4). The core of this edifice is a stone pavement covering, during its final iteration, 1.6 × 8.5 m, oriented about 349 degrees, and resting atop a 0.2-m-high earthen platform with indistinct boundaries. The stone surface supports no discernible features and is bounded on the south and the east by stone walls that are 0.15–0.2 m wide and extend 0.25 m into and below the supporting fill but do not rise above floor level. The latter constructions are fashioned of unmodified stones set on end.

What was probably the formal entry to Str. 144-11's summit was marked by a plaster surface measuring approximately 1.25 × 2.1 m, located immediately west of the pavement and slightly south of its center point. The plaster here was resurfaced at least once; the earlier preserved version was painted red and polished, while its successor, which rests on 0.01 m of earth, was too heavily eroded to determine its original appearance. A dense concentration of *Pachychilus* sp. shells, mixed with other artifacts and organic materials,

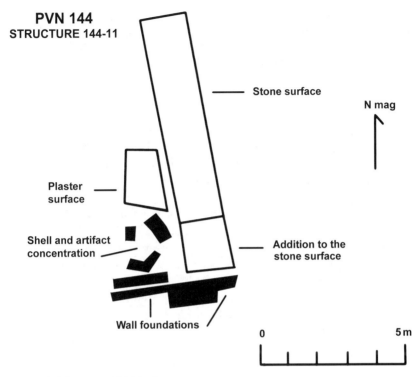

FIGURE 4.4 *Structure 144-11, plan*

was found 0.15 m south of the plaster floor (Feature 1). Feature 1 measures 0.8 × 1.1 m, is maximally 0.15 m thick, and is bounded by three low, discontinuous stone walls that form a rough circle around this material.

The 63 *bajareque* fragments retrieved from the environs of Str. 144-11 imply that walls of this material formerly bounded portions of the edifice. Approximately 70 percent of the recorded pieces came from the vicinities of the footings that border the pavement's east and south flanks. Such a pattern suggests that these foundations formerly supported perishable walls. The relative paucity of *bajareque* elsewhere on the building tentatively indicates that Str. 144-11's north and west sides were left exposed to view.

The generally open character of Str. 144-11's summit, and the absence of any obvious domestic furniture upon it, distinguish this building from the more obvious residences represented by Strs. 144-1 and 144-2. The artifacts encountered during excavations at Str. 144-11 also diverge somewhat in their frequencies, although not in their forms, from those that make up the assemblages of the latter two buildings (table 4.1).

The number of pottery sherds recovered from clearing Str. 144-11 is relatively high, about 30 p/em^2. Not only is this a large figure for Site PVN 144, but the distribution of forms is skewed markedly toward bowls (77% of form-classifiable rims; table 4.2). Admittedly, the sample of categorized rims is small (N=22), but the discrepancy contrasts starkly with the nearly equal distribution of bowls and jars noted for Strs. 144-1 and 144-2. Pottery vessels therefore figured significantly in the activities conducted on and around Str. 144-11, and most of those containers were likely used in serving foods and liquids. Incensario frequencies fall within the range noted at Strs. 144-1 and 144-2. Insofar as these items functioned in the performance of religious devotions, small-scale rites were conducted at all three locales.

The frequency of chipped stone tools at Str. 144-11 (0.9 p/em^2) corresponds well with the figures obtained from Strs. 144-1 and 144-2. Once again, most of the items are made from imported obsidian (60% of the collection), followed by perlite and chert (26% and 4% of the assemblage, respectively) (table 4.3). Ninety-six percent of the analyzed obsidian is in blade form, while three of the perlite pieces are small nodules apparently used as sources for flakes produced by direct percussion. The remaining perlite and chert fragments appear as flakes. Whereas some casual fashioning of perlite flake tools likely occurred in Str. 144-11's environs, there is no sign of obsidian blade or chert flake manufacture here. The sorts of tasks in which these implements were used parallel those inferred for Strs. 144-1 and 144-2 (table 4.4). Once again, cutting is the most commonly recognized activity, followed by nearly equal frequencies of scraping and whittling. A single small projectile point fashioned on an obsidian blade was also retrieved from Str. 144-11. Behaviors involving chipped stone implements, therefore, were apparently pursued at roughly equivalent levels of intensity in all three locales.

The absence of ground stone tools at Str. 144-11 tentatively indicates that certain steps in food processing were not pursued here, or at least not to any significant degree. What does stand out in the comparisons is the marked preponderance of shells, largely *Pachychilus* sp., recovered from Str. 144-11. Nowhere in the patio do the numbers even approximate those recorded in these excavations (43.7 p/em^2). The vast majority (2,054, of which 2,052 are *Pachychilus* sp. shells) come from Feature 1 on Str. 144-11's west side. Here, the density is roughly 1,867 p/em^3. Associated with the shell in Feature 1 are 183 sherds, 25 bones, 13 fragments of chipped stone, 2 pieces of *bajareque*, and 5 incensario sherds. This mix of materials suggests that Feature 1 was a trash deposit. Even if that were the case, certain aspects of the midden mark it off as something more than a collection of domestic debris: its location, on the plaza-facing side of Str. 144-11 immediately adjoining the building's formal entryway; its composition, dominated by snail shells; and its segregation

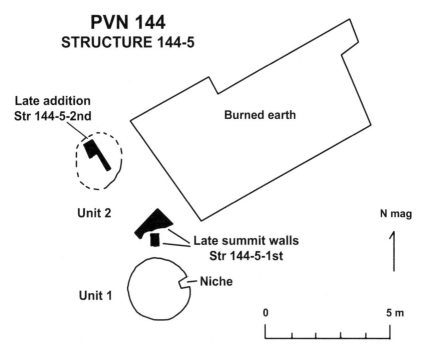

PVN 144
STRUCTURE 144-5

Late addition
Str 144-5-2nd

Burned earth

Unit 2

N mag

Late summit walls
Str 144-5-1st

Niche

Unit 1

0   5 m

FIGURE 4.5 *Structure 144-5, plan*

from other parts of the building by the low walls that encircle the deposit. It may be that Feature 1 contains materials associated primarily with processing *Pachychilus* sp. shells, and this was one of the purposes to which Str. 144-11 was devoted. The goal would likely have been to extract the animal from its casing, with that meat incorporated in meals on its own or as part of soups or stews. There is no clear evidence of burning in the vicinity of Feature 1, so any cooking likely took place elsewhere in the building or in the nearby plaza. The prominent location of Feature 1 vis-à-vis Str. 144-11 and the plaza hints at the importance of snail processing in the activities conducted in both areas.

Structure 144-5, situated between Strs. 144-2 and 144-18, closes off the northwest corner of the plaza (figure 4.5). Excavations here revealed two distinct building phases, with the functions of each markedly different. Structure 144-5-2nd (the earliest known version of the edifice) is a 0.59-m-high earthen platform, into the summit of which were built two circular, flat-bottomed basins (Units 1 and 2). Unit 1, the better preserved of the pair, measures 2.4–2.5 m across the top (narrowing to a diameter of 1.2 m at the base), is 0.45 m deep, and has a niche set into its east wall 0.2 m above the base (figures 4.6 and 4.7). The niche is 0.22 m wide, 0.25 m deep, and extends 0.36 m from the wall of

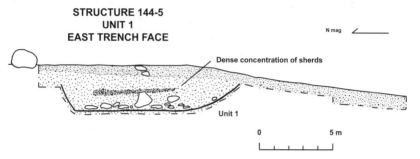

FIGURE 4.6 *Structure 144-5, section through the Unit 1 basin*

the basin into the down-sloping flank of the declivity. Unit 1's walls consist of a 0.02-m-thick layer of fire-hardened earth, to which a few fragments of white plaster still clung when uncovered during excavation. Unit 2, 3.35 m north of Unit 1, was poorly preserved. Based on the surviving fragments of this construction, it appears to have been nearly identical in form and dimensions to its southern neighbor. Unit 2's reconstructed diameter at the orifice is around 2 m, whereas it is 0.42 m deep; if there was a niche associated with Unit 2, it was not preserved. Both of these basins occupied nearly identical stratigraphic positions and were almost certainly in use at the same time.

Beginning 1 m east of Units 1 and 2, Str. 144-5-2nd's earthen summit floor showed evidence of intense burning. The limits of this feature were not ascertained, although the fired surface covered at least 4.7 × 9.65 m. No other superstructure constructions were noted, implying that the summit was featureless and left largely open.

Several stages of renovations mark significant shifts in the use of this edifice. During the first of these episodes (included in Str. 144-5-2nd), Unit 1 was filled by a 0.2-m-thick layer of flat-laid rocks and earth, which, in turn, was buried by 0.04–0.1 m of earth mixed with what appears to have been midden materials (figure 4.6). Approximately 0.2 m of soil was introduced into Unit 2 at about this time and supported a 0.12-m-high stone wall that projected 1.35 m south into the basin from its reconstructed north margin. This construction was 0.1–0.4 m wide (narrowing from north to south) and left a 0.15-m gap between it and the southern, down-sloping edge of Unit 2. Whatever transpired within the northern basin at this time involved firing intense enough to alter the 0.06 m of earth immediately underlying the newly erected wall.

It seems likely that the fire-altered summit floor lying east of Units 1 and 2 was still exposed at this time. In fact, we cannot determine with any certainty

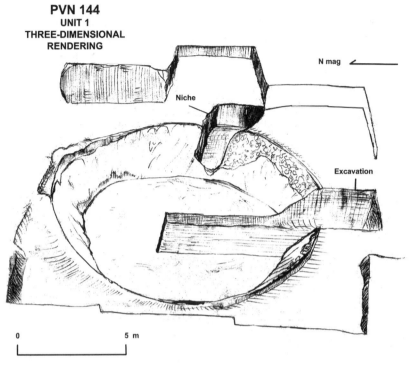

PVN 144
UNIT 1
THREE-DIMENSIONAL
RENDERING

FIGURE 4.7 *Structure 144-5, three-dimensional rendering of the Unit 1 basin. The trench dug through the basin's east wall and floor is shown here (original drawing by Heather Ogston).*

when within Str. 144-5-2nd's construction sequence this floor was created, except to say that it predates the final modifications made to the edifice.

Significant changes to the building resulted in the creation of Str. 144-5-1st. During this span Units 1, 2, and their associated constructions were covered by an earthen fill that ultimately raised Str. 144-5-1st's height to 0.94 m. The fire-reddened summit floor lying east of Units 1 and 2 was also enveloped by earth fill at this time. Capping the final summit are two casually constructed stone walls that were likely parts of a superstructure. Unfortunately, this construction was so disturbed that we could not reconstruct its form and dimensions.

The functions served by Str. 144-5 during the various stages of its use are difficult to determine. The basins are virtually unprecedented in the Naco valley architectural corpus during any period. The firing of the walls of Units 1 and possibly 2 implies that their uses required the creation of hard, relatively impermeable surfaces. The intensity of this burning is suggested by the altering of the soil bordering Unit 1; no comparable modification of the environing earth was noted in Unit 2, but its poor state of preservation means such alterations cannot be excluded. The plaster, patches of which are preserved on Unit 1's interior, may have also formalized the appearance of the basin and contributed to the integrity of its surfaces. No clear signs of burning are associated with the use of either basin; the firing of Units 1 and maybe 2 was apparently associated with their construction and was not a by-product of their function.

Structure 144-5-2nd's pits would have been excellent storage facilities for durable goods. Their hard earthen walls could have repelled pests and retained food and perhaps liquids. The utility of these constructions as storage receptacles was enhanced by the addition of plaster on at least Unit 1's surfaces. No signs of the putative curated commodities were noted, in part because of the subsequent modifications visited on the edifice.

During the next phase, it appears that Unit 2's newly raised floor became a locus for burning that altered that earthen surface to a depth of 0.06 m. One possibility is that Unit 2 was converted into a pit kiln or oven, with the north–south–running interior wall part of a baffle designed to direct heat within the circular space. Unit 1, in contrast, seems to have been transformed into a place for trash disposal. The wide array of artifacts found here, including food-processing tools (three grinding stones along with three obsidian blades with evidence of having been used in cutting) and organic materials that likely figured in ancient meals, implies that the basin was the ultimate resting place for debris that resulted from preparing and serving food. This detritus may have been derived from cooking that went on in the northern basin.

The summit associated with Units 1 and 2 in their various iterations was extensive, open, and modified through firing. It is unclear whether the burning recorded over this exposed 43.4 m² resulted from activities pursued on it or was part of an effort to formalize this surface. Repeated use of the summit as an area for cooking may have produced the observed effect. Although it remains unclear when within Str. 144-5-2nd's history the platform's summit was burned, it likely remained unencumbered by superstructure construction until the final phase. In general, Str. 144-5-2nd lacks the architectural markers of a domicile. Any food preparation conducted in and around Unit 2, therefore, was probably not controlled by, or pursued for the primary benefit of, one particular house group residing on Str. 144-5-2nd.

By the final occupation stage, Units 1 and 2 had been buried, and Str. 144-5-1st seems to have become a platform supporting a superstructure defined by stone foundations that likely sustained perishable upper walls. Assigning artifacts to this interval is complicated by the absence of clear floors and well-defined building perimeters that would facilitate distinguishing between material derived from terminal debris and architectural fill. It is possible, therefore, that objects from these two contexts were intermingled following the platform's abandonment and were combined during excavation and analysis. Bearing this caveat in mind, something can be inferred of Str. 144-5-1st's uses from the range of artifacts tentatively associated with its final occupation (table 4.1).

The sherd density recorded at Str. 144-5-1st is comparable to the figures noted at the two known residences, Strs. 144-1 and 144-2. Unlike the form distributions identified at the first two domiciles, the Str. 144-5-1st assemblage is skewed heavily toward bowls, much as was the case at Str. 144-11 (table 4.2). This patterning implies that whereas ceramic vessels were employed in roughly similar numbers at Strs. 144-5-1st, 144-2, and 144-1, bowls assumed a larger importance in the activities pursued around and on the first of these edifices.

Frequencies of shell and bone at Str. 144-5-1st are a bit high when compared with those recorded at Strs. 144-1 and 144-2, although they are not nearly as elevated as those noted for Str. 144-11. These organic remains suggest that food was processed and consumed at this locale, much as it was in the neighboring domiciles to the east. The activities in question, however, did not apparently involve the intense or frequent use of grinding stones, no examples of which could be unambiguously assigned to the building's final phase. Similarly, although chipped stone implements were recovered here, their densities are lower than those recorded at Strs. 144-1, 144-2, and 144-11. The collection is once more dominated by obsidian blades (72%), whereas six perlite flakes and one core of this material are also found (table 4.3). The assortment of activities in which these implements figured conforms to the same pattern seen elsewhere; that is, cutting is the most commonly identified task, followed by scraping and whittling (table 4.4). If anything, whittling seems less well represented here than it is in other excavated portions of the settlement. No projectile points were recovered from Str. 144-5-1st.

These patterns imply that the full range of domestic chores was not enacted on Str. 144-5-1st. Attention apparently focused on serving, rather than storing, foods and liquids. The processing of grain was also not practiced here to any significant degree; nor was whittling a major component of the daily round.

It is difficult to account for the relatively high densities of *bajareque* fragments at Str. 144-5-1st, especially given the paucity of stone foundations associated with the building's final phase. One possibility is that the platform's superstructure walls were largely erected directly on the earthen summit without benefit of rock footings. It is just as likely, however, that some of these foundations were obliterated by recent activities that disturbed the extant footings or that a portion of the recovered *bajareque* derived from destroyed buildings that were incorporated in the platform's latest fill.

PVN 144

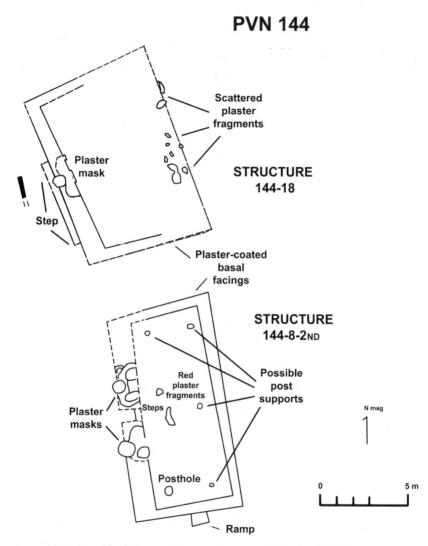

FIGURE 4.8 *Plan of final phase architecture, Structures 144-8 and 144-18*

Community Buildings

Structure 144-8, together with Str. 144-18, which is 2.9 m to the north, is on the west side of the main patio (figure 4.8). The first recorded activity at this locale was the burning of the earth on which Str. 144-8 would be erected. This firing altered the underlying soil to a depth of 0.04–0.07 m. Structure 144-8 began its use-life as an extensive surface-level building (Str. 144-8-3rd)

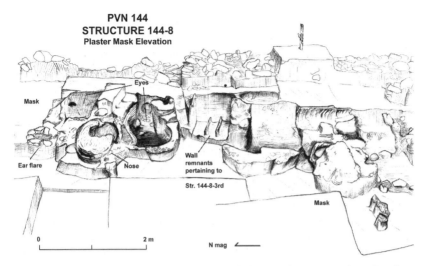

FIGURE **4.9** *Elevation of Structure 144-8's west side showing the stucco masks and evidence of earlier (Structure 144-8-3rd) construction (original drawing by Heather Ogston).*

covering 7 × 12.5 m. It was bounded by perishable walls 0.12–0.25 m wide set on stone foundations and, at least over their surviving bases, covered with a thin white plaster on the exterior. A 0.9-m-wide doorway in the south wall provided access to the interior. At least parts of the building's floor were covered by more plaster. Although the evidence is somewhat unclear, Str. 144-8-3rd was apparently divided into northern and southern rooms by an east-west–running perishable wall. The northern enclosure covers 34.5 m², while its southern counterpart encompasses 31.6 m². No evidence of built-in furniture was recorded, although large portions of Str. 144-8-3rd's interior were not fully exposed.

This early edifice was converted into a platform (Str. 144-8-2nd) that stood 0.6 m high, covered 87.5 m² at its base, and was bordered by stone facings battered back at an angle of approximately 30 degrees. The best-preserved, bottommost portions of these facings were coated with a white lime plaster. A 0.85-m-wide plaster-coated ramp provided access to the summit from the south, this incline having been built over the site of Str. 144-8–3rd's doorway. Formal access to Str. 144-8-2nd, however, was apparently achieved by ascending a 0.7-m-wide pair of plaster-coated steps built near the midpoint of the platform's west flank. These diminutive risers are bordered by two stucco masks built on stone armatures that represent a being distinguished by a pronounced bulbous nose, two flanking goggle-shaped eyes, bulging cheeks, and ear flares (figure 4.9). The masks are canted back at a slope of 33 degrees and measure

2.4 m north-south by 1.6 m east-west. They were frequently refurbished, having been resurfaced more than fifty times (Douglass and Mooney 2001).

The summit covers 51.7 m² and is surfaced in limestone plaster, the central 3.4 m² of which was painted red. The remaining portions of the summit floor were apparently left white. Structure 144-8-2nd's superstructure was delimited by sizable poles set at intervals of 2.5–4.5 m along its perimeter. No footings for perishable walls were noted; nor are there any signs of built-in features, such as benches or room dividers. The summit, in short, was extensive and roofed. Whether it was bounded by perishable walls remains unknown.

The final version of the platform (Str. 144-8-1st) retained its basic shape and access features but now stood 1.1 m high. The summit had been heavily damaged prior to excavation but seems to have been extensive (50.8 m²) and floored with a white plaster. Although we cannot be as certain in reconstructing the form of Str. 144-8-1st's superstructure as we are with the better-preserved earlier version, extant remains tentatively suggest that the summit now consisted of a large, featureless room. The sizable quantity of burned daub fragments found in terminal phase deposits implies that the superstructure was bounded by perishable walls.

Widespread disturbance suffered by Str. 144-8 prior to excavation means that tying materials recovered from this building to specific construction phases is very difficult. We have adopted a conservative stance in making such assignments (listed in table 4.1). No objects could be definitively assigned to Strs. 144-8-3rd and 144-8-2nd.

Despite the uncertainty attendant on associating artifacts with distinct phases of Str. 144-8's use, it is clear that this building yielded very few pottery sherds compared with most other constructions investigated at Site PVN 144. At 2 p/em², this is by far the lowest density noted in any portion of the main plaza except for Str. 144-18. Even if all the sherds, regardless of context, recovered from Str. 144-8 were included, the number would only rise to 5 p/em².

Modern activity on Str. 144-8 and in its vicinity may have inadvertently removed some pottery fragments, along with other artifacts, from the investigated area. Whereas this possibility is likely, it seems implausible that the impact of these disturbances alone was sufficient to reduce sherd yields to the noted levels. Figures for chipped stone artifacts, although low, were not dramatically different from those recorded elsewhere around the plaza, and the quantities of *bajareque* fragments were actually higher than those noted in other patio locales. It is unlikely that ceramic pieces were selectively removed from Str. 144-8 in the course of recent activities, leaving other artifact categories relatively undisturbed. While sherd densities were probably higher prior to the modifications visited on Str. 144-8, therefore, they were likely lower than those attested to at other, better-preserved Site PVN 144 buildings. This pattern implies that ceramic vessels were less intensively used in and around Str. 144-8-1st than they were at most of the other investigated edifices.

The proportion of bowl and jar rims in the Str. 144-8-1st assemblage matches that seen for Strs. 144-5-1st and 144-11 (table 4.2). In all three cases, bowls comprise over 70 percent of the collection, implying that serving food, drink, or both played a larger role than did storing these commodities at the edifices in question. While the Str. 144-8-1st figures must be treated with caution, the pattern identified here is suggestive and tentatively implies that, despite their different forms and dimensions, Strs. 144-5-1st, 144-8-1st, and 144-11 hosted activities in which the serving of comestibles played a significant part.

Incensario fragments, pieces of chipped and ground stone, and organic remains such as bone and shell are likewise relatively rare here. The composition of the chipped stone tool assemblage also diverges from that seen elsewhere at the settlement (table 4.3). On the one hand, obsidian blades do not dominate the collection to the extent seen at other buildings. These implements comprise slightly more than half of the total assemblage (58%), whereas perlite and chert are, correspondingly, more common than seen elsewhere (32% and 10% of the collection, respectively). In addition, very few of the analyzed fragments were apparently used, with only one blade showing evidence of cutting. Three casual perlite cores were also found here (table 4.4). The Str. 144-8 assemblage is characterized, however, by a locally unusual concentration of small projectile points made on obsidian blades (four in all). It is not so much that Str. 144-8-1st yielded more of these implements than any other building but rather that their proportions are unusually high (36% of all blades were fashioned into points here, versus 15% for Str. 144-2, the investigated building with the largest number of points at Site PVN 144).

This pattern tentatively points to several conclusions. Obsidian was, for whatever reason, less readily used at Str. 144-8-1st than it was in other portions of the settlement; perhaps it was not considered appropriate for the activities conducted there. Further, those scraping, cutting, and whittling tasks in which chipped stone implements were employed elsewhere around the main plaza apparently figured little in the activities pursued on this extensive edifice. In contrast, either projectile points were used relatively often here or this area was a favored place for storing and displaying them. Similarly, the relatively dense concentration of perlite cores at Str. 144-8-1st may point to the fashioning of simple flake tools in the immediate area. Most of those implements, however, were probably used in other locales, as indicated by the paucity of perlite flakes (three in all) in the analyzed collection.

The one artifact class abundantly represented in the Str. 144-8-1st excavation collections is *bajareque,* which at 3 p/em^2 is the highest density for this material noted anywhere at the settlement. The general prevalence of these burned wattle-and-daub fragments in all contexts implies that walls in the three construction phases were fashioned primarily of this material. It may also suggest that these constructions were regularly burned, possibly prior to initiating the next building effort.

Overall, materials associated with Str. 144-8-1st, and with Str. 144-8 in general, point to the conduct here of a select range of domestic and ritual activities, all at fairly low levels of intensity. The absence of clear domestic furniture, especially benches, coupled with the artifact data implies that Str. 144-8-1st and its predecessors were not used as residences. Instead, the large rooms found in each of the edifice's iterations tentatively indicate that the building served throughout its history as a gathering place for substantial numbers of people. The formal entrance—complete with flanking sculptures—provided for Strs. 144-8-1st and 144-8-2nd, and the use of plaster for flooring and exterior surfacing in all three versions, hint at the importance of these meetings to those involved. The general paucity of artifacts associated with Str. 144-8 in at least its final manifestation implies that the gatherings did not involve activities, such as food preparation, that left behind considerable material residues.

Structure 144-18, immediately north of Str. 144-8, was the tallest structure recorded at Site PVN 144. Although it stood roughly 2.5 m high when originally mapped in 1978, by 1996 most of Str. 144-18's summit had been planed off, and much of the edifice's east side was razed down to the base. Consequently, little can be said about Str. 144-18's building history and uses, although its final basal dimensions and overall form can be reconstructed (figure 4.8).

During the surviving construction stage, Str. 144-18 was a stone- and earth-filled platform that covered 7.7 x 10.7 m and was bounded on all sides by stone walls coated with limestone plaster. Extrapolating from the relatively well-preserved western flank, these basal facings were canted back at an angle of approximately 33 degrees, much like the bottommost portions of Strs. 144-8-2nd's and 144-8-1st's perimeter walls. Formal access to the summit was likely from the west, where what may be the bottommost riser of a staircase projects 0.35 m beyond Str. 144-18's basal line. This possible staircase is located south of the building's center line and is bounded on the north by a stucco mask that covers 1.2 x 2.6 m. Although heavily damaged, this feature has the pronounced nose seen on the masks that border Strs. 144-8-2nd's and 144-8-1st's western stair. Most likely, all three masks were originally very similar in construction and appearance, probably representing the same entity. No comparable mask was noted on the southern edge of Str. 144-18's putative stair. Fragments of limestone plaster, some of them painted red, were found on and around surviving portions of the platform. The summit may have originally been floored with this material, as was the case in the last two known versions of neighboring Str. 144-8.

Overall, Str. 144-18 resembles its southern counterpart in the use of a stucco mask to mark a formal western entry and possibly plaster flooring in its summit room(s). The sloping basal zones of the platform's perimeter facings also link it to building practices seen at Strs. 144-8-2nd and 144-8-1st.

The range of materials found in terminal debris contexts around Str. 144-18, as well as their relative densities, generally match those observed for Str. 144-8-1st. Frequencies of pottery sherds are once again fairly low, as are those of incensarios, chipped and ground stone, and bone and shell. Unlike the case for Str. 144-8-1st, the prevalence of *bajareque* in the Str. 144-18 assemblage is relatively muted, more in keeping with the densities of this material recovered elsewhere around the patio. The sample of nine form-classified rims (six of which are from bowls) retrieved from Str. 144-18's environs is too small to serve as the basis for advancing even tentative inferences concerning the relative importance of food serving and storage in the suite of activities conducted here.

Structures 144-8-1st and 144-18, therefore, can be jointly distinguished from other buildings at the settlement by what they lack. They also stand out for what they share in their chipped lithic assemblages (table 4.4). The distribution of activities represented in Str. 144-18's analyzed blade collection closely matches the pattern inferred for Str. 144-8-1st. Specifically, signs of scraping, cutting, and whittling are in this case totally absent, with the one clear tool form a single diminutive projectile point made on an obsidian blade (comprising 16% of the blade assemblage). In addition, as with Str. 144-8-1st, obsidian is not nearly as dominant in the lithic collection here as it is elsewhere at the site; 29 percent of the assemblage consists of this material, while perlite and chert make up 67 percent and 4 percent of the assemblage, respectively (table 4.3). The recovery of two cores, one perlite and the other chert, from Str. 144-18's environs also points to the fashioning of casual flake tools in the area. Unlike Str. 144-8-1st, however, the thirteen perlite flakes found here may indicate that at least some of those tools were also employed nearby.

To be sure, we are working with a sample heavily impacted by the recent destruction of the investigated edifice. All we can say, and that with trepidation, is that the surviving artifacts associated with the final use phases of Strs. 144-18 and 144-8 point to the performance of the same restricted array of domestic and ritual behaviors at the same low levels of intensity in both cases. Structure 144-18's greater height, however, may suggest that it served somewhat different purposes than did Str. 144-8-1st.

FIGURE 4.10 *Structure 144-19, section*

Trash Deposit

Structure 144-19 appears on the surface as an amorphously shaped earthen mound that stands 0.45 m high and covers roughly 7 m × 15 m (figure 4.10). It is located in the main plaza, about 15.5 m northeast of Str. 144-8. The loosely consolidated, dark brown soil that constitutes Str. 144-19's core (Unit 1) contains sizable quantities of artifacts (tables 4.1 and 4.3). This deposit is 0.49 m thick at its approximate center and extends for 11.1 m northeast-southwest (the northwest and southeast sides of the feature were not uncovered). Unit 1 lacks clear margins demarcated by boundary walls, its edges simply petering out. The large amount of cultural material found within Unit 1 (72 p/em^2, 200 p/em^3), coupled with its amorphous shape and lack of clear construction, implies that it was not the hearting of a building but rather an accumulation of trash generated by activities that occurred in the main plaza. Presumably, this debris would have eventually been removed outside the patio, but the residents never completed that chore before the settlement was abandoned. In fact, the Unit 1 trash may have been intentionally left in place for a time as a tangible reminder of the events that produced it.

The Unit 1 artifact assemblage stands out in comparison with the material recovered from other parts of the main plaza in several respects. First, there is, by local standards, a very high concentration of pottery sherds here. The preponderance of bowl rims within the small form-classified sample (table 4.2) weakly suggests that the majority of ceramic containers represented by the recovered sherds were used to serve food and drink. Incensario fragments are also unusually well represented. In fact, a little under half (43%) of all incense burner pieces recovered from terminal debris contexts around the main plaza were found in Unit 1.

The relatively large chipped lithic collection generally conforms to patterns recorded elsewhere at Site PVN 144. Obsidian blades dominate the Unit 1 collection (84%), with perlite and chert far more sparsely represented (10% and 6%, respectively) (table 4.3). Once again, cutting is the most commonly represented activity, followed by scraping and whittling, in that order (table 4.4). Scraping is somewhat better represented here, however, than is the case elsewhere at the settlement. The three small projectile points found in these excavations comprise 9 percent of the analyzed obsidian blades from Unit 1, a relatively high figure that still falls easily within the range seen throughout the main plaza except at Strs. 144-18 and 144-8-1st.

While some bone, including a fragment of antler, was retrieved from this deposit, Unit 1 is notable for its complete lack of shell. Especially obvious is the absence of the carapaces of *Pachychilus* sp. that are nearly ubiquitous in Roble phase deposits, especially in middens, throughout Site PVN 144. Also missing are representatives of the ground stone artifact class. It appears, therefore, that grinding foodstuffs and processing crustaceans and snails for meals did not commonly take place within the main plaza, although the products of those efforts may have been consumed there.

Bajareque densities within Unit 1 are high; only those recorded at Strs. 144-5-1st and 144-8-1st within the main plaza show more elevated levels. The relative prevalence of these pieces may hint at the former existence of perishable constructions that were set up in the plaza, at least some of which were burned and their remains included with the rest of the trash.

Taken together, these figures strongly imply that the behaviors in which the recovered materials functioned generally mimic those seen at other excavated locales around the patio. Those activities involving pottery vessels, incense burners, and chipped stone may have been more intensively pursued here than elsewhere, whereas those in which snails and grinding stones were involved seem to be underrepresented.

These figures imply that Site PVN 144's principal patio was an area in which a limited range of activities was carried out at high levels of intensity. At least some of these behaviors involved the use of relatively large numbers of ritual objects, specifically incense burners, as well as ceramic serving containers and chipped stone tools.

Main Plaza Summary

There is strong evidence for the differential distribution of activities among various locales associated with the main plaza during its final period of construction and use. Two sizable residences, Strs. 144-1 and 144-2, bordered the patio's northern margin, each containing central benches that overlooked ample rooms. These edifices' large sizes, coupled with the evidence for plaster floors in Str. 144-2, imply that they were homes to people of elevated rank within the Site 144 community. Artifacts associated with these constructions point to the performance of the same domestic chores using the same materials in each of them.

A pair of community buildings flanks the plaza on the west (Strs. 144-8 and 144-18). Structure 144-8 underwent at least three building episodes, rising from an extensive surface-level edifice to an approximately 1.1-m-high platform. Throughout these renovations, Str. 144-8 was characterized by ample, plaster-floored rooms that contained no surviving built-in furniture. The western entrance to its last two versions (Strs. 144-8-2nd and 144-8-1st) was also flanked by two of the three stucco sculptures recorded in the Naco valley during any period (the third is on neighboring Str. 144-18). Structure 144-18's poor state of preservation when investigated makes assessment of its form and functions difficult. What we can ascertain from the extant architectural fragments is that the platform's final version was sizable (ca. 2.5 m high), that it was decorated with at least one stucco mask on the west, and that the summit and at least parts of the basal facings were coated with lime plaster. The relative paucity of artifacts retrieved from both buildings, taken together with their distinctive architectural arrangements, suggests that they were not residences. Instead, their extensive, largely unencumbered rooms likely served as venues for meetings of influential individuals from Site PVN 144 and perhaps Naco and Site PVN 306. The importance of such putative gatherings was highlighted by the elaborate ways these facilities were decorated.

Structures 144-5 and 144-11 were, at least during some episodes in their histories, devoted to the performance of a limited range of specific activities. Structure 144-11, on the plaza's eastern edge, consists of one sizable, largely open and featureless room sitting atop a 0.2-m-high earthen platform. Associated with this enclosure is what appears to be a formally prepared trash deposit composed almost exclusively of large quantities of *Pachychilus* sp. shell. Whatever else was going on at and around Str. 144-11, the processing of riverine snails was significant to the building's function. The location of the midden, overlooking the main plaza and adjoining Str. 144-11's formal entrance, implies that these activities were accorded a place of some prominence and may have been closely linked to events that transpired in the plaza.

Structure 144-5 seems to have begun its use-life (Str. 144-5-2nd) as an extensive earthen platform, into the western portion of which were built two flat-bottomed basins lined with fired earth and, at least in one case, plaster. Structure 144-5-2nd's ample summit was apparently open, featureless, and burned over much of its extent. Although the building's functions are unclear, it seems likely that the pits were used to store food, liquid, or both. The adjoining summit may have been a staging ground for processing these comestibles, its burned surface possibly resulting from the lighting of many cooking fires over a protracted span. Subsequently, the northern basin was converted into a firing facility, an oven or kiln, while its southern analog was used as a trash receptacle. Burning on the summit may have continued during this interval. By the time Str. 144-5-1st was erected, all evidence of the basins and the fired earth summit was buried beneath a mantle of fill. Structure 144-5-1st was not apparently converted into a residence. Instead, it seems to have served some specialized function associated with food serving.

Although very different in form, Strs. 144-11 and 144-5 seem to have been associated with aspects of food storage and preparation throughout their known histories. It is possible that at least some of the meals derived from these activities were consumed in the main plaza. The debris from one or more of those feasts, represented by Unit 1 of Str. 144-19, contains a disproportionately high density of ceramic containers, most of which may have been bowls suitable for food serving. These gatherings were apparently accompanied by rituals, as signified by the locally unprecedented concentration of incense burners in that same deposit.

The dimensions of Strs. 144-8 and 144-18, along with the scale of food processing represented by Strs. 144-5-2nd and 144-11, seem out of proportion to the size of the domestic unit that resided around the plaza. These facilities were almost certainly designed to accommodate and feed more people than likely lived in nearby domiciles. As is argued in chapters 6, 8, and 10, these edifices and the plaza they define probably supported gatherings of those who participated in different ways in a single network that encompassed all occupants of Naco and Sites PVN 306 and PVN 144.

Site PVN 144's main plaza, therefore, was a locus of residence for a few and a gathering place for many. A particularly influential subset of those living in the basin may have convened in the rooms of Strs. 144-8 and 144-18, while all members of the broader community periodically assembled in the plaza itself. Whereas the former meetings generated few tangible remains, the latter apparently combined feasting with ritual. Supporting those large-scale meals were specialized facilities in which food and drink could be stored and processed at considerable scales. Consequently, the main plaza seems to have served as a point of intersection in which people participating in the multiple networks of house, household, site, and settlement cluster convened to enliven and reinforce their membership in extensive webs, in part by eating and worshipping together.

NON-PLAZA MATERIAL PATTERNS

Excavations conducted outside the main plaza took the form of fifty-six test pits, eight of which were dug within an equal number of surface-visible artifact scatters; the remaining forty-eight probes were set in areas beyond the patio that lacked signs of obvious construction or occupation. In two of the latter tests, Subops. 144AE and 144AM, relatively dense concentrations of Roble phase materials comparable to those found within most artifact scatters were uncovered. Materials from Subops. 144AE and 144AM are hereafter included when discussing the artifact scatters. No architecture was revealed by these tests, although artifacts, mostly of Roble phase date, were dispersed over an area measuring approximately 41,000 m².

The artifact scatters visible on ground surface average 3–6 m in diameter, and the investigated examples are uniformly thin (at most, 0.5 m thick; only the Subop. 144AE deposit is over 0.4 m thick). They contain large quantities of cultural material (417 to 2,119 p/em²; table 4.1) set in fine-grained soils that range in color from dark to yellowish brown. Such densities indicate that these artifact scatters represent middens, while their shallowness suggests that they accumulated over relatively short periods of time. Tests dug beyond these concentrations revealed much lower artifact frequencies (no materials at all were recorded in thirteen probes), indicating that each artifact scatter was relatively distinct and not part of a continuous sheet midden. Analyses of material recovered from excavations in ten of these trash deposits suggest that their contents resulted from a varied set of overlapping, but not uniformly distributed, activities.

Turning first to what is not well represented in the studied collections, only a few fragments of ground stone and incensarios were recovered from the deposits. In a sense, this is hardly surprising, as members of these artifact classes are rarely unearthed in most excavated contexts at Site PVN 144. Still, representatives of other material categories were commonly found in the studied deposits. Hence, the paucity of incense burners and grinding implements here is likely a result of the relative unimportance of grain processing and ritual in the activities of those who generated the investigated trash.

In general, ceramic frequencies are high in all but one of the studied deposits, ranging from 295 to 936 p/em² (Op. 484, Midden 1 yielded no ceramics). These figures far exceed the numbers obtained from the Site PVN 144 main plaza, where the greatest ceramic density is attested to within Str. 144-19's Unit 1 (61 p/em²). There is no clear patterning in sherd densities across the excavated middens save that Artifact Scatter 16, with the highest concentration of chipped lithics (73 p/em²), also has the lowest density of pottery fragments (295 p/em²). Operation 484, Midden 1 represents an even more extreme expression of this negative correlation; no pottery sherds were found here, while the density of chipped stone was the second highest among the artifact scatters (40 p/em²). Such patterning may hint at some specialization in the suite of activities that employed stone tools in the immediate areas of both deposits. Very likely, those jettisoning trash within Op. 484, Midden 1 were exclusively engaged in tasks that employed lithic implements. Otherwise, sherd densities do not seem to correlate in any identifiable way with the frequencies of other artifact classes.

Three principal patterns are identified in the distribution of vessel forms in the studied collections: those in which bowls predominate (Artifact Scatters

16 and 21), one in which jars are more numerous (Op. 144AE), and two cases where the major form categories comprise nearly equal proportions of the assemblages (Artifact Scatters 18 and 19; table 4.2). Based on these data, it appears that ceramic vessels were widely and fairly intensively used throughout the area surrounding the main plaza, the behaviors in which they functioned involved serving and storing comestibles, and the relative importance of these two general activities varied across the investigated area.

Densities of shell, most deriving from *Pachychilus* sp., are generally far greater in the recorded artifact scatters than in plaza contexts. The only exception is Feature 1 on Str. 144-11's west side. Here, shell densities fall above the upper end of the range of variation noted for the excavated trash deposits (table 4.1). Outside of this general contrast between plaza/non-plaza settings, there are notable differences in shell densities among the investigated middens. They range from a low of 6 p/em^2 (Artifact Scatter 16) to a high of 1,964 p/em^2 in Op. 484, Midden 1. Such variation once again hints at behavioral distinctions among the people who deposited debris in these distinct middens. Whereas everyone who used the excavated trash deposits seems to have been consuming meat from snails and, to a lesser extent, freshwater clams, they may not all have been doing so to the same extent.

Patterning in the chipped stone tool and debris collections demonstrates both unity in the materials represented and dissimilarity in the density of lithic items and the degree and nature of tool use across the investigated middens. Imported obsidian, primarily in the form of blades, is the most commonly represented raw material identified in all studied collections (table 4.3). Locally available perlite and chert, usually in the form of flakes, appear in much smaller numbers, if at all. In fact, obsidian dominates these assemblages more decisively than is the case within the main plaza; three of the seven analyzed midden collections had nothing but obsidian in them, and obsidian comprised 73–94 percent of each of the remaining four studied assemblages. Whatever else this pattern might signify, it suggests that foreign obsidian was easily available to those living and working in the environs of the Site PVN 144 main plaza.

The density of chipped lithics within the investigated collections does differ markedly. This variation falls out in these general categories: middens with 11–17 p/em^2 (Artifact Scatters 18 and 27 and Op. 484, Midden 2), those with 24–29 p/em^2 (Artifact Scatters 17, 19, and 21 and Subop. AE), and two examples with 40 and 73 p/em^2 (Op. 484, Midden 1 and Artifact Scatter 16, respectively); the Subop. 144AM deposit alone yielded no chipped lithics. It appears, therefore, that there was considerable variation in the intensity and frequency of the tasks that employed chipped stone tools.

The manner and extent to which these implements were used also differ across the investigated middens (table 4.4). Tools found in Artifact Scatters 16 and 21 exhibit the characteristic pattern found in most other excavated contexts at Site PVN 144, in which cutting is the most commonly attested form of use, followed by scraping and whittling. The chipped implements retrieved from Artifact Scatters 17 and 19, on the other hand, showed no signs of use or significant modification. Interestingly, the densities of chipped stone tools and debris in Artifact Scatters 17, 19, and 21 are very similar (ranging from 27 to 29 p/em^2). It does not appear, therefore, that the absence of observable use-wear correlates with differences in ease of access to the relevant raw materials. Based on the available evidence, therefore, it seems that chipped lithics were deposited in trash deposits in approximately equal frequencies in both those areas where the tools were clearly employed in a variety of tasks and those where they were used little, if at all. The possibility that the seemingly pristine lithics recovered from Artifact Scatters 17 and 19 are the residues of stone tool production is negated by the lack of other evidence for such fabrication there. These two deposits may therefore represent the detritus of activities in which chipped stone implements were employed for such short durations that signs of use were not inscribed indelibly on their surfaces.

Frequencies of burned wattle-and-daub fragments also vary among the investigated middens, from none recorded in Artifact Scatters 16, 144AE, and 144AM and Op. 484, Midden 2 to a high of 118 p/em^2 in Artifact Scatter 21. The remaining deposits yielded numbers ranging from 2 to 8 p/em^2. The behavioral implications of these differences are unclear. Most probably, *bajareque* fragments signal the presence of perishable buildings in the immediate vicinity of the trash deposits in which they were found. Those scatters that lack wattle-and-daub pieces might therefore not have been associated with any standing architecture. Just as likely, however, the observed discrepancies reflect whether nearby buildings were burned prior to abandonment.

The excavated deposits described here represent discrete collections of trash that resulted from activities pursued in their immediate environs. Although the behaviors involved varied somewhat from place to place, they all fell within the general domain of domestic chores involving ceramics, lithics, and various forms of fauna. Most likely, therefore, the studied artifact scatters are the material residues of distinct house groups, the members of which engaged in much the same range of tasks using the same sorts of materials, to somewhat different degrees. The one possible exception is Op. 484, Midden 1, with its high preponderance of chipped lithics and faunal remains but no ceramics. If this sample fairly represents the range of behaviors conducted nearby, then its skewed patterning points to the pursuit of a specialized set of activities in its immediate vicinity, possibly the processing of meat primarily from riverine snails.

GENERAL SUMMARY

Patterns noted in the form and distribution of Roble phase architecture and artifacts at Site PVN 144 point to differences in the behaviors of the site's occupants. In general, however, these variations are relatively continuous, with few definitive breaks. It appears that everyone at the settlement used much the same portable objects for much the same purposes, although the behaviors in question varied somewhat in their intensities and scales. For example, rituals that employed incensarios are attested to at all investigated structures around the main plaza and at four of the areas associated with as many investigated middens beyond that patio. The dense concentration of incense burner fragments in the Str. 144-19, Unit 1 deposit within the plaza, however, implies that this extensive open space was a major center for religious observances involving relatively large numbers of incensarios wielded, presumably, by considerable numbers of people. Similarly, *Pachychilus* sp. shells are found widely within and outside the main plaza but are particularly concentrated at Str. 144-11 on that patio's east side and in five of the artifact scatters beyond the plaza. Such a distribution suggests that processing snails for consumption was likely occurring throughout Site PVN 144 but was especially concentrated in a few locales.

The observed material patterns, therefore, hint at a situation in which intra-site unity was encouraged in part by common participation in the same range of basic domestic and ritual activities that employed the same array of materials. Differences among people were marked not by their engagement in tasks in which few others took part. Instead, distinctions were signified by variations in the scale and intensity with which widely shared actions were pursued by those residing in different parts of the settlement. The relative uniformity of material remains and the behaviors in which they were employed, therefore, were likely underlain by values and understandings at least nominally shared by all members of the Roble phase Site PVN 144 community.

More pronounced interpersonal differences are expressed through site planning and architecture. One such distinction is between those who lived around the main plaza and others who resided beyond it. The latter, represented now solely by their middens, did not live in plaza-focused clusters. Instead, the artifact scatters identified on the surface and through excavation seem to have been dispersed across the landscape with no clear or coherent plan. This statement must be treated as provisional. We already know that some middens were not visible on ground surface (for example, those revealed in Subops. 144AE and 144AM). Still, concerted efforts to locate, through survey, artifact scatters near those we did identify failed to reveal them, suggesting that settlement away from the main plaza was widely dispersed (a pattern also noted at Roble phase Site PVN 306, where it was far easier to recognize artifact scatters). It is likely, therefore, that most of Site PVN 144's Roble phase residents lived in discrete houses, relations among which were not signaled by their proximity.

Site PVN 144's main plaza represents a larger, more inclusive form of organization. The arrangement of its component buildings around a central patio implies that those who resided here shared a sense of themselves as members of a distinct household composed of at least two houses, materialized in Strs. 144-1 and 144-2. The close spacing of these residences bespeaks comparably intimate social connections, a relationship confirmed by their conduct of nearly identical activities using the same forms of material culture.

Not all of the structures surrounding this space were residences, however. Two were apparently set aside to host gatherings of some importance to the community-at-large (Strs. 144-8 and 144-18), while two more were seemingly devoted to the conduct of specialized activities including, but probably not limited to, food and liquid storage (Str. 144-5-2nd), food processing (Strs. 144-5-2nd's second version and 144-11), and possibly pottery firing (Str. 144-5-2nd). The goods produced and curated in these locales almost certainly exceeded the needs of the patio's immediate residents, who in any case were apparently supporting themselves through their own labor. Instead, the large scale of these behaviors, coupled with their conduct overlooking the plaza, implies that their products were intended for use by the relatively large numbers of people who convened in that extensive open space. Evidence provided by Str. 144-19, Unit 1 suggests that such putative gatherings involved religious ritual and feasting.

What we hypothesize from the information in hand is that by the Roble phase, Site PVN 144 was a focus for activities by which multiple overlapping sociopolitical networks were enacted. At the smallest scale, these webs included those sharing a common residence, whose ties were instantiated and reaffirmed every day through regular and oft-repeated interactions. Domiciles associated with the middens identified beyond the patio, as well as Strs. 144-1 and 144-2 on that plaza, were focal points of such webs. The common projects in which these individuals cooperated involved domestic chores, including food preparation, storage, and consumption, as well as religious rites pursued at fairly low levels of intensity.

Participants in several of these house nets comprised one household, the members of which lived in close proximity to each other on the margins of the central plaza. As with the houses, this net was enacted through intense participation in daily tasks, this time by near neighbors. A wider, site-wide network was enlivened through activities pursued in and around the main plaza. This large open space could accommodate sizable numbers of people and was easily reached through wide passages between the surrounding buildings. As noted earlier, however, the plaza likely also hosted gatherings of local worthies and their clients drawn from throughout the settlement cluster composed of Naco, Site PVN 306, and Site PVN 144. Once gathered, the reality and emotional significance of the connections that linked different houses, households, and sites were created and reinforced through common participation in rites of intensification that involved shared meals and religious devotions. Food and beverages for those feasts may have been derived from storage facilities set on the plaza (Str. 144-5-2nd) and prepared at prominent places surrounding that arena (Strs. 144-11 and 144-5-2nd). By juxtaposing sites of storage, processing, and consumption within a dramatic setting hedged round with substantial edifices at the settlement, abstract ties of affiliation could have been made vibrantly and vitally real to those taking part (Goffman 1974; see chapter 8).

Coordination of these large-scale tasks may have been facilitated by the network of local leaders drawn from Strs. 144-1 and 144-2, Site PVN 306's EPP, and Naco's northeast principal plaza (see chapters 3 and 5), who gathered periodically in the ample, lavishly decorated settings provided by Strs. 144-8 and 144-18. Given the sizes of the rooms provided for such purposes, it seems that the emphasis was on including numerous people in the decision-making process. If the artifacts associated with these edifices are any guide to the behaviors that took place within them, the putative meetings do not seem to have been occasions for lavish feasting. That sort of behavior was apparently reserved for the larger gatherings in the plaza to the east.

This reconstruction undoubtedly simplifies a complex reality. One factor that likely disrupted this seamless interlocking of parts was power. Although questions of power are reserved for chapter 6, the nets described in the present chapter were not based solely on egalitarian principles. The two recorded domiciles on the main plaza are also the most substantial residences known for the site. The considerable effort that went into building and, in the case of Str. 144-2, decorating these edifices sets them apart from the largely perishable buildings associated with the middens beyond the plaza. The activities pursued in the ample and imposing spaces provided within Strs. 144-1 and 144-2 may have been roughly the same as those conducted elsewhere at the center, but they were enacted in settings that distinguished them and their practitioners from everyone else. Similarly, as large as the rooms within various iterations of Str. 144-8 were, they could not have held all members of the settlement cluster's population. Consequently, it seems likely that certain Naco cluster residents were regularly singled out to be participants in gatherings that transpired in relatively lavish surroundings while others were excluded from them. No matter who was invited, the guest list encompassed a subset of all those who inhabited the valley, a network of influential people operating within a broader web of interacting houses and households. The common project that united these influential individuals most likely involved the acquisition, maintenance, and display of some forms of power. We return to this point in chapter 6.

Site PVN 144, therefore, provided venues for the instantiation of variably overlapping interaction nets, the members of which had differing affiliations expressed in distinct contexts. Every day, people actively participated in the lives of their individual houses. They were also involved in a more extensive net that linked them to others within and beyond the site, although the significance of these more abstract ties may have been brought home only occasionally during large-scale ceremonies held in the main plaza. Intersecting these general networks were affiliations that at least periodically singled out individuals who together played significant roles in coordinating the actions of large numbers of people, possibly the society-at-large, in common actions. To be sure, these are just the bare bones of what was certainly a multilayered structure. Even this skeletal rendition of ancient reality, however, suggests the complex and dynamic interplay of interpersonal interactions that once enlivened Site PVN 144's Roble phase occupation.

FIVE

Activity Patterning at Roble Phase Naco

The site of Naco has long been identified in the ethnohistoric and archaeological literature as a major political and population center that served as an entrepôt in interregional exchange (e.g., Chamberlain 1966; Strong, Kidder, and Paul 1938; Wonderley 1981). Direct investigation of the site prior to 1977, however, was limited to test excavations undertaken over the course of ten days in 1936, during which five constructions in Naco's center were cleared to varying extents (Strong, Kidder, and Paul 1938: 27–34). Anthony Wonderley's systematic mapping and excavation at Naco during 1977 and 1979 provided a far more comprehensive account of the settlement's history of occupation, as well as the nature and extent of its Late Postclassic settlement (Wonderley 1981, 1985). In all, Wonderley excavated nine structures in the site core, five beyond that area, and four shallow middens (three outside the core and one within it) and conducted two additional tests away from architecture in Naco's epicenter (Wonderley 1981). One additional probe was dug within a midden situated 1.3 km southeast of the architectural core along the west bank of the Rio Naco (Wonderley 1981). Based on this work, Wonderley identified three facets of Late Postclassic occupation at Naco and reconstructed changes in behavioral patterns within the settlement and the connections its residents enjoyed with those living beyond the site's boundaries. This report (1981), coupled with Wonderley's later publications on the work (1985, 1986), defines current understandings of Naco's place within the late prehistoric Mesoamerican world.

In brief, Wonderley argues that Naco was an indigenous settlement that, during what he defined as the middle facet of the Late Postclassic (AD 1250–1450), covered approximately 160 ha and was dominated by foreign interlopers—most likely Chol speakers—who originated at the base of the Yucatan peninsula. Bearing a "Mexicanized Maya" culture, these immigrants introduced new ceramic and architectural styles along with a locally unprecedented emphasis on the exploitation of riverine resources. The resulting synthesis of autochthonous and foreign elements resulted in a culture that differed markedly from its predecessors in the eponymous basin. The migrants were apparently attracted to the valley by its strategic location athwart one of the premier trade routes linking Mesoamerica to the west and north with Central America to the south and east. Once established as a commercial center, Naco grew rapidly to encompass 160 ha. Wonderley's relatively large sample of excavated middle facet contexts did not reveal strong evidence of political centralization or hierarchy. Materials of all sorts, including elaborately decorated ceramics and imported obsidian blades, were widely distributed across the center, suggesting more or less equal access to valuables by all of the inhabitants. The concentration of larger-scale, elaborately decorated constructions around two neighboring plazas in the site core hints at the privileged command over labor some of those inhabitants enjoyed. Denizens of the site core may also have consumed greater quantities and varieties of meat than did their counterparts who lived beyond the epicenter. These political divisions might have correlated with ethnic distinctions. Material features associated with "Mexicanized" cultures, such as ground platform abrasions on obsidian blades, side-notched projectile points, and ceramic comales, seem to have been concentrated within the immediate vicinity of the site center. These political and ethnic distinctions, however, were muted.

The late facet (AD 1450–Conquest) possibly marked a shift in rulership with the arrival of a new cadre of foreign trader-warriors, this time from the Pacific Coast of Central America. The proposed change is signified by the appearance of new bichrome and polychrome ceramic types, the designs of which, Wonderley argues, are not outgrowths of indigenous Naco valley decorative traditions. Constructions raised now in the site core also reflect novel building styles, marked especially by the appearance of thick white plaster summit surfaces, construction fill composed of boulders, and platform facings made of stone slabs set horizontally and vertically. The form and location of an I-shaped ballcourt erected immediately off the southwest corner of the southwest principal plaza also resemble similar complexes associated with the

"Mexicanized" Maya of the Postclassic highlands and lowlands. The fact that three edifices in Naco's architectural core show signs of burning at roughly this interval suggests that the transition from the middle to late facet occupation in central Naco may not have been entirely peaceful. This newly constituted polity was what the Spanish encountered in 1523, cursorily recorded, and rapidly destroyed.

Much additional research into Late Postclassic developments has taken place in the Naco valley and beyond since 1979. At the time Wonderley wrote, we had only a rudimentary grasp of the basin's prehistory, let alone an understanding of the multifarious foreign transactions in which its denizens engaged at any point in the valley's 2.5 millennia of prehispanic settlement. We will bring this newly acquired data to bear on Wonderley's results in an attempt to make sense of his pioneering investigations within currently evolving interpretive frameworks. This reinterpretation is not meant as a criticism of the earlier work; in fact, Wonderley's monograph (1981) provides an excellent basis for rethinking his discoveries. What we offer instead is a new perspective on developments at Roble phase Naco that contextualizes these events and patterns in processes revealed by research conducted since 1979 throughout the valley and Southeast Mesoamerica generally.

In pursuing this comparison, we will collapse behavioral and material patterns from middle and late facet Naco into one composite picture of the settlement dating to the Roble phase. There are several reasons for this strategy. First, according to Wonderley (1981), late facet Naco retained the same basic form and size as its immediate predecessor, with most changes attributed to this span relating to modifications made on several buildings in the site core and the addition of the ballcourt. Second, relatively few pure late facet contexts were sampled during the 1977 and 1979 investigations, with most information on activity structuring coming from studies of more common middle facet remains scattered across the center (Wonderley 1981). Wonderley felt confident using the middle facet data as bases for interpreting Late Postclassic behavioral patterning at Naco in general, and we follow his lead here. Finally, in our own investigations at Sites PVN 306 and PVN 144, we were unable to distinguish between middle and late facet occupations. It is our opinion, based on the enlarged database, that the shifts in architectural and ceramic styles used to define these intervals at Naco are relatively minor and do not describe temporally significant behavioral transformations applicable to the entire valley. For example, the bichrome and polychrome ceramics whose advent heralds the late facet at Naco comprise a very small proportion of the entire Naco assemblage and are found largely in the environs of the main plaza. As Wonderley argues (1981), these minority taxa may represent a functionally specific subcomplex of the Late Postclassic assemblage tied to events that transpired in the vicinity

127

of Naco's largest buildings. As we see it, however, their appearance cannot be restricted to a specific portion of that span. The same case can be made for the modes on utilitarian ceramics Wonderley advances as temporally diagnostic of the late facet. Without clear stratigraphic sequences, in short, it is not possible consistently and reliably to distinguish among facets within the thirteenth-through early–sixteenth-century occupation of the Naco valley.

ACTIVITY PATTERNING IN THE MAIN PLAZAS

By the mid-1970s, Roble phase Naco was almost completely submerged beneath the modern town of the same name. This growth has accelerated since then, and now nearly every part of the late prehistoric center has been incorporated into a modern house lot. Consequently, even the most substantial of the settlement's Roble phase edifices have been damaged, and the many middens once identifiable from artifact scatters on ground surface have vanished. These modern modifications had greatly altered the appearance of prehistoric Naco by 1977 and almost completely obliterated it thirty years later. Comparing material and behavioral patterning at Naco with the patterns recorded at Sites PVN 144 and PVN 306, therefore, is difficult because in the 1970s, as well as now, Naco was not as well preserved as were the last two centers when they were investigated. Still, some sense of the overall arrangement of buildings and relations among activities can be inferred for Roble phase Naco.

Southwest Principal Plaza

As is the case with Sites PVN 144 and PVN 306, Naco is dominated by an architectural core defined by relatively substantial platforms that, in this case, bound two adjoining plazas set in a southwest-northeast line (figure 5.1). The southwest member of the dyad is largely open on the north and contains within its bounds Str. 4F-1 (figure 5.2; Strong, Kidder, and Paul's Mound 6). At 4 m high, this edifice is at least twice the size of the next largest platform recorded at the center (Strong, Kidder, and Paul 1938: figure 3). As Wonderley notes, however, about half of the observed height was likely made up of tumbled stones from the superstructure, which had been removed prior to his investigations. The building itself was heavily damaged on its west side but was relatively well preserved on the east face as of 1979. Structure 4F-1 started off as a "plaster-coated earth column in the form of a wheel with eight cogs" (Wonderley 1981: 56). The building measured 4 m across, stood 1 m high, and had a featureless summit. Sets of two to three steps may have been located in each of the interstices between the cogs; this was the case in the two uncovered instances. The early column was renovated three or four times, culminating in

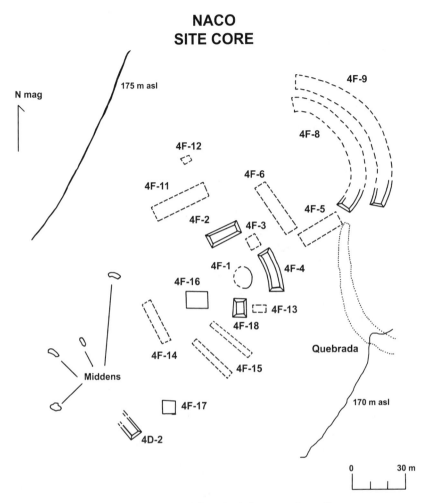

FIGURE 5.1 *Roble phase Naco site core (after Wonderley 1981, figure 5)*

a circular, plaster-coated platform measuring 11.3 m across. A plaster-covered "skirt" slopes up to the platform's edge, while a stone-faced circle with at least five stone "bastions," or cogs, projecting out from it was raised atop the basal platform (Wonderley 1981). The surface of the circle between the bastions is battered back toward the summit. The circular superstructure was at least partly surfaced with stones and contained a 0.6-m-high plaster-coated bench. Traces of red, yellow, tan, and blue pigments recovered from the summit suggest that the single superstructure room was brightly painted. Steps mounted Str. 4F-1 on the north and the west.

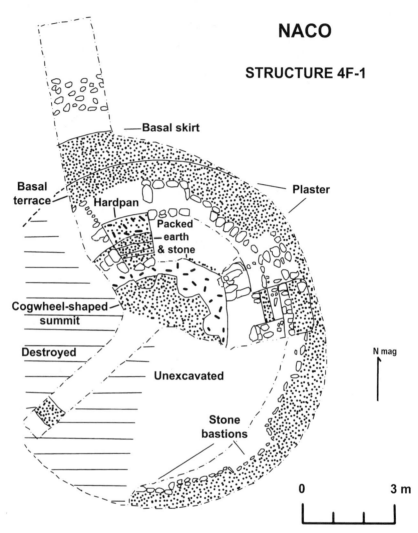

NACO

STRUCTURE 4F-1

Basal skirt

Basal terrace

Hardpan

Packed earth & stone

Plaster

Cogwheel-shaped summit

Destroyed

Unexcavated

Stone bastions

N mag

0   3 m

FIGURE 5.2 *Structure 4F-1 plan (after Wonderley 1981, figure 6)*

Structure 4F-1 generally resembles Str. 306-19 found within Site PVN 306's western principal plaza (WPP). This building was also characterized early in its history by eight arms projecting from a central core, a feature it retained with decreasing physical salience throughout its use-life. Structure 306-19's final version was, like Str. 4F-1's last stage, roughly circular, bordered by a plaster skirt that sloped up to the main body of the platform. The frequent and extensive use of plaster on Str. 306-19 also parallels the application of this material on Str. 4F-1. Structure 306-17, on the south margin of the WPP, had a more straightforward circular form. It too, however, was framed in its final iteration by a basal sloping zone that rose toward the platform. Structures 306-17 and 306-19 are somewhat smaller than Str. 4F-1's final version; the first two are 1.03 m and 0.8 m high and their platforms measure 8 m across and 9.9 m × 6.9 m, respectively. There are other differences as well. The Site PVN 306 examples apparently supported monuments, at least one of which was of carved stone, and neither evinced signs of the summit bench or painted superstructure surfaces seen in Str. 4F-1. Associated artifacts were sparse in all three cases, suggesting that any detritus generated in the course of activities pursued in and around the buildings was carefully cleared away.

Even allowing for the observed differences, there are enough formal similarities among the three edifices to suggest that they expressed similar concepts, most likely related to beliefs concerning Quetzalcoatl/Ehecatl (Wonderley 1981; see also chapter 8); were foci of public gatherings centered on open plazas located in the western portions of major site cores; and represented relatively significant investments of both skilled and unskilled labor in their construction. Structures 4F-1, 306-17, and 306-19, therefore, likely played similar roles in community religious events.

The six excavated buildings delimiting Naco's southwest plaza (Strs. 4F-2/4, 4F-7, 4F-14, and 4F-16) are generally platforms with earthen (Strs. 4F-2, 4F-4) and cobble fills (Strs. 4F-3 and 4F-7) capped with plaster surfaces, at least some of which are painted red (Wonderley 1981). They stand 0.4–2 m tall, cover 5.5–165 m² basally, and lack clear evidence for formal superstructures. Although most of the edifices are square or rectangular, Str. 4F-4 on the northeast side of the plaza has a crescent shape, its concave face looking to the southwest. The plaza they define was apparently surfaced with earth and covers 1,020 m². Few artifacts of any sort were found during investigation of any of these buildings except for Strs. 4F-14 and 4F-16.

Excavation of Str. 4F-14 on the plaza's southwest side revealed an artifact-rich deposit composed of dark-colored earth and measuring 5 m northeast-southwest and 0.34 m thick at its deepest point. The cultural material included in this lens was predominately composed of pottery sherds, many from decorated incense burners, and was burned; charcoal flecks were recorded throughout the deposit (Wonderley 1981). A possible rock pavement located on the northeast edge of the aforementioned stratum suggests to Wonderley that Str. 4F-14 was originally a surface-level building, possibly a community or men's house (Wonderley 1981). While this interpretation remains plausible, we are struck by the similarity of Str. 4F-14 with Strs. 144-19 and 306-182, both of which turned out on excavation to be trash deposits containing high proportions of ceramic incense burners. In addition to the prevalence of incensarios, all three collections lacked the otherwise ubiquitous *Pachychilus* sp. shells and were located on the western margins of relatively open plazas. We hypothesize, therefore, that Str. 4F-14 is yet another example of debris likely resulting from activities that occurred within the plaza on the western edge of which it was piled prior to removal.

Structure 4F-16 (Mound 9 in Strong and colleagues' nomenclature) is a 0.5-m-high conical eminence measuring about 15 m across and situated on the southwest corner of the southwest plaza. Very limited excavations here by William Duncan Strong and his colleagues revealed an ashy black soil that yielded numerous artifacts along with "freshwater mussel shells" (Strong, Kidder, and Paul 1938: 32; see also the summary in Wonderley 1981: 38–40). The fragments of two presumably human skulls found here may have been from post-Conquest burials (Wonderley 1981). Wonderley interprets Str. 4F-16 as a perishable surface-level structure comparable to Str. 4F-14. We suggest instead that both Strs. 4F-14 and 4F-16 are trash deposits composed of debris produced during activities conducted in the southwest plaza. In this sense, Str. 4F-16's location and general contents call to mind Str. 306-83. The latter, situated off the southwest corner of the WPP, was an extensive trash lens composed of large numbers of artifacts associated with faunal remains.

The general form and dimensions of Naco's southwest main plaza closely resemble Site PVN 306's WPP. In each case an extensive open area is bounded by substantial platforms that do not seem to have been residences. The latter interpretation is indicated by the structures' open summits, lack of built-in domestic furniture, and general paucity of artifacts. The centerpiece of both plazas is an edifice with a circular basal platform above which rises a cogwheel construction, both elements heavily coated with plaster. These distinctive buildings are situated in the eastern portion of their respective plazas. While the central edifice(s) was kept scrupulously clean, something of the nature of the activities performed on and near it is suggested by artifact-rich trash deposits on the plazas' west and southwest sides. The high proportion of pottery incense burners found in Strs. 4F-14 and 306-182 points to the importance of ritual in the gatherings hosted in the western plazas of Naco and Site PVN 306. The Str. 144-19, Unit 1 deposit seems functionally equivalent to these Naco and Site PVN 306 collections, although the former lies on the west edge of a residential patio. The general rarity of faunal remains associated with these incensarios—especially the notable absence of *Pachychilus* sp. shells, which are so common in most investigated middens—also characterizes Strs. 4F-14, 144-19 (Unit 1), and 306-182. In each case there seems to have been a shared commitment to segregate some debris associated with public religious observances from the detritus of meals, or at least of most forms of meat. Remnants of such feasts were identified in the deposit glossed as Str. 4F-16, where numerous "plain potsherds" (Strong 1935: 58, quoted in Wonderley 1981) were found together with faunal remains. Structure 306-83 yielded comparable materials and in a similar position to that occupied by Str. 4F-16, that is, off the southwest corner of the WPP.

Apparently, in both Naco and Site PVN 306, large open spaces distinguished by unusual and elaborate architectural forms were venues for religious observances carried out in conjunction with large-scale feasting. The detritus generated by these activities was, to some extent, segregated prior to removal. Building sizes are somewhat greater at Naco than at Site PVN 306, and plaster seems to have been used more intensively on buildings in the former's southwest plaza. Such variations might imply that those who commissioned Naco's central constructions enjoyed greater control over labor than did their eastern neighbors. These differences were apparently not great.

Northeast Principal Plaza

Wonderley excavated two buildings, Strs. 4F-8 and 4F-9, on the northeast side of Naco's northeast main plaza, a space encompassing 1,380 m² (1981). These platforms comprise two nested half circles open on the southwest, where they face into the plaza. They are 0.9–1.5 m high, encompass about 105 m² along their basal dimensions, and are composed of earth fill. Little is known of the platforms' superstructures, although the penultimate version of Str. 4F-8 apparently consisted of "a rectangular building (1.9 × 5.9 m) with flanking red plaster patios and a western entrance" (1981: 84). Wonderley interprets at least this version of Str. 4F-8 as an "upper class" residence (1981: 84). It is difficult to establish the uses to which the platform's final version and Str. 4F-9 were put, as their summits are featureless and most of the artifacts uncovered during their investigation came from fill. One possibility the excavator tentatively advances is that the last versions of Strs. 4F-9 and 4F-8 were large storage platforms analogous to those found at late prehistoric Cozumel (Wonderley 1981; see also Freidel and Sabloff 1984: 190–191).

Strong and his associates extensively cleared portions of Str. 4F-5 (Mound 1 in their system; Strong, Kidder, and Paul 1938: 32, 34; summarized in Wonderley 1981: 36–38). This earthen platform defined the southeast flank of the northeast plaza, covered approximately 204 m², and stood 1 m high. Structure 4F-5 was apparently capped with several contemporary plaster floors tinted a dark red. Superstructure walls were fashioned of *bajareque*, the surfaces of which seem to have been painted in varying colors, including red, yellow, and blue-gray. Large quantities of artifacts, including two pieces of European glazed wares, were recovered during summit clearing. While the picture is far from clear, a good case can be made that Str. 4F-5 served as a fairly elaborate residence for a house group.

Naco's northeast plaza in some ways resembles Site PVN 306's EPP. Both were bordered in part by relatively large and complexly embellished habitations. The case was made that those who lived around the EPP constituted a household, and the same was apparently the case for the residents of Str. 4F-5 and at least the early version of Str. 4F-8. Nevertheless, the extensive crescent-shaped constructions represented by late Str. 4F-8 and Str. 4F-9 have no clear parallels at any other known Naco valley site dating to the Roble phase or otherwise.

Architectural Excavations beyond the Principal Plazas

Wonderley (1981) excavated five buildings (Strs. 4F-11, 4D-2, 6F-3/4, 6F-5, and 6D-1) located outside Naco's main plazas. Strong and his associates also partially cleared the ballcourt (Str. 4F-15) that lies directly off the southwest corner of the southwest plaza (1938: 33; summarized in Wonderley 1981: 40–41). Structures 6F-5 and 6D-1 were apparently not actual buildings but trash deposits that protruded slightly above ground surface. These will be considered in the discussion of the middens Wonderley investigated at Naco.

Structures 4F-11 and 4D-2 lie 50 m northwest and 100 m southwest of the main plazas, respectively. They are earthen platforms measuring 455 m² by 1.75 m high and 84 m² by 0.8 m high, in turn. Structure 4D-2's functions could not be inferred from extant architectural features or the few artifacts found with it. The identification of two parallel channels, 0.42 m and 0.52 m wide, 0.2–0.23 m deep, and running at least 3.85 m long east-west on Str. 4F-11's eastern summit, may point to the use of at least part of this building as a sweatbath (Wonderley 1981). No comparable features were recorded elsewhere in the contemporary Naco valley.

Structure 6F-3, lying 160 m northeast of the principal plazas, is a 1-m-high circular eminence that had a diameter of approximately 15 m (Wonderley 1981). This entity apparently consisted entirely of cultural debris that combined numerous artifacts with bones and snail shells (table 5.1). No architectural features were noted here. The deposit, in turn, covered an earthen-floored, surface-level building defined by foundations consisting of large, un-shaped stones (Str. 6F-4). This earlier construction measured 2 m by at least 7.5 m and was apparently completely open on the north. Based on the organic material embedded in Str. 6F-4's floor and the artifacts associated with the building, including several grinding implements, Wonderley argues that the edifice served as a residence (1981). In a very general sense, Str. 6F-4 resembles Str. 144-2; both are domiciles, built in similar ways, and open to the north.

TABLE 5.1 Density by excavated square meters of materials recovered from Roble phase contexts at Naco (after Wonderley 1981)

Structure/ Operation (Op.)	Pottery Sherds	Chipped Obsidian	Shell/Bone	Ground Stone	Bajareque	Other
4F-14	151	2.5	0/3g	0.08	—	—
6D-1	48	0.3	—	—	—	—
6F-3*	154	9.9	24g/3g	0.4	1	2 g.s., 0.3 chert flake
6F-5	25	0.6	10.4g/0	0.2	—	—
Op. 63	142	3.3	663g/0.5g	0.3	—	0.3 sw
Op. 69	123	9.7	662g/78g	0.2	—	—
Op. 72	52	2.4	0/4g	—	—	0.2 chert flake
Op. 75	426	19.4	1,325g/13g	0.4	0.4	0.5 g.s.
Op. 76	266	8.7	980g/21g	—	—	0.3 chert flake
Op. 77	150	8.7	3,271g/21g	0.4	—	0.3 g.s.

Key:
g.s.: grooved ceramic sphere; sw: spindle whorl
*These figures are estimates based on the inference that 8 m² were excavated in Str. 6F-3; material Wonderley associated with Str. 6F-4 is excluded in these computations.
Sufficient information from Strong and colleagues' excavations at Str. 4F-16 was not available for inclusion in table 5.1.

Although Wonderley believes overlying Str. 6F-3 was a formal platform, we think it is more likely a trash deposit that accumulated above an abandoned building near the end of Naco's prehispanic occupation.

It is hard to say how these constructions relate to other Roble phase Naco valley edifices located beyond site epicenters. The only examples with which to compare them are Strs. 306-86, 306-72, 306-78, 306-79, and 306-130 (see chapter 3). All but Strs. 306-72 and 306-78 in this set were arguably residences, a function Str. 6F-4 may have also served. Otherwise, Strs. 4D-2 and 4F-11 were seemingly special-purpose buildings that lacked clear signs of domestic activities. Structures 306-72 and 306-78, modest platforms lying south of Site PVN 306's main group, might also fall in this category. They, like Str. 4D-2, also yielded very few artifacts, suggesting that whatever occurred around them generated relatively little debris; at least they were kept very clean. All we can say, however, is that buildings raised outside the Naco and Site PVN 306 main plazas served multiple poorly understood purposes, of which residence is but one possibility.

Information available on the ballcourt (Str. 4F-15) is derived solely from records provided by Strong and his colleagues (Strong, Kidder, and Paul 1938: 33; summarized in Wonderley 1981: 40–41). The alley is I-shaped, is oriented

310 degrees, measures 27 m long by 10.15 m wide, and is bordered by vertically set stone slabs that rose 0.5–0.8 m above the earthen playing surface. These boundary walls were fronted by a 0.3-m-wide "coping" of horizontally laid stones and backed by what seems to have been stone fill. The full height of the platforms that define the ballcourt on the northeast and the southwest is unknown; they almost certainly rose higher than the 0.8 m represented by the walls delimiting the alley. The southeastern end zone was also bordered by vertically set stones, but without the "coping," and covered 4.25 m northwest-southeast by 18.4 m northeast-southwest. The alley surfaces and walls were apparently not covered with plaster; nor were many artifacts recorded from excavations in this area.

To date, the Naco ballcourt is the only construction of this sort recorded from the Roble phase Naco valley. Its likely association with ritual implies that Naco's late prehistoric denizens, or a segment of them, alone engaged in the relevant observances. The court's modest dimensions, however, suggest that its importance in local religious observances was signaled more by its distinctive form and location adjoining the southwest plaza than by the grand scale on which it was constructed. Downplaying building size may have been one way to ensure that the architectural foci of religious activities, such as Str. 4F-15, did not overwhelm the rites conducted around them. The goal may have been to insinuate concepts associated with ballcourts and round structures within rites that embodied local premises rather than conducting the latter in the shadow of the former (see chapter 8).

Midden Excavations beyond the Principal Plazas

In addition to architecturally focused excavations, Wonderley investigated four middens, one (Operation 69) within 300 m of the main group and the remainder (Operations 75–77) outside that radius (1981). These trash deposits closely resemble those studied at Sites PVN 144 and PVN 306; that is, they consist of shallow (averaging 0.2 m thick) layers, in this case of brown sandy clay, that contain high densities of artifacts and faunal remains. The latter primarily consist of *Pachychilus* sp. shells. On the surface, these material scatters often appeared as slight (0.1–0.3 m high) mounds encompassing 2–3 x 5–6 m. Wonderley interprets these strata as middens, likely produced by people living in perishable constructions somewhere in the near vicinity, a view with which we heartily concur. The distribution and density of material recovered from the investigated deposits are presented in table 5.1.

As noted earlier, Strs. 6F-5 and 6D-1 seem to have been middens as well. The former is 140 m northeast of the site core and comprises a 0.44-m-thick brown clay covering an estimated 35 m² (Wonderley 1981). This deposit yielded 303 sherds, 7 obsidian blades, 2 mano fragments, and 10.4 g of *Pachychilus* sp. shells. The absence of unambiguous architectural features here, coupled with the mix of artifacts and shells derived from the clay, suggests that Str. 6F-5 is yet another pile of detritus swept into a low mound (see also Strs. 4F-14, 4F-16, and 6F-3). A possibly comparable deposit is represented by Str. 6D-1, situated 330 m southeast of the main group (Wonderley 1981). Here, digging revealed a 0.05- to 0.15-m-thick earth level resting atop a 0.5-m-high rise in the underlying culturally sterile, gravel-rich red clay. No clear architectural features emerged in the course of this work, although 357 sherds and 2 obsidian blades were retrieved from the excavated soil. Once again, it appears that Str. 6D-1 is a debris lens containing artifacts associated with activities conducted somewhere in the immediate area.

In addition to these tests dug within Naco, Wonderley, in collaboration with Urban, excavated four 1 m² test pits about 1.3 km southeast of the main group (Operation 63; Wonderley 1981). These probes revealed a moderately extensive, if shallow (0.17 m thick), artifact-rich deposit on the west bank of the Naco River. Based on disparities in artifact contents between Operation 63 and the middens dug within the site proper, Wonderley believes the former qualifies as debris generated by special-purpose, non-domestic chores pursued outside Naco. This interpretation is suggested by the relatively low quantities of obsidian found in Operation 63 vis-à-vis their greater prevalence in most investigated Naco trash deposits, the relative paucity of Nolasco Bichrome vessels in the former collection, and the preponderance of jars among utilitarian types in Operation 63. It is our experience at Sites PVN 144 and PVN 306 that such differences fall within the range of variation attested to across middens investigated at these centers. We have therefore included Operation 63 in the discussion of activity patterning within and near Roble phase Naco.

Overall, the same set of artifacts appears in all of the investigated trash deposits, suggesting that all house group members residing beyond the main plazas in Naco engaged in comparable domestic tasks involving ceramic vessels, chipped stone tools, faunal remains, and, to a large extent, grinding stones. Variations in the frequencies of these items among the excavated middens were noted. As was the case at Sites PVN 144 and PVN 306, there are no clear correlations between the frequencies of different classes of material. For example, Operation 75 yielded the largest concentrations of pottery sherds and obsidian blades but not of faunal remains. The highest density of the latter is attested to in Operation 77, which has nearly one-third the density of ceramics and half that of obsidian blades seen in the former collection. It is unlikely, therefore, that variations in the density measures outlined in table 5.1 directly or simply reflect differences in the sizes of the house groups linked to each midden. Rather, they probably express inter–house group distinctions in the intensities in which people living in different parts of the settlement engaged in essentially the same tasks, employing the same items of material culture.

Structures 6F-5 and 6D-1 may constitute something altogether different. Both deposits exhibit consistently low ceramic and chipped stone frequencies when compared with the other midden assemblages and stand out for their very low concentrations of faunal remains, especially shells of *Pachychilus* sp., which are otherwise very common in house group trash at Naco. Most likely, Strs. 6F-5 and 6D-1 consist of detritus generated by a limited array of domestic tasks that did not include processing meat to any great extent. Both deposits may also have accumulated over fairly short periods, thereby accounting for their relatively low densities of both ceramics and obsidian blades. Consequently, Strs. 6F-5 and 6D-1 do not seem to be residues from the full range of chores pursued in most house groups. They might not, in fact, be materials jettisoned from nearby residences but instead collections of garbage swept up in the course of cleaning general activity areas in the immediate vicinity.

BEHAVIORAL AND MATERIAL SIMILARITIES
AMONG ROBLE PHASE NACO VALLEY SITES

As with Sites PVN 144 and PVN 306, Naco's Roble phase population was apparently organized into numerous individual house groups and one household. The former occupied dwellings scattered across and beyond the settlement. Some of these domiciles were made completely of perishable materials (those associated with Str. 6F-3 and Operations 63, 69, and 75–77), while others had at least stone foundations (Str. 6F-4). No isolated residential platforms were identified among the investigated buildings, although they may simply not have been excavated. The one household at Naco, like its counterparts at Sites PVN 306 and PVN 144, occupied the most elaborately decorated and substantial domiciles known from the center (the northeast principal plaza). We will turn to the possible political significance of this pattern in chapter 6. The unusual form of Strs. 4F-8 and 4F-9 within the northeast plaza may tentatively suggest that substantial quantities of goods were stored here.

Relatively few artifacts were recovered from clear terminal debris contexts associated with residences in the northeast principal plaza. Some material that was possibly derived from this occupation was uncovered in Operation 72, a trench measuring 1.5 m × 3 m dug in the open area between Strs. 4F-8 and 4F-9 (Wonderley 1981). While the density of material recovered here does not match that of most Naco middens, artifacts were sufficiently diverse and plentiful as to suggest that they qualify as debris related to activities conducted in the near vicinity. These remains do point to the conduct of at least some prosaic chores that employed ceramic vessels and obsidian blades in the area. Uncertainty concerning the source of this debris, whether it comes from nearby Strs. 4F-8, 4F-9, or elsewhere, renders its interpretation problematic.

The excavated middens, on the other hand, contain a wide array of comparable material, pointing to the performance of much the same activities across house groups at the center and within the Naco valley generally. It is quite likely, therefore, that one factor that united members of different domestic webs within the larger Naco community was the repeated performance of basically the same tasks employing essentially the same materials by all residents of the center. Such mechanical solidarity (Durkheim 1984) was noted at Sites PVN 144 and PVN 306, where very similar ceramics, stone tools, and faunal remains were also found both in domestic middens and associated with substantial residences. All inhabitants of the Roble phase Naco valley, therefore, may have derived some sense of common identity from their oft-observed daily engagement in the same round of domestic chores completed using very familiar sets of materials.

Localized domestic nets were also enmeshed within wider bonds of loyalty that encompassed all of the Naco site's occupants. The southwest principal plaza was a venue where most, perhaps all, of the center's population gathered periodically to celebrate public rites enacted in the context of large-scale feasts. These observances focused on structures whose unusual forms set them apart from constructions associated with the mundane realm of domestic chores (Strs. 4F-1 and 4F-15). The rituals celebrated within the southwest principal plaza involved the same kinds of ladle incense burners employed in religious observances conducted in domestic circumstances. As at Sites PVN 306 and PVN 144, there does not appear to have been a suite of ritual gear used exclusively in public gatherings. The same case can be made for community-wide commensality; the food shared within domestic groups and the utensils on which it was served were employed on a grander scale in general convocations. We consider the political significance of these replications in chapter 8.

The same general activity patterns are noted at Naco and Sites PVN 306 and PVN 144. Similarities between the first two of these large centers are especially close. Both have comparably extensive western plazas that seemingly accommodated large numbers of people who gathered in them to conduct religious rites and share food using much the same sets of materials. Even more striking, the architectural foci of these activities have very similar forms; that is, round structures, sometimes supporting cogwheel constructions. Further, the debris generated by performances conducted within the western plazas was disposed of in much the same ways; incensario fragments were largely isolated from food remains in deposits on the patios' western flanks, whereas most of the more prosaic residues of feasting were tossed off the plazas' southwest corners. It is highly likely, therefore, that very similar processes of network creation, reinforcement, and reproduction were employed in both Naco and Site PVN 306.

The case for Site PVN 144 is somewhat different. Here, there are no obvious special-purpose religious edifices; nor was a plaza set aside for public gatherings. Rites of network intensification instead took place within a space defined in part by substantial domestic buildings. Even here, however, there is good evidence for the enactment of settlement-wide affiliations through ritual and feasting, the debris from which is largely culled of food remains and concentrated on the west side of the plaza (Str. 144-19, Unit 1). Apparently, the same processes of network formation operated at centers of varied sizes, although their physical expressions accommodated differences in population size and leaders' capacities to commission special-purpose constructions.

In all three investigated sites there is also a clear link between ritual foci and the residences of the only household recognized at each center. At Naco and Site PVN 306, the nexus of large-scale religious activity lies immediately west of the household, whereas at Site PVN 144 the household surrounds the plaza where public gatherings were convened. Such close juxtapositions of households and venues where community solidarity was enacted imply that participants in each center's largest domestic web played significant roles in the rites of intensification conducted nearby (see chapter 8).

BEHAVIORAL AND MATERIAL DIFFERENCES AMONG ROBLE PHASE NACO VALLEY SITES

In addition to the many behavioral and material parallels noted among the three investigated centers, there are several ways in which they differ. Each center has constructions with no known parallels at the others. The large crescent-shaped platforms, ballcourt, and possible sweatbath (Str. 4F-11) distinguish Naco's large-scale building efforts, just as Strs. 144-5-2nd, 144-8, 144-18, 306-17, and the relatively large, isolated residences at Site PVN 306 set those settlements apart. More thorough excavation at the three sites may have eventually revealed functional and formal analogs for all of these edifices in each center. Although possible, we doubt this is the case. The Naco ballcourt, for example, has a singular form that is relatively easy to see from the surface, but nothing like it was recorded at the better-preserved Sites PVN 306 and PVN 144. It is therefore very likely that each center provided venues for certain behaviors that were not replicated at its near neighbors.

This is the case for activities that required specialized architectural forms. It may also have been true among individual house groups, although in this instance the differences are more subtly expressed. For example, the frequency of

TABLE 5.2 Density by excavated square meters of obsidian artifacts classified by general form at Roble phase Naco (after Wonderley 1981)

Structure/Operation (Op.)	Obsidian Blades	Obsidian Polyhedral Cores	Obsidian Flakes
4F-14	2.0	0.2	0.3
6D-1	0.3	—	—
6F-3*	8.0	1.0	0.9
6F-5	0.6	—	—
Op. 63	3.0	—	0.3
Op. 69	9.0	0.5	0.2
Op. 72	2.0	0.2	0.2
Op. 75	16.0	3.0	0.4
Op. 76	8.0	0.7	—
Op. 77	8.0	0.7	—

*These figures are estimates based on the inference that 8 m^2 were excavated in Str. 6F-3; material Wonderley associated with Str. 6F-4 is excluded in these computations.

Sufficient information from Strong and colleagues' excavations at Str. 4F-16 was not available for inclusion in table 5.2.

obsidian blades in Site PVN 306 and PVN 144 trash deposits is often greater than that attested to in Naco, reaching as many as 33 p/em^2 and 47 p/em^2, respectively. The latter figure is almost three times the highest measure of blade frequency obtained from Naco. Insofar as these results are not purely a result of sampling error, they suggest considerable variation in the intensities of blade use within and across all three settlements, with Naco's residents somewhat less involved in such tasks than were their near neighbors to the northeast. These results are particularly interesting in that blade cores occur in higher frequencies in Naco middens than they do elsewhere in the Roble phase basin (table 5.2). This point is covered further in chapter 7. Suffice it to say for the present that loci of intense blade production were not necessarily areas of intense blade use. Rather, many of the blades made in certain house groups were seemingly intended for use elsewhere, with some of these consumers likely living outside the site where the tools were made.

Naco is also distinguished by a general paucity of obsidian and chert flakes, as well as the nuclei from which they were struck. As was mentioned in chapter 3, we did not recognize perlite as a distinct material category prior to 1992. Items glossed as "obsidian flakes" in collections analyzed before that date, therefore, would likely have been identified as perlite after it. Even bearing this point in mind, however, it is hard to escape the impression that obsidian blades not only dominated Naco's late prehistoric lithic assemblage, but almost completely comprised it. Obsidian/perlite and chert flakes tend to be less common than obsidian blades at Site PVN 144, where Str. 144-18 is the only exception to the pattern. At Site PVN 306, however, there are fifteen instances where flakes outnumber blades, including eleven buildings (Strs. 306-8, 306-20, 306-21, 306-72, 306-78, 306-79, 306-86, 306-124, 306-125, 306-130, and 306-174) and four middens (Str. 306-83, Operations 306AL/BQ, 306AX/BK, and 306BV). Blades may have been easier to obtain at Naco than elsewhere in the valley, where people supplemented these tools with simple flakes made using hard-hammer percussion. The latter interpretation is seemingly belied by the aforementioned high densities of obsidian blades in some Site PVN 144 and PVN 306 middens. Alternatively, flakes might have been employed for different purposes than blades, with the observed distribution reflecting more functional distinctions than those of access. In either case, Naco's Roble phase denizens were neither making flake tools nor using them as much as were their compatriots at Sites PVN 144 and especially PVN 306.

Similarly, ceramic sherds are found in far greater densities within middens at Sites PVN 144 and PVN 306 than in Naco trash deposits. As was the case with obsidian blades, there is some overlap in these figures, and variations in frequency measures within sites are often as great as those between them. Nonetheless, it is potentially significant that the highest numbers were derived from sites outside Naco. Such discrepancies may reflect differences in the sizes of domestic groups that used specific trash deposits or, for the reasons cited earlier in this chapter and in chapters 3 and 4, variations in the intensities with which tasks that involved ceramic storage and serving vessels were pursued within different domestic webs. Unfortunately, the Naco data outlined by Wonderley do not contain figures on the relative proportions of jars and bowls. It is thus not possible to compare directly Wonderley's findings with those obtained from Sites PVN 306 and PVN 144. We can therefore identify discrepancies in pottery densities but advance little further in understanding their roots in behavioral variation.

Figures for incensarios are not available for Naco; most of the recovered fragments are difficult to distinguish from Nolasco Bichrome bowls, and items from both functional classes were grouped together in the original analyses (Wonderley 1981). Wonderley does make reference to the general prevalence of incense burners in different deposits, especially where they are particularly common (e.g., Str. 4F-14), and these accounts provide a qualitative sense of censer distributions. It is important that many of the ladle censers recovered from Roble phase contexts at Naco were slipped white and painted with red designs identical to those appearing on Nolasco Bichrome bowls. Such decorated censers were not nearly as common at Sites PVN 144 and PVN 306; incense burners from the last two sites closely resemble Naco forms but are largely undecorated. Such distinctions may reflect significant differences in the ways the occupants of the three settlements viewed incensarios and how they were incorporated into local belief systems.

Despite the considerable overlap in activities among the three sites, therefore, each differs to some extent in the presence of certain behaviors unique to a settlement, the intensities at which generally prevalent tasks were pursued, or both. The result is a complex mosaic of similarities and differences presumably resulting from variations in the extent to which members of different webs operating at domestic and site-wide scales engaged in unique or generally prevalent tasks. The overall impression is one of populations residing in distinct locales who, in the course of enacting the same basic cultural themes in mundane and exceptional circumstances, introduced some variations on those leitmotifs. The reasons underlying such differences relate to the ways networks were structured by the various agents who created and sustained these interconnections in pursuit of specific goals. We will return to these points in the succeeding chapters.

Power in the Roble Phase Naco Valley

In this chapter we review the evidence for differential control over labor among population segments who resided at Sites PVN 144, PVN 306, and Naco. Once again, we argue that people achieve political preeminence not as individuals but as parts of groups whose members are united in their pursuit of common goals. What we are looking for in the Naco valley's late prehistoric archaeological record is evidence for those networks and some indication of how successful their participants were in achieving prominence or in undermining the pretensions of others. Chapters 7–9 take up the issue of what resources members of different webs employed in their political contests. For the moment, however, we are primarily concerned with describing any hierarchies that might have existed at Naco and Sites PVN 306 and PVN 144 during the fourteenth through early sixteenth centuries.

ARCHITECTURAL VARIATION

Taken together, four levels of architectural elaboration pertain to residences at Sites PVN 144, PVN 306, and Naco. At the uppermost end are the four domiciles identified in Site PVN 306's eastern principal plaza (EPP) (Strs. 306-21,

306-123, 306-128, and 306-11), as well as Strs. 4F-5 and early 4F-8 on Naco's northeast principal plaza. What distinguishes the first four habitations is their size; they are all stone-faced, earthen platforms that stand 0.46–1.33 m tall. The constructions in question are also extensive by local standards, covering 63–184 m² (based on a combination of excavated data and surface indications). At Naco, Str. 4F-5 stood 1 m high and encompassed approximately 204 m²; the dimensions of Str. 4F-8's penultimate version are not given in published reports. At least five of these buildings, and probably all six, required considerable labor to erect and would have stood out on the landscape as prominent reminders of their occupants' preeminence.

Within this grouping there may be a further division based on the input of additional labor used to fashion surfaces of stone, plaster, or both. Stone pavements top terraces or summits on Strs. 306-21, 306-123, and 306-128, while the tops of Strs. 306-21 and 4F-5 were capped with white plaster. Early Str. 4F-8 was also flanked by two "patios" coated with plaster. In the case of the two Naco buildings the plaster was painted red, and there are signs that the walls of Str. 4F-5's superstructure were decorated with hues of red, yellow, and blue-gray (Wonderley 1981). Apparently, those who resided in these edifices were able to command the large workforce needed to raise and maintain their domiciles along with the skilled labor, in some cases, to process and apply lime plaster to them.

On the more modest end of the continuum of residential buildings are Strs. 306-79, 306-86, and 306-130. These are 0.27- to 0.48-m-high earthen platforms or terraces that measure 71–400 m² (based on excavated finds and surface configurations) and are bounded by stone facings. They lack any signs of formalized stone or plaster pavements. Each of these edifices apparently stands alone; at least no other constructions of comparable sizes are found in their immediate vicinities.

Slightly further down on the architectural scale are Strs. 144-1, 144-2, and 6F-4. The first two edifices are sizable (encompassing at least 60–87 m²) but were built directly on ancient ground surface. Structure 6F-4 was not completely cleared; its uncovered portion measures 15 m². Stone is used in these buildings, although not as facings. Instead, rock walls served as foundations for perishable upper constructions fashioned of sticks and clay daub. Additional steps were taken to prepare Str. 144-2 for use. Here, the earthen floor was fired—apparently to harden it—and then covered, at least in part, with white plaster. No such treatment was identified within Strs. 144-1 and 6F-4, suggesting a slight difference in these house groups' abilities to muster skilled labor for their respective constructions.

Only hints were found of the simplest constructions erected at Sites PVN 144, PVN 306, and Naco. These are the buildings made of perishable material that are inferred to have existed near the numerous middens that surround the principal plazas. Their presence is indicated primarily by the pieces of burned daub found within the trash deposits. Given the absence of clear platforms in the immediate environs of the middens, we presume that those residing near them lived in structures set on ground surface. The general paucity of stones of any size in these deposits tentatively indicates that the *bajareque* walls did not rest on substantial footings but instead rose directly from ground level.

POWER AND ARCHITECTURE

Several inferences can be drawn from these observations. First, people who lived in the Roble phase Naco valley were divided by their ability to control the labor needed to fashion their domiciles (see also Pugh 2009: 187–188; Rosenswig and Masson 2002). A few could activate networks large enough to transport the earth and rocks used in raising extensive platforms of varying heights and to pave parts of their surfaces with stones, plaster, or both. Next on the scale are those who could marshal the labor to fashion more modest platforms with fewer architectural elaborations. The most common form of residences consisted of surface-level buildings.

Second, considerable variation is seen within the four categories of residence outlined here. Structures 306-21 and 4F-5, for example, are larger and more lavishly outfitted with stone or plaster floors than any other known Roble phase domicile. Structure 306-11, at 1.2 m tall, may be next in line, although excavations here were not sufficiently extensive to determine how the platform's surfaces were floored. The three seemingly isolated domiciles at Site PVN 306 also diverge in their heights and overall dimensions. Finally, buildings erected on ground level ranged from fairly substantial examples with stone foundations and plastered floors to those in which perishable walls apparently rose directly from the ancient surface. In short, the proposed architectural categories based on platform height, extent, and decorative elaboration most likely demarcate a continuum in the amount of skilled and unskilled labor invested in their construction (Pugh 2009: 188). A larger excavated sample might reveal a more unbroken progression in measures for these variables.

Third, even allowing for such continuity, there are variations in the size and degree of elaboration of the residences that comprise one household. Structure 306-21, as noted, stands out on both measures within the EPP. The differences between Strs. 144-1 and 144-2 are more subtle, although the latter's fired and plastered floors set it apart in labor investment from its near neighbor. Distinctions between Strs. 4F-5 and early 4F-8 are less obvious, but the first does appear to have been the larger of the pair. Insofar as power is reflected architecturally, those residing within the three known households may well have enjoyed different degrees of political prominence.

Fourth, distinctions in the magnitudes of labor investments along this continuum are not great in any absolute sense. Variations in the dimensions of Roble phase domiciles are real and bespeak house groups' differing abilities to mobilize networks of supporters in construction projects. The political ranks this variation implies, however, were not apparently distinguished by major power differences, at least as these distinctions were conveyed by the sizes of domiciles that pertained to different house groups.

Fifth, architectural differences at Sites PVN 306, PVN 144, and Naco almost certainly reflect variations in the stability of residential patterns. The more labor devoted to constructing a house group's residence, the more likely its members were to remain in that spot for a protracted span. The three construction stages reconstructed for Str. 306-21 provide the clearest example of such continuity. Unfortunately, digging was not pursued far enough in the other studied Site PVN 306 platforms to determine their building sequences. In addition, Strong and his colleagues' report on their work at Str. 4F-5 is not sufficiently clear to indicate whether the building was the result of multiple construction efforts (Strong, Kidder, and Paul 1938: 32, 34; Wonderley 1981). At the other end of the scale are the surface-level edifices erected beyond the principal plazas. The shallowness of the trash deposits associated with them points to relatively short occupations in each locale. It appears, therefore, that the higher up the power hierarchy a house group was, the more prone it was to reside in one place for fairly long periods (see also Blanton 1994; Tourtellot 1988).

One likely reason for this residential stability is an equivalent commitment to those with whom the domestic space was shared (Blanton 1994; Tourtellot 1988). Investing in substantial domestic architecture rooted the inhabitants to a specific place and materialized their connections with those who lived in the immediate area. It is no accident, therefore, that the most impressive domestic constructions at Naco and Site PVN 306 are grouped around the EPP and the northeast principal plaza, respectively. These sizable edifices made tangible the devotion of each of their respective house groups to the household of which they were a part. Similarly, the largest known domiciles at Site PVN 144 adjoin each other on the north flank of that settlement's principal plaza. Although they did not represent labor investments on the scale of the EPP and northeast principal plaza constructions, Strs. 144-1 and 144-2 were relatively large and elaborately outfitted by the standards of that site. The investment of such locally unprecedented effort in their erection embodied these house groups' enduring connections to the household they comprised.

The fact that some individual house groups made comparable, if more physically muted, claims to place is suggested by the isolated platforms excavated at Site PVN 306. The networks to which their members belonged are less clearly expressed than is the case for the households at Naco and Sites PVN 306 and PVN 144. They may have been foci of larger domestic webs whose other participants lived in more modest, less physically salient and permanent constructions. Such putative nets might then have been materialized through the residences of their most powerful members, with the remaining participants in the domestic network lacking the resources to raise comparable expressions of their presence and importance. Middens scattered in the vicinities of Strs. 306-79, 306-86, and 306-130 could point to the existence of the latter's physically fleeting habitations. It is impossible at this point, however, to draw such connections with any confidence. The shallowness of trash deposits and the general absence of substantial residences outside the main plazas of the investigated sites indicate that most house groups at all three settlements were fairly mobile and did not enshrine their interconnections through substantial investments in constructions.

POWER, NETWORKS, AND ARCHITECTURE

The networks through which power was obtained, conveyed, and defended at Roble phase Naco valley centers were instantiated and expressed in part through construction projects of varying scales (see also Pauketat and Alt 2003). At both settlements, prominent households mobilized the productive efforts of their respective webs to raise domiciles that were locally prominent in size and degree of elaboration. Based on the dimensions of these constructions, the labor pool drawn on for their erection almost certainly included those who lived outside the plaza they surround. It may have involved all residents of the site. By building large, members of the prominent household instituted projects in which all network participants cooperated (Joyce 2004; Pauketat and Alt 2003). Insofar as social webs come to life in the context of shared endeavors, the process of building substantial domiciles was crucial to the maintenance of webs focused on particular households. The tangible outcomes of these efforts would have also served as persistent reminders of the nets mobilized to build the edifices surrounding the principal plazas (Joyce 2004; Pauketat and Alt 2003; Trigger 1990). In process or finished, therefore, sizable domiciles grouped around plazas instantiated and reproduced the power of the households who commissioned and lived within them.

The networks centered on isolated residential platforms were likely smaller than those actualized in the construction of their counterparts within dominant households. The labor devoted to the erection of such domiciles as Strs. 306-79, 306-86, and 306-130 was relatively sizable and not replicated in other residences within the immediate area. Raising these edifices likely involved the contributions of more than their residents. Consequently, each of these domestic platforms was the nexus for webs that included individuals who inhabited far less physically prominent dwellings. The fact that only one such residence could be built by members of these nets, combined with the relatively small sizes of the resulting constructions, point to the less powerful positions of their leaders vis-à-vis the occupants of the EPP and Naco's northeast principal plaza. The absence of clear structure clustering in these cases may also suggest that Strs. 306-79, 306-86, and 306-130 were not parts of households in the same ways as those residing around the latter plazas and Site PVN 144's patio. Instead, they may have exerted power through webs that reached directly out to individual houses located at varying distances from the main residence.

We know very little about the constructions raised by the majority of Roble phase Naco valley residents, save that they were fashioned using easily acquired materials, primarily wooden posts and clay. Such constructions, no matter how small, were unlikely to have been built by single individuals. Rather, their erection required mobilizing support among members of the immediate house network and possibly beyond. These buildings, no less than their much larger counterparts, were embodiments of the webs in which their occupants participated. The small sizes of the nets they materialized point to the restricted power the members exercised and highlight their relative difficulty in making tangible claims to specific portions of a settlement.

Those who lived in such relatively impermanent dwellings also contributed to the construction of the more sizable residences on the main plazas and, at Site PVN 306, of their isolated counterparts. In a sense, therefore, even individuals who resided in the most modest constructions were rooted to specific areas, those connections materialized in physically salient architecture. Such ties, however, were expressed in the dwellings of others who likely mediated relations between people and place.

There is no evidence that the house and household networks at Sites PVN 306, PVN 144, and Naco nested neatly within each other. Instead, we argue that competition among house groups for labor resulted in a situation wherein web loyalties frequently overlapped. For example, each site was dominated by a primary household whose members drew on considerable numbers of people to build their residences. Variations in the dimensions and elaborateness of these domiciles imply that there were power differences among a household's constituent house groups. Each of these entities residing on the EPP, Naco's northeast principal plaza, and Site PVN 144's main plaza may have drawn on its own web for construction projects. Those who occupied the largest, most lavishly outfitted domiciles would therefore have commanded the most extensive net. In this way, a household might ultimately control the labor of all residents at a settlement but not through the operation of a single unified network. Instead, each prominent house group in a household could have fashioned its own web of supporters, webs that might well have overlapped in membership.

Counterbalancing these competitive tendencies within households were the close spacing of the residences of their component house groups around principal plazas and their members' common participation in a wide range of tasks. These patterned and regular interactions bespeak a shared identity and considerable cooperation. As such, intra-household power contests were probably suppressed, and their actions were coordinated to some degree. In fact, it may have been the ability to separate themselves from the rest of the community and to cooperate in securing labor that contributed to the political prominence of the household as a group. Still, it would be a mistake to impute too much unity of purpose and action to these domestic networks.

Webs focused on the isolated residential platforms at Site PVN 306 were, for whatever reasons, not integrated directly within the dominant households. Their members may have owed allegiance to those who resided around the EPP, but that connection did not give them access to residential space on that plaza. These house groups were therefore also probably contesting for labor among themselves and with members of the dominant household. Variations in the sizes of isolated residences hint at the differential success their occupants enjoyed in these contests. Nevertheless, the apparent inability of those residing in Strs. 306-79, 306-86, and 306-130 to forge their own households implies that they were at a competitive disadvantage in marshaling labor compared with the occupants of the EPP. For whatever reasons, they had not developed the means of ensuring coordination among other house groups in political projects, an obstacle paramount households at all three sites had overcome. From this perspective, Strs. 306-79, 306-86, and 306-130 were nodes within a site-wide political network in which power was concentrated at relatively low levels. They occupied a subordinate position within the net focused on the core domestic group that occupied the EPP. Still, the fact that those who lived on isolated residential platforms could achieve even a modicum of political preeminence hints at their active roles as competitors for power within a site-wide net.

The residents of perishable surface-level buildings were less favorably positioned within political webs. Each of these house groups was a focal point of its own network through which labor was marshaled to fashion domiciles among, presumably, other tasks. The relatively insubstantial character of these constructions bespeaks comparably small domestic webs with limited memberships. As such, these house groups appear to have been the most powerless of all social segments at Sites PVN 144, PVN 306, and Naco. Their political positions, however, may have been less disadvantageous than this assessment suggests. Members of even the smallest house group were also participants in webs that included the most preeminent members of their community. After all, if labor was mobilized through networks, then those who committed their productive efforts to building projects must ultimately have been participants in the same web as those who commissioned these endeavors. There are many ways to structure relations within a network of unequals, varying in the degree to which distinctions among their members are clearly drawn. The evidence from Sites PVN 306, PVN 144, and Naco suggests that whereas such divisions were maintained, they were not marked.

As noted earlier, measures of architectural size and elaboration are fairly continuous across all three sites. Further, even the largest residences at the settlements are not massive in any absolute sense. These observations indicate that power, far from being concentrated in a few hands, was diffused among members of different house groups, and the amount of labor any one of these entities could command was limited. Hierarchical distinctions were therefore subtly conveyed and power was dispersed and widely contested in the investigated settlements.

This ongoing rivalry would have worked to the advantage of those whose labor was in such demand. They could potentially have shifted network allegiances based on the advantages offered by different contestants. The situation, of course, may not have been that fluid. At the very least, would-be elites commanding labor within webs would have had to take into account the sensibilities of those who might find the blandishments of rival claimants attractive. Excessive demands for work, or insufficient generosity in rewarding that effort, could have yielded disaffection by, and loss of support from, web participants (discussed later in this chapter). In a situation where other house groups were competing for adherents to their own nets, ensuring supporters' consent and contentment would have been crucial.

We hypothesize, therefore, that political power was exercised and reproduced through the operation of hierarchically structured networks focused on specific house groups. The most successful of these entities were those that found ways of organizing within households whose members presumably pooled their efforts to guarantee some degree of persistent control over the actions of subordinates. Nevertheless, there was no unified, well-defined hierarchy within any one site by which power over labor was exercised. Instead, leaders of different house groups contended for adherents even within the paramount households. Consequently, the adherents of house groups who were the objects of this competition were able to play competing magnates against each other. How much freedom they enjoyed in choosing among web allegiances is unclear. The relatively small sizes of even the largest residences at Sites PVN 144, PVN 306, and Naco imply that demands on subordinates' productive capacities were limited. Political relations in the investigated late prehistoric

Naco valley settlements, therefore, may well have been structured according to hierarchical principles. The inability of rival factions to resolve their claims on the labor of the majority, to institutionalize ranked access to those productive efforts, meant that the degree of inequality was limited.

VALLEY-WIDE POWER NETWORKS

Along with political divisions within Naco valley sites, there were marked differences in the power of their respective elites. The levels of support commanded by households at Site PVN 306 and Naco were greater than those exercised by the residents of Site PVN 144's main plaza. Consequently, the webs focused on leaders at Naco and Site PVN 306 were almost certainly more extensive, involving more people, than those centered on Site PVN 144's paramount household. It may be, in fact, that some of the labor invested in Naco and possibly Site PVN 306 constructions was drawn in part from Site PVN 144's inhabitants, who occupied subordinate positions in webs operating out of the larger settlements.

Relations between residents of Naco and Site PVN 306 are less clear than those of either center with Site PVN 144. Naco is far larger than its northeast neighbor (160 ha as opposed to 35 ha). If area covered positively correlates with the number of people who occupied that space, then it appears that Naco's rulers were more successful at attracting followers to their settlement (de Montmollin 1989; Roscoe 1993). The sizes and degrees of elaboration exhibited by large-scale buildings in the two settlements are, however, roughly equivalent. The magnates in both cases, therefore, seemingly mobilized labor within networks of about equal size and enjoyed comparable levels of success in fashioning political nets among the basin's Roble phase populations. Naco's paramount household apparently attracted more people to its settlement than did the leaders at Site PVN 306 but may not have been better able to command their labor than were potentates at the latter center.

It is also possible that what we defined as Sites PVN 306, PVN 144, and Naco were treated by their residents and Spaniards alike as parts of the same extensive community glossed with one name (Gasco and Berdan 2003). Several lines of evidence tentatively support such a view. First, the apparent physical isolation of these sites may be more apparent than real. It was difficult within the basin, as it is throughout southern Mesoamerica, to identify Roble phase settlement (Wonderley 1985: 267; see also Voorhies and Gasco 2004: 12–13). As noted in chapters 3 and 4, the most common signs of habitation dating to this span are artifact scatters that usually only appear on open ground in newly plowed fields. As these conditions rarely pertained when survey was carried out, it is highly likely that late prehistoric occupations are underrepresented in our sample. In fact, the apparent nucleation of people around Naco may in part be a result of the disrupted nature of the terrain there, cleared as it was for housing and plowed for commercial cultivation. These remains might be part of a more extensive settlement within which population was more or less evenly distributed over the roughly 5 km separating Naco from Sites PVN 144 and PVN 306.

Second, no two of the sites are located more than 3 km from each other, and they all demonstrate strikingly similar material and behavioral patterns (chapters 5, 7, and 8). There is no doubt that their occupants were in close contact throughout the Roble phase and were organized in comparable ways in pursuit of analogous goals that employed identical elements of material culture. Such close similarities imply that the boundaries we drew in delimiting Sites PVN 144, PVN 306, and Naco were arbitrary and porous.

What we class as different sites, therefore, may simply represent three physically prominent nodes within a single settlement cluster, the residents of which participated in one overarching political network. Residents of Naco's northeast principal plaza may have enjoyed a slight advantage in power contests, but the amount of labor they controlled through their networks was apparently little greater than that wielded by their contemporaries residing around Site PVN 306's EPP. Just as power was diffused within sites, it was not clearly centralized across the broader Naco settlement zone. This entire area was apparently characterized, therefore, by ongoing, largely unresolved political competitions that involved people of different ranks, all of whom participated to some degree in the same cultural and economic webs.

How was the unity of this network maintained despite competition between the two dominant households that anchored opposite ends of the settlement cluster? We argued in chapter 2 that nets of any sort exist only to the extent that the ties uniting their members are enacted at least periodically. Close material and behavioral similarities throughout the Naco settlement zone strongly indicate that some degree of inter-site solidarity was maintained, but where and how such feelings were enlivened is far from clear.

One possible locale for performing such rites of intensification is Site PVN 144's main plaza. It lies between the Naco and Site PVN 306 paramount households and contains the strongest candidates for buildings that acted as gathering places for influential community members (Strs. 144-8 and 144-18; Str. 306-20 may have served a similar set of purposes, although the evidence is less clear). The dimensions of the rooms that grace Strs. 144-8 and 144-18 and their elaborate decorations, including at least three stucco masks that bounded entrances to them, set these two edifices apart from other recorded contemporary buildings in the basin. No other residential compound includes facilities for hosting meetings of comparable sizes in similar grandeur. In addition, constructions devoted to processing (Str. 144-11) and possibly storing and cooking food (Str. 144-5-2nd) are recorded only on Site PVN 144's main plaza. This area may have been devoted to a mix of activities, including residences for those of intermediate social status (Strs. 144-1 and 144-2) and hosting large-scale gatherings accompanied by feasts. The recovery of ritual paraphernalia from within the patio (Str. 144-19, Unit 1) and renderings of deities on Strs. 144-8 and 144-18 imply that these convocations and celebrations were conducted in a context that linked the sacred with the profane. Such assemblies also maintained status distinctions between those who gathered in lavishly decorated public buildings and the rest, who collected together within the neighboring plaza. Even as affiliations encompassing the entire settlement cluster were affirmed, divisions between leaders and the led were reproduced.

Site PVN 144, therefore, was a site for constructing unity within both a specific household and the broader settlement cluster of which it was a part. We return to these points in chapters 8 and 10.

POWER AND VALUABLES

There is very little evidence that those who commanded labor also enjoyed privileged access to valuable commodities (see also Masson 1999, 2000b: 178–179; Rice 1984; Voorhies and Gasco 2004: 182; but compare with Pugh 2002–2004). The latter are often identified in archaeological contexts using some combination of these factors: complexity of the manufacturing process, skills required to transform the relevant raw material into finished goods, and the object's foreign origin (Feinman, Upham, and Lightfoot 1981; Helms 1979, 1988, 1992, 1993; Hirth 1993; Kenoyer 2000: 91–92; Smith 1987, 2003a: 118). Using these criteria, very few goods qualify as "valuable" in Roble phase Naco valley assemblages. The most common examples are imported obsidian cores and the blades knapped from them, along with white-slipped, red-painted ceramic vessels made within the valley (Nolasco and La Victoria Bichromes; see chapters 1 and 8). In both cases, the items in question are found far more commonly in the middens scattered around the principal plazas than within these elite precincts (see also Masson 2000b: 151–153; Smith 1994: 153; Smith and Smith 2000: 225). At Site PVN 306, densities of obsidian blades range from 0 to 0.6 p/em^2 among domiciles within the EPP, 0 to 0.4 p/em^2 across the isolated residential platforms, and 1.7 to 33 p/em^2 within the ten excavated middens (six of these yielded figures between 10 and 33 p/em^2). The same pattern holds at Site PVN 144, where blades are found at rates of 0.4–1.3 p/em^2 among the two residences on the main plaza and at densities of 8–47 p/em^2 in those middens that have relatively large analyzed collections. Approximately 2 blades were found per excavated m^2 in the one investigated deposit arguably from a domestic context in Naco's northeast principal plaza, whereas six of the eight excavated middens beyond the core had density figures of 3–16 p/em².

The distribution of red-on-white ceramics at Sites PVN 144, PVN 306, and Naco parallels the pattern noted for obsidian blades. Looking exclusively at domestic contexts, Site PVN 306's EPP has the lowest proportion of these decorated taxa (0.003%; N=1,145). In fact, only Str. 306-123 yielded fragments of Nolasco and La Victoria Bichromes (they comprise 0.03% of the analyzed sample of 875 sherds retrieved from this edifice's terminal debris contexts). No bichromes were found among the 270 studied sherds from Strs. 306-79, 306-86, and 306-130.

Turning to the next lowest rung in the architectural hierarchy, Nolasco/La Victoria Bichromes make up 3 percent (N=776) and 2 percent (N=574) of the analyzed ceramic collections from Strs. 144-1 and 144-2, respectively. As was the case with obsidian blades, however, decorated ceramics are more prevalent in the domestic trash deposits of both settlements. At Site PVN 306, fragments of red-on-white–painted vessels comprise 1–11 percent of the analyzed midden collections, with six of the investigated deposits having figures that fall between 6 and 7 percent. Overall, Nolasco/La Victoria Bichromes make up 7 percent of all analyzed sherds from domestic trash deposits here (N=7,587). Red-on-white–painted sherds comprise 2–8 percent of the ceramics from the five Site PVN 144 middens that were sufficiently analyzed to provide reliable results. In general, these bichromes comprise 5 percent of the 1,583 ceramic fragments studied from these contexts.

The frequency of elaborately decorated pottery vessels (table 6.1) in the middens located outside Naco's main plazas is striking (Wonderley 1981). Figures here range from 7 to 21 percent, with six of the collections yielding proportions of elaborately decorated ceramics of 13–21 percent. These numbers greatly exceed the measures obtained from analogous contexts at Sites PVN 306 and PVN 144. Some of this discrepancy results from the inclusion of incense burners in the general Nolasco taxon at Naco. Still, insofar as the slipping and painting of these vessels heightened their value in the eyes of those who used them, the distribution noted earlier indicates that such esteemed items were easily available to members of the humblest house groups at Naco. The low proportion of elaborately decorated ceramics from Operation 72 in the northeast principal plaza (3%) matches the pattern noted at Sites PVN 306 and PVN 144, where the putative elite residences yielded lower proportions of elaborately decorated pottery than did their humbler counterparts. Once again, however, the order of magnitude is different, with far higher percentages of decorated containers in the Operation 72 collection than at either of the other investigated paramount households. Everywhere, however, valuable

TABLE **6.1** Proportions of elaborately decorated ceramics by excavated Roble phase contexts at the Site of Naco (Wonderley 1981)

Structure/Operation (Op.)	Nolasco Bichromes	All Elaborately Decorated Ceramics	Sample
4F-14	47	47	1,590
6D-1	13	13	357
6F-3	14	14	1,218
6F-5	14	14	303
Op. 63	7	7	142
Op. 69	13	13	702
Op. 72	2	3	235
Op. 75	16	16	992
Op. 76	8	9	799
Op. 77	21	21	439

ceramics somehow made their way into the hands of non-elite consumers in greater quantities than was the case for their presumed social betters.

The two most prevalent valuables, therefore, seemed to have flowed away from those with power and toward their humbler counterparts living in the most modest constructions at all three centers (see also Smith 1994: 153; Smith and Smith 2000: 226; cf. Pugh 2002–2004). The significance of this pattern is considered in chapters 7 and 8, where we argue that the widespread distribution of esteemed and eye-catching items was integral to elite political strategies. Blades and decorated pottery were among the resources leaders deployed to circumscribe their networks of supporters and motivate participation in the nets thus defined. It is important to bear in mind that however well these schemes worked to capture labor, they resulted in the extensive dispersal of valuables among the lowest-ranking members of the population resident at the three investigated centers. We cannot say how Roble phase Naco valley elites might have distinguished themselves from the rest of the population through the ostentatious display of such perishable materials as cloth and less ephemeral items such as jewelry that did not end up in trash deposits. What is clear is that the creation of hierarchy and concentration of power required the provision of considerable material inducements to those who bore the burden of supporting claimants to high status. Apparently, that weight was lightened by the regular dissemination of esteemed items.

SEVEN

Crafts and Power

Competitions for power can be waged through the strategic manipulation of key physical resources. Among these assets are those fashioned by craft specialists. Insofar as some participants in a network gain privileged control over raw materials needed to fashion items desired by all, techniques essential to the production process, the means by which finished items are distributed to consumers, and the use of these objects, they can advance claims to power over others (Costin 1991, 2001; Hayden 1995; Schortman and Urban 2004b). Those who regulate any strategic point(s) in the production-distribution-consumption cycle of a generally desired good can reward those who comply with their demands by granting them access to that item and punish resistance by denying access. They do so by admitting individuals to, or excluding them from, networks enacted through the exchange and use of craft items. Such connections may be as crucial to a person's sense of self as they are to his or her physical survival (e.g., Ekholm 1972; Friedman and Rowlands 1977; Peregrine 1991).

Chapter 6 presents a case for the existence of a muted political hierarchy within the Roble phase Naco valley. In this chapter we examine to what extent elites gained and reproduced their power by insinuating themselves within those processes by which certain tangible assets were acquired, fashioned, distributed, and consumed.

Production is broadly defined as the transformation of raw materials into finished items for use by the manufacturer, exchange with others, or both. Distribution, in turn, deals with the mechanisms by which completed goods are passed to those who will use or consume them. Obviously, these processes are interrelated. Each step in the cycle, however, may be implicated in the projects by which different networks are enacted and the goals of their members realized. The manner in which production, distribution, and consumption instantiate these interpersonal ties and are related to political struggles varies by industry and, within any one industry, over time.

The discussion that follows is organized according to these crafts for which there was evidence at Roble phase Sites PVN 144, PVN 306, and Naco: knapping obsidian blades, fashioning flake tools of chert and perlite through hard-hammer percussion, manufacturing ceramics, and spinning/weaving. Each case will be examined to determine who was involved in the processes of production, distribution, and consumption; how networks were embodied through the structuring of these three processes; and the extent to which such nets were implicated in contests for power. Primary attention is paid to blade knapping, the craft for which we have the most information. The implications of these findings for the organization of power and the construction of hierarchy at Roble phase Sites PVN 144, PVN 306, and Naco are summarized in the concluding section of this chapter.

OBSIDIAN BLADE KNAPPING

Evidence for fashioning obsidian blades here is seen in the distribution of those polyhedral cores and core fragments from which the implements were detached. Relying on such diagnostics means we cannot necessarily identify workshops where stone tools were made (e.g., Moholy-Nagy 1990). In fact, the recovery of most cores from trash deposits implies that the observed distribution reflects the general areas where blade nuclei were jettisoned or lost. Assuming that these find-spots are not far removed from the places where blades were manufactured and the cores stored, it is possible to use the available information indirectly to infer who was involved in fabricating blades, at what scales and levels of intensity, and in what contexts they worked.

Contexts and Intensity of Production

There are very slight indications of blade knapping at Site PVN 144; two polyhedral core fragments that were reused as sources of flakes detached by direct percussion, one recycling flake from a comparable nucleus, and an exhausted polyhedral core were found scattered among three middens situated beyond the main plaza. In addition, one distal core rejuvenation flake comes from Str. 144-2. These materials are not strong indicators of blade production at these locales, as all but one of the examples were likely employed as flake tools or sources for them. The one exception, the exhausted nucleus, was probably lost prior to its conversion into a flake core, as it was no longer a source of blades. In short, the few signs of blade manufacture identified at Site PVN 144 could well represent materials recycled from workshops located at unknown distances from their find-spots. They are therefore not necessarily indicative of blade production in or near the settlement.

Sixteen polyhedral cores not subsequently modified by other uses were found in Roble phase contexts at Site PVN 306. Although one of these nodules was encountered near a building (Str. 306-20 in the western principal plaza [WPP]), the rest were derived from middens not clearly linked to specific edifices. The distribution of these trash deposits hints at two potential patterns of obsidian blade production across the center. Two cores were located within and directly southwest of the WPP (including the one found in the environs of Str. 306-20). This association suggests that at least some blades were fabricated in the course of feasts and rites conducted within the center's primary focus of religious devotion (see also Wells 2003). The majority of the polyhedral cores, however, were scattered over five discrete middens lying north and east of the principal plazas; they were not identified in trash deposits south and west of this architectural core, nor were they retrieved from all of the investigated northern middens. Insofar as the observed distribution accurately mimics the patterned spread of polyhedral cores within Site PVN 306 during the Roble phase, blade knapping was an activity pursued in domestic and public contexts by a limited array of specialists, most of whom resided in humble constructions north and east of the site's architectural core.

The distribution of polyhedral obsidian cores at Naco indicates that blades were also fashioned primarily by artisans who lived in architecturally modest house groups. Five of the middens excavated beyond the main plazas but within Naco proper yielded fragments of blade cores, indicating widespread participation in fabricating these tools. Here, as at Site PVN 306, it seems that blade knapping was carried out primarily by people who were not members of the elite household and who operated largely beyond the direct supervision of those luminaries.

There is no evidence at Naco or Site PVN 306 that those who fabricated blades always enjoyed privileged access to their products. The Subop. 306AX/BK midden, for example, yielded the highest density of polyhedral cores at this center but not the largest concentration of blades (1.2 cores and 12 blades p/em², respectively). Along the same lines, the Subop. 306AC/AE deposit had the highest blade density at the site (33 p/em²) but no sign of the cores from which these implements were removed. The correlation between frequencies of nuclei and blades is somewhat clearer at Naco. Here, Operation 75 is characterized by the greatest frequency of cores (3 p/em²) and of blades (16 p/em²) recorded at the settlement. Middens with lower densities of polyhedral nuclei have correspondingly fewer blades (see table 5.2). What is striking in this case, however, is that despite the relatively high densities of blade cores at Naco, the items removed from these nuclei are often more common in middens from Sites PVN 144 and PVN 306, where evidence for blade knapping is not as prevalent. Within Naco, therefore, blade and blade core frequencies are roughly correlated, but the relationship does not hold across contemporary sites.

The frequency and density of polyhedral nuclei are nowhere high in any absolute sense. Based on the available evidence, therefore, it seems that no one group of artisans was working full-time in this industry. Instead, the considerable demand for obsidian blades throughout the Naco valley was likely met by the combined efforts of multiple groups of artisans working on their own. The ubiquity of blades everywhere, even at Site PVN 144 where there is no strong evidence for their manufacture, indicates that these implements flowed in relatively sizable volumes along networks that linked producers with consumers within and across settlements. How these exchanges were organized remains an open question.

Modes of Distribution

One possibility is that market transactions were the means by which blades were acquired (Berdan 2003b: 94; Berdan et al. 2003: 101–102; Braswell 2003b: 156; Masson 2000b: 188–189; Smith 2005). As Ken Hirth and others have argued (1998; also see Dahlin et al. 2007), relatively even distributions of goods within sites and across regions may be diagnostic of transactions mediated through face-to-face exchanges at established locales. The open WPP at Site PVN 306, Naco's southwest principal plaza, and the central plaza at Site PVN 144 may have provided venues for such interchanges. Nothing beyond the easy accessibility of these spaces, however, supports such a view. Outside these weak possibilities, there are no clear signs of a marketplace at any Naco valley settlement. Given the ephemeral nature of these economic venues throughout Mesoamerica (e.g., Dahlin et al. 2007; Jones 1996), however, our inability to identify them here is not surprising.

Through barter within markets or not, producers and consumers likely negotiated the transfer of blades largely on their own, without elite interference. This inference is based on the location of artisans' domiciles outside

TABLE 7.1 Distribution of obsidian sources represented in the sample of items from Roble phase contexts at Site PVN 306 subjected to X-ray diffraction analysis

Source	Proportion	Number
Ixtepeque	33	7
La Esperanza	24	5
Unknown	43	9
Sample total		21

paramount households. By distancing themselves physically from this nexus of political power, knappers materialized their relative independence from direct elite control over their craft, an arrangement in which local notables must at least implicitly have acquiesced (Costin 1991, 2001). Knappers and consumers, therefore, were free to use the exchange of blades as a means of establishing and sustaining networks that served their own economic and social purposes.

It is important to bear in mind that however widely it was distributed within Naco, Sites PVN 144, and PVN 306, obsidian was imported from varying distances outside the Naco valley (tables 7.1 and 7.2). Given the paucity of detritus resulting from shaping cores, this material likely arrived in the basin in the form of polyhedral nuclei. Acquisition of the cores would have been a difficult process, requiring, among other skills, the ability to negotiate considerable cultural, linguistic, and purely physical distances and differences. The candidates most likely to have spanned these divides are local elites and merchants.

At present, it is difficult to decide whether local rulers or traders played the greater role in acquiring polyhedral nuclei. The Late Postclassic Mesoamerican world was spanned by merchants operating at various spatial scales and transporting considerable volumes of goods. The pochetca based in the Mexica empire are only the best known of these entrepreneurs (Berdan 2003a; Berdan et al. 2003; Hassig 1985; Pollard 1993). Anthony Wonderley argues that Naco was, in fact, home to an enclave of Pipil warrior-traders who had only recently ensconced themselves in the valley prior to the arrival of the last group of military adventurers, the Spanish (1981). He bases this interpretation on changes in material styles that have an arguably foreign inspiration. While this interpretation is plausible, we argue in chapter 8 that the observed stylistic shifts were more likely initiated by local lords with local goals in mind.

Even discounting the presence of foreign overlords does not preclude the possibility that itinerant merchants were active in the Naco valley during the fourteenth through sixteenth centuries. The stucco masks that adorn Strs. 144-8 and 144-18 (see chapter 4) may represent God M, a deity the Maya associated with merchants (Douglass and Mooney 2001; see also chapter 8). If this is the case, and if this supernatural figure retained its original meanings within its new context, then the masks may point to the presence of foreign traders within the Roble phase Naco valley. It is just as likely, however, that the basin's

TABLE 7.2 Sources of obsidian attested to among specimens analyzed visually from Roble phase contexts at Site PVN 144

Structure/Artifact Scatter (AS)	Ixtepeque	La Esperanza	Other
144-1	54	—	4
144-2	48	—	—
144-5-1st	18	—	—
144-8-1st	11	—	—
144-11	20	—	—
144-18	6	—	—
144-19, Unit 1	27	1	4
AS 16	44	1	4
AS 17	14	—	2
AS 18	11	—	—
AS 19	15	—	—
AS 21	15	1	—
AS 27	8	—	—
Subop. 484, Midden 1	28	—	1
Sample totals	319	3	15

residents adopted this symbol and turned it to their own purposes (a point pursued in chapter 8). Exotic iconography, therefore, requires contact with the distant lands from which the motifs and ideas were derived but not necessarily the presence of resident foreigners (Masson 2000b: 41). There is no clear sign of the latter anywhere in the Naco valley during the fourteenth through sixteenth centuries. In the absence of such evidence, we suggest that parochial elites—either on their own or in association with traveling merchants—played the central role in acquiring goods from afar, including polyhedral obsidian nuclei.

Elites and the Acquisition of Polyhedral Cores

The rationale for arguing that elites played significant roles in acquiring polyhedral cores comes down to motive and opportunity (Clark and Parry 1990). Members of paramount households comprise the population segment best positioned to deal effectively with outsiders. They could have used the networks under their control to mobilize goods given in exchange for imports and had the time to master the symbolic structures deployed in communicating across cultural and linguistic boundaries. The brief reference in Spanish accounts to Naco *caciques* who could apparently speak Nahuatl is but a tantalizing glimpse of such symbolic virtuosity (Pagden 1971: 407; Wonderley 1981). The manipulation of foreign-inspired motifs in ceramics and architecture outlined in chapter 8 further indicates just how deeply valley magnates were involved in interregional discourses.

Elites were also highly motivated to monopolize foreign contacts and the goods obtained through these transactions. Imports are, by definition, locally uncommon. Their rarity and association with whatever potency is linked to distant realms enhance their value in the eyes of local residents (Helms 1979, 1992, 1993). By controlling exclusively the parochial dissemination of foreign valuables, notables would have put themselves in an excellent position to convert equals into subordinates dependent on elite largesse for goods they desired but could only obtain from a single source. Those seeking power, therefore, would move to exclude the majority from participation in networks by which contacts with providers of esteemed imports were secured. Whether blade cores were obtained by leaders who traveled to other realms or from visiting merchants, we argue that the creation of hierarchy and centralization of power depended on the control of these transactions by paramount lords (Kipp and Schortman 1989).

Blades, Cores, and Networks

What we can surmise from the extant evidence is that, whatever modalities of exchange may have pertained:

1. Obsidian blades were made by specialists living at Naco and Site PVN 306.

2. Demand for these tools was relatively high among all segments of known Roble phase Naco valley populations.

3. This call for blades was not met by the formation of a few large-scale workshops but rather by the efforts of part-time specialists, each of whom fabricated blades in relatively low volumes.

4. The context of production was largely domestic, although these artisans occasionally fashioned blades during public gatherings in Naco's and Site PVN 306's ritual foci.

5. Recovery of most blade cores at Naco and Site PVN 306 from areas well removed from the centers' monumental plazas implies that obsidian tool production and its subsequent distribution were not carried out under close elite supervision.

6. The ubiquity of blades at all three excavated sites, regardless of where knapping took place, strongly suggests that the mechanisms by which these tools were moved were relatively efficient and open to all.

7. Acquisition of the polyhedral cores from which blades were knapped required the ability to muster the economic, social, and cultural capital needed to acquire these valuables from afar.

8. Such transactions were probably the only aspect of the obsidian blade production-distribution-consumption cycle that was monopolized by those who could mobilize such assets—that is, elites.

Following from these observations, there appear to have been several major networks involved with, and made manifest by, the distribution of obsidian blades and cores. One of these involved the interactions through which consumers acquired blades from knappers. Given that blades were used for a variety of mundane tasks, these transactions had strong economic implications. Houses and households depended on these commodities to meet basic needs. The decision to use imported items in such quotidian pursuits is an interesting one. Locally available perlite and chert were adequate substitute sources of tool stone; the former was used exclusively as such throughout the valley's Middle Preclassic occupation (1200–400 BC; Urban and Schortman 2002). It is likely, therefore, that obsidian blades had more than pragmatic significance to their users. Rather, the foreign origin of blades probably enhanced the implements' social significance, imbuing the mundane chores in which they were employed with meanings derived from their exotic and perhaps supernaturally charged sources (Helms 1979, 1988, 1993). Knappers and consumers were therefore participants in networks that had considerable economic and social significance to their participants.

For the most part, these webs were not hierarchically structured. Production of blades was dispersed away from architectural expressions of power, access to these tools was widespread and relatively even, and there is no sign that processes of distribution were centrally monitored or controlled. Consequently, extant evidence indicates that most of the local networks instrumental to obsidian exchanges were organized according to heterarchical principles in which manufacturers and consumers were linked directly to each other both economically and socially (Crumley 1979).

The precise nature of such heterarchical premises is difficult to reconstruct. The occurrence of cores in multiple domestic contexts indicates that several social groups were involved in fabricating blades. These tools, therefore, may have moved along different interaction webs, each focused on specific knappers. Given the uniformity of raw materials used in, and artifacts manufactured by, different artisans, it is impossible to distinguish among the products of distinct knappers. Consequently, we cannot parse out individual networks involving specific producers. It is also difficult to reconstruct how blade production and exchange were interwoven with other social and economic processes in constituting the shared projects that defined network membership. The transactions through which blades moved may have created only transitory links among artisans and consumers based on such shifting considerations as quality and cost. Alternatively, particular knappers and specific clients might have been united by enduring social ties, of which blade exchanges were just one tangible manifestation. The first scenario tends toward a market-based approach, whereas the second perspective imagines a situation in which transactions among individuals primarily expressed and reproduced long-lasting social relations. The utilitarian and social significance of the tools involved implies that the networks through which they moved so widely and easily were founded on both economic considerations and social commitments.

Complicating this situation are the polyhedral cores recovered from Site PVN 306's WPP and Naco's southwest principal plaza in apparent public contexts. Whether the resulting blades were employed solely within these locales or were taken away by participants in the gatherings for use elsewhere is unknown. What is clear, however, is that at least some blade fabrication was not embedded within social and economic networks focused on specific craft workers who resided within particular house groups. Blades fashioned and distributed outside these networks were likely implicated in other webs that incorporated other people, possibly including all those who attended rites and feasts conducted in public ritual spaces. The association of cores with ritual may also point to the sacralization of the ties in which some blades were used and disseminated.

While most intra-valley blade exchanges may have been founded on heterarchical premises, it is important to remember that elites also used blades. The only sign that notables might have produced such implements themselves is the one polyhedral core recovered from Operation 72 in Naco's northeast principal plaza. As the behavioral significance of the deposit uncovered in Operation 72 is unclear, this evidence cannot be used to make a strong case for blade knapping in elite residential contexts. Thus local notables must have developed some means of obtaining blades from non-elite craft workers for their own uses. It is highly likely that the passage of blades between knappers and rulers enacted tributary relations rather than those founded on equal exchanges. Since labor was apparently successfully co-opted by the valley's magnates for construction projects, it is reasonable to infer that other resources would have been incorporated in this upward flow of tributary services. The intra-valley distribution of blades, therefore, gave tangible expression to networks organized along heterarchical and hierarchical principles, depending on who was involved in the interactions and what their relative power positions were.

The second network involves the passage of polyhedral nuclei from the local agents who acquired the cores to those who would knap blades from them.

As discussed earlier, the interlocutors who commanded the requisite knowledge of foreign symbol systems to establish enduring ties with distant partners were probably valley magnates operating alone or in concert with merchants.

We hypothesize, therefore, that whereas production and distribution of blades within the Roble phase Naco valley were for the most part structured along heterarchical lines, the cores essential to this industry flowed through intra-valley webs that were hierarchically arranged. This is the step in the cycle of blade production-distribution-consumption most vulnerable to control by those seeking power. Individuals or groups who monopolized access to cores ultimately determined the flow of blades to all occupants of the Roble phase valley. Given the widespread dependence on these implements, or at least the high esteem their ubiquitous distribution implies, such oversight could have been a source of substantial power. Failure to follow the monopolists' dictates could have led to exclusion from the raw materials needed to make tools central to performing daily chores. Just as important, failure to obtain nuclei would have translated into an inability to enact social ties through the exchange of blades.

The final network related to blade production considered here involves the long-distance ties through which cores moved. As argued earlier, the participants in this web likely combined itinerant traders with the leaders of different polities. The resulting net ultimately connected the Naco valley to the Ixtepeque and La Esperanza obsidian flows from which the nuclei were derived (tables 7.1 and 7.2). At this remove, it is impossible to say how many different notables from distinct realms were involved in these transactions and the extent to which the composition of the networks changed with time. The widespread distribution of obsidian blades within Sites PVN 306, PVN 144, and Naco attests to the reliability and regularity of these interchanges. Such ease of access to imported obsidian in a valley located great distances from the flows implies that whatever the precise structure(s) of the webs through which cores moved, they were fairly stable over time.

Our knowledge of Late Postclassic societies in Southeast Mesoamerica is, at best, spotty. The potential exchange partners of Naco valley elites, and their degrees of sociopolitical elaboration, cannot therefore be specified in any detail. This uncertainty means that reconstructing the hierarchical or heterarchical structures of interregional interaction webs can be carried out only on the most general level. Bearing these limitations in mind, there are several reasons to suggest that transactions linking notables and merchants occurred among equals. First, Naco and Site PVN 306 are large, complexly organized centers focused on monumental constructions that bespeak the power their leaders wielded within their own domains (see chapter 6). If, as seems likely, Naco, Sites PVN 144, and PVN 306 together comprised one extensive community, then this center was certainly on the level of other known Late Postclassic capitals within southern Mesoamerica. The fact that Naco was singled out in early Spanish accounts as one of the most preeminent commercial entrepôts in northern Central America further implies that its rulers were not economically or politically subordinate to any of their contemporaries.

Second, there is no evidence for a dominant southern Mesoamerican polity whose rulers exerted dominion over considerable territorial expanses. The boundaries of the Mexica empire stopped well short of the Naco valley. Closer to hand, the political unit based at Mayapan in northern Yucatan never extended beyond a limited portion of the peninsula and was in disarray by AD 1451 (Kepecs and Masson 2003; Pugh 2003). Spanish chronicles of the Conquest period in the early sixteenth century mention complex polities in the nearby Sula Plain, whose residents were active participants in long-distance exchanges (Chamberlain 1966). Many of these same accounts, however, also treat Naco as the capital of a seemingly independent realm (Chamberlain 1966). Late Postclassic Southeast Mesoamerica, along with much of the contemporary neighboring Maya lowlands, therefore, comprised a fragmented political landscape divided among numerous small domains, each ruled from towns of modest sizes (Marcus 1993; Scholes and Roys 1948). In these circumstances no single set of rulers could dictate the terms of exchange to its benefit or to the detriment of others. Hence, elites from Naco and Site PVN 306 almost certainly interacted with their compatriots in contemporary realms on an equal footing. Obsidian cores, along with other goods, therefore, were likely transmitted among partners who were united by social bonds of cooperation and who communicated using mutually intelligible symbols. Some aspects of that symbol system are discussed in chapter 8.

Summary

Processes of obsidian blade production, distribution, and use within the Roble phase Naco valley were linked through the operation of at least three interconnected networks characterized by dramatically different memberships and structures. The cores essential to blade knapping were secured by a small group of elites at Site PVN 306 and Naco, who forged connections with their counterparts in other realms—either directly or through intermediaries—who could supply this item on a regular and predictable basis. As no one within these webs could consistently dictate the terms of exchange to their partners, ensuring reliable supplies of cores in sufficient quantities would have required creating social bonds that linked the participants as peers in enduring, fairly stable relations. These ties were bolstered through elites' participation in a common symbolic system tied to the supernatural (Smith 2003b; chapter 8).

Obsidian cores moved from local notables to artisans at Site PVN 306 and Naco within webs that incorporated people of different social ranks. In fact, elite monopolies over the provision of such nuclei may well have formed a basis for the underlying inequalities. The blades these knappers produced were then distributed throughout the Roble phase Naco valley within networks enacted in part by such exchanges. For the most part, these connections were organized heterarchically among social equals (cf. Pugh 2002–2004). Thus the movement of blades materialized important interpersonal ties even as it ensured ready access to a widely used tool important in meeting daily needs. Transfer of blades to elite members of the webs probably took the form of tribute payments in which goods and services moved up, and defined, hierarchies. Here again, the passage of blades made tangible social relations, although now of an unequal nature.

The widespread distribution of blades across Sites PVN 306, PVN 144, and Naco suggests that these connections were persistent and ultimately tied all known residents of the valley to each other. Through networks organized along hierarchical and heterarchical lines, therefore, a tool implicated in a wide array of quotidian tasks was dispersed among all recorded segments of Roble phase Naco valley society. In the process, relations of equality and inequality operating on local and interregional scales and over roughly two centuries were regularly produced and reproduced.

PERCUSSION FLAKE INDUSTRY

This manufacturing stream is characterized by the fashioning of relatively simple, multi-purpose tools by hard-hammer percussion applied directly to nuclei of locally available chert, perlite, and in some cases exhausted polyhedral obsidian cores. Unlike blade knapping, this procedure required no specialized knowledge or skill set. Further, sources of chert and perlite are readily available throughout the Naco valley and would have been easily accessible to most, probably all, of its Late Postclassic occupants. There were few obstacles, therefore, to general participation in this craft.

Casual cores of perlite and chert were recovered from middens at Site PVN 306 (Subop. 306AR/BL, 306AX/BK, 306BI, and 306-83; three, two, one, and two cores, respectively), as well as in the vicinity of Str. 306-21, the monumental platform that divides the EPP and the WPP (two cores).

Diagnostics of the percussion flake industry overlap with those of the obsidian blade manufacturing stream at Site PVN 306. The same trash deposits that produced casual cores outside the principal plazas also yielded blade nuclei, and both blades and flake tools were apparently fashioned in the WPP, probably in the context of rituals and feasts. Blade and flake industries at Site

PVN 306 were therefore not parts of mutually exclusive practices. On the contrary, their pursuit coincided to a considerable degree in both domestic and public contexts.

The major difference between blade and flake production is that the latter was also conducted at Site PVN 144. Here, the fashioning of casual tools took place in much the same locations noted at Site PVN 306: in rural contexts (Artifact Scatters 17 and 27 and Op. 484, Midden 1) as well as near focal points of public gatherings (Strs. 144-5-1st, 144-8-1st, 144-18, and 144-11). Structures 144-8-1st and 144-18 are interpreted as venues where influential members of the Site PVN 144 community, and perhaps the entire Naco settlement cluster, met. Structures 144-5-1st and 144-11 are also thought to have been related to public activities conducted in the plaza they border on the east and the northwest, respectively. In the case of Str. 144-11, the implements fashioned were likely used in processing meat derived from snail shells (*Pachychilus* sp.) that was intended for consumption during communal events.

The patterned distribution of blade and percussion nuclei implies that the manufacture of stone tools generally was implicated in at least two different networks within the Roble phase Naco valley. One was centered on domestic groups, while the other was enacted within public rites that most, perhaps all, community members attended. As with blades, the flakes chipped off nodules in public settings may have figured in practices that forged a sense of unity within a network that included all those living at Sites PVN 306 and PVN 144 and in their vicinities.

Implements fashioned in more purely domestic contexts were almost certainly used by the manufacturers and exchanged with other participants in their social networks. This case has been made for blades. It may also have applied to flake tools at Site PVN 306, where the nearly isomorphic distribution of perlite, chert, and polyhedral obsidian cores suggests that the people who made implements from these nuclei were members of the same social groups; at least they deposited their trash in the same locales. The movement of blades and flake implements, therefore, probably materialized the same social webs.

At Site PVN 144, on the other hand, flake tools were apparently fashioned and used primarily, although not exclusively, in public settings, whereas obsidian blades made elsewhere were widely distributed throughout the settlement. The ways in which the use and exchange of flake implements instantiated network relations at Site PVN 144, therefore, may well have differed from those seen at Site PVN 306. At the very least, it seems that these tools were less integral to enacting ties between specific knappers and consumers at Site PVN 144 than they had been at Site PVN 306. In contrast, they may have been used mostly in performances that united all members of the former community. How webs materialized through the exchange of blades mapped onto those made tangible through flake tool production, exchange, and use is unclear.

The totals of perlite and chert flakes combined are outnumbered by blades at Site PVN 144 everywhere except at Str. 144-18. The situation at Site PVN 306 is more complex. Here, flakes outnumber blades in most architectural contexts, including those associated with the site core. The ratio is reversed in middens situated beyond the EPP and the WPP except at Subops. 306AL/BQ and 306AX/BK, where flakes are more numerous. There is no clear correlation at Site PVN 306 between locales of apparent flake tool production and the prevalence of these implements. Rather, it seems that flakes moved toward areas where they were used intensively and that these places were not necessarily the same spots where blades were called for to the same extent. At Site PVN 144, either the activities in which flakes were so intensively used at Site PVN 306 were not conducted at the same scales, or blades were employed in place of flakes in the pursuit of these common tasks. The prevalence of blades, as opposed to flakes, at Site PVN 144 is especially notable, as there is no sign of the former's manufacture here.

As was the case for blade production, the networks enacted through flake tool exchange likely operated on heterarchical principles. There is no sign that flake tool manufacture and distribution were centrally controlled. Instead, artisans resident in dispersed domestic groups or periodically congregating in public plazas apparently took responsibility for negotiating transactions involving these casual tools. Elite needs for percussion flakes may have been met by tribute payments.

Naco is distinguished from its neighbors by the nearly complete absence of evidence for the manufacture and use of flake tools. As noted in chapter 3, those of us working in the valley did not identify perlite as a distinct material category until 1992. The absence of nodules of this material in Wonderley's collections, therefore, is at least in part a result of our joint failure to discern perlite's significance in ancient manufacturing processes. Nevertheless, chert had long been recognized as a tool stone, and flakes of this material were retrieved from the Naco investigations. It is difficult, therefore, to escape the impression that cores other than those used in fashioning blades are completely absent from Naco collections and that flakes of all materials are very rare. The significance of implements made using hard-hammer percussion techniques in the economic and social transactions of Naco's residents, therefore, was apparently slight.

POTTERY PRODUCTION

Evidence for the manufacture of ceramic vessels is sparse and ambiguous throughout the Roble phase valley. The clearest sign of participation in the

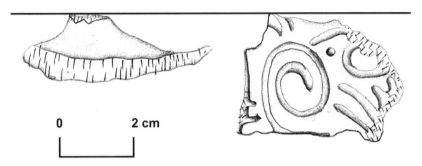

0   2 cm

FIGURE 7.1 *Ceramic mold for pottery production*

craft comes in the form of two fragments of fired clay molds, used to craft pottery bowls, found in the Subop. 306AR/BL midden east of Site PVN 306's main group (figure 7.1). No firing facilities were clearly identified here or anywhere else at Roble phase Site PVN 306; nor is there evidence of ceramic manufacture at Naco.

Tools for pottery production were not identified at Site PVN 144. Here, however, the ceramic-lined pits that comprised Str. 144-5-2nd (Units 1 and 2) might have served as facilities for firing ceramics. The better preserved of these declivities, Unit 1, has walls that were subject to intense heat, creating a hard, impermeable surface on its base and flanks (Unit 2, immediately to the north, was too badly preserved to determine if it had also been subject to the same treatment). At 2–2.5 m in diameter and 0.42–0.45 m deep, Str. 144-5-2nd's pits could have been sizable kilns. They might just as easily have been storage containers, however. The latter view is suggested by the fragments of white plaster found adhering to the sides of Unit 1's earliest version and the fact that this basin was seemingly fired during its construction and not as part of its use.

A better contender for a firing facility is the second iteration of Unit 2. Fully 0.2 m of earth now filled the bottom of the northern of the two pits and supported a stone wall that projected 1.35 m south from the construction's north edge. Burning was so intense within this newly reconstituted facility that it altered the pit's earthen floor to a depth of 0.06 m. Clearly, during this interval Unit 2 was used to fire something; the north-south–running wall that bisects its interior possibly served as a baffle designed to direct the flow of heat (see also Masson 2000b: 82–85). As noted in chapter 4, Unit 2 may now have been a kiln or an oven. The seemingly domestic nature of the debris that accumulated in adjacent Unit 1 to the south at this time tentatively suggests the second view. This is especially the case because the southern deposit lacked clear evidence of pottery manufacture, such as distinctive tools and quantities of sherds from vessels that failed during firing. If this detritus was a by-product of activities conducted in Unit 2, then the latter was probably a large-scale cooking facility. The possibility that Unit 2 served as a kiln cannot be precluded, however.

The burned earthen surface that covers at least 43.4 m² east of Str. 144-5-2nd's Units 1 and 2 may well be tied in to the use of these pits. Once again, while intense and likely repeated burning is attested to here, the sources of those fires are not clear. Both fashioning pottery and cooking remain possibilities.

It may well be that pottery vessels were fashioned at all three of the investigated settlements. Variations in paste among locally made decorated wares (especially the Nolasco and La Victoria Bichromes) strongly imply that at least two workshops were employing an equal number of distinct clay recipes involved in fashioning these widely used ceramic containers. Since we did not identify the location of the relevant production areas, it is impossible to infer the networks linking production, distribution, and consumption of pottery vessels.

OTHER INDUSTRIES

The remaining evidence for specialized manufacture is scant. Ceramic spindle whorls were found in small numbers dispersed across middens (Subops. 306AB/AD [five pieces] and 306AX/BK [one fragment]) and architectural contexts at Site PVN 306 (Strs. 306-21 and 306-72, with one spindle whorl coming from each of these locales; figure 7.2). A fragment of a sherd reworked as a disk, which might have also served as a spindle whorl, was recorded from the Subop. 306AB/AD trash deposit. Spindle whorls were not identified from excavated late prehistoric contexts at Site PVN 144 and Naco, although one of these items was retrieved from the Operation 63 midden located outside the latter center. The spinning of thread, likely associated with weaving, therefore, was apparently pursued at low levels of intensity across Site PVN 306, within the principal plazas (Str. 306-21) but primarily in domestic contexts outside the core. Based on the distribution of the sole tool we could link to this activity, there is little evidence for anything more than occasional participation in the craft.

Grooved, fired clay spheres, often called "net weights" in the literature (e.g., Masson 2000b: 121; Rice 1987: 204–208), that were derived from clear Roble phase contexts were found in middens at Site PVN 306 (Subops. 306AR/BL, 306AX/BK, and 306AC/AE; yielding 11, 1, and 4 pieces, respectively) and Naco (Operations 6F-3, 75, and 77; 17, 2, and 1 examples were found in each case, in turn). The functional significance of these items is uncertain. They have been linked to weaving and fishing by various authors (e.g., Rice 1987:

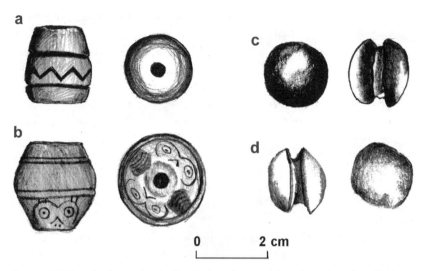

FIGURE 7.2 *Sample of ceramic spindle whorls and grooved fired clay spheres from Roble phase Naco valley contexts*

204–208; Voorhies and Gasco 2004: 79–81; Wonderley 1981). However they were used, these spheres seem to have been exclusively employed by people who lived well outside the monumental cores of Naco and Site PVN 306. Those who deposited trash in the Subop. 306AR/BL and Operation 6F-3 middens appear to have been particularly committed to the activities in which the grooved spheres were implicated. As with spindle whorls, "net weights" were not found at Site PVN 144.

SUMMARY OF CRAFT WORK

Several patterns stand out in an overview of Roble phase manufacturing activities at Sites PVN 144, PVN 306, and Naco. First, production took place in both private domestic settings and public ritual contexts. Diagnostics of spinning/weaving, obsidian blade knapping, and the manufacture of flake tools from perlite and chert were recovered in the WPP and from shallow middens unassociated with surface-visible architecture at Site PVN 306. It is likely that the same artisans who worked from their residences also fashioned goods during public events. The more limited evidence of manufacture at Naco follows the same general pattern. At Site PVN 144 the few extant diagnostics of production are concentrated mostly within the main plaza, where the knapping of flake tools was probably carried out in the course of large-scale gatherings convened there.

Second, in no case was manufacturing volume high. The complex skills required to make some items, in particular obsidian blades, may have required at least part-time specialization (Clark 1987). In this case at least, considerable effort was likely invested in learning and practicing essential manufacturing techniques. Still, there is no sign that any Roble phase Naco valley artisans engaged in their crafts full-time. Rather, the needs of these communities for all manner of locally fashioned items were almost certainly met through the occasional fabrication of goods by a scattered cadre of craft workers producing to meet their own requirements and those of their neighbors.

Third, the evidence for craft production overlaps in several locales at Site PVN 306 and Naco. Most examples of this situation are found in middens outside site cores (Subops. 306AR/BL [blades, flake tools, spinning/weaving, pottery, use of "net weights"], 306AX/BK [blades, flake tools, spinning/weaving, use of "net weights"], and 306AB/AD [blades, spinning/weaving] and Operations 6F-3, 75, and 77 [blades, use of "net weights"]). Structure 306-21 also evinced signs of flake tool manufacture and spinning/weaving. In the last case, however, the items that signaled participation in crafts may have been associated more with activities conducted within the WPP and not at Str. 306-21 specifically.

Fourth, the only segment of the manufacturing stream in any known industry that was possibly monopolized by a single segment of the population involved the acquisition of polyhedral obsidian cores by elites residing at Naco and Site PVN 306. As argued previously, magnates who ruled from these centers were likely intermediaries in the transactions by means of which these essential assets were disseminated in the Roble phase Naco valley. Local notables, therefore, could have indirectly but effectively controlled the access of all valley inhabitants to a highly valued resource.

Fifth, manufacturing, as dispersed as it was, was centered primarily on Site PVN 306 and Naco. Even a moderately large center such as Site PVN 144 yielded only scant signs of specialized production. It may have been the case, therefore, that such items as obsidian blades and cloth were ultimately obtained within the Roble phase Naco valley from craft workers laboring at Site PVN 306 and Naco.

POWER AND CRAFTS

Processes of manufacturing, distributing, and consuming craft goods were incorporated within complexly related webs of interpersonal relations that ultimately linked all denizens of the Roble phase Naco valley. By insinuating themselves at crucial points in these three operations, enterprising members of specific factions could structure these interconnections to their advantage.

Hence, power would flow toward those who effectively manipulated the production, distribution, and use of generally needed or highly valued goods.

Evidence for such maneuverings is, at best, subtly expressed in the available data. Elites alone obtained polyhedral obsidian cores from distant sources by dint of their own efforts or through merchant intermediaries. These nuclei were essential to the manufacture of blades all members of the basin's population needed or wanted to conduct basic quotidian tasks and engage in public rites. Further, the exchange of blades materialized social webs through which, ultimately, all members of houses and households were linked. Control over the local dissemination of cores thus had far-reaching social, economic, and ideological consequences for people of every rank. Such a monopoly would certainly have provided a strong motivation to acquiesce to the monopolists' demands.

Power based on managing the distribution of obsidian cores in the basin, however, would have been fragile at best. On the one hand, there is no evidence that elites were in a position to control the acquisition of other goods essential to local manufacturing processes. The perlite, chert, clay, and, presumably, cotton used in the other known industries were easily obtained by those who lived in the Naco valley. Further, the skills used to fashion flake tools, pottery, and cloth were relatively simple and could have been mastered by most house and household members. The production streams described earlier, therefore, provided few opportunities for centralized monopolies.

Elite pretensions based on control over the acquisition and distribution of polyhedral nuclei were also threatened by the fragility of inter-societal exchange networks (see also Renfrew 1982). These webs were no stronger than the individual strands that comprised them. A disruption in any one of these connections would have reverberated throughout the web, to the disadvantage of all participants. As discussed in chapter 8, efforts were made to strengthen these interconnections by promoting common participation within a shared symbolic system. Nevertheless, the challenges of maintaining regular and reliable social connections across physical and political boundaries would have been considerable. Coupled with the threats to hierarchy posed by factions at home, sustaining political advantages based on a monopoly over the local dissemination of obsidian cores would have been difficult indeed.

A major question remains concerning how centralized control of the distribution of polyhedral nuclei translated into power over all members of a society. Certainly, artisans who received cores would have been indebted to their noble patrons for such "gifts." The challenge would have been to transform this dyadic relation of inequality into hierarchical connections that extended outside an artisan's house group and, as seen in the case of Site PVN 144, beyond the boundaries of the center where production occurred.

We hypothesize that artisans, even though they operated outside direct elite supervision, were integral to these magnates' political machinations. By encouraging a few house groups, but not all, to engage in specialized manufacture, notables who ruled from the paramount households of Naco and Site PVN 306 created nodes in local networks where debt and social obligations were concentrated. Certainly, those seeking power had only limited control over these processes because their oversight of production was restricted. Elites could, however, favor certain house groups with "gifts" of polyhedral cores along with, presumably, the knowledge required to knap blades from them. These select social entities might then have been encouraged to expand their involvement in crafts, adding such specialties as percussion flaking of perlite and chert nodules as well as spinning/weaving and pottery manufacture. As fabricators of widely desired objects, each of these house groups enjoyed an edge in creating interpersonal social webs and materializing the existence of these nets through the exchange of the goods they produced. Other members of such nets would have owed the specialists something in return, if only because reciprocation was essential to maintain membership in the web; networks cannot exist in the absence of such interchanges. This is equally true of the relations between craft workers and their elite patrons, except that in this case goods and services flowed up the hierarchy rather than among more or less equals.

We suggest, therefore, that notables used their control over craft workers to tap into the flow of items and labor passing through the nets in which those artisans played important roles. In return for access to such key assets as obsidian cores and manufacturing skills, artisans redirected to elite projects some of the social and economic resources owed them as members of distinct webs instantiated through the exchange of specialized manufactures. Such assets included the provision of tribute in the form of labor and goods.

This strategy would not have worked nearly as well if craft production had been conducted in a few large workshops. Such concentration of manufacturing activities on a sizable scale could potentially vest the power to create and manipulate social networks in the hands of strategically placed artisans. Unless the manner in which goods were made in, and distributed from, such production loci was tightly controlled by elite patrons, the craft workers could pose a serious threat to elite pretensions. By dispersing manufacturing activities widely, competition among craft specialists for adherents was ensured and the ability of each artisan to fashion networks in opposition to elite agendas accordingly diminished. Of course, the proliferation of different artisans posed its own problems. Primary among these would have been the need for magnates continually to negotiate social and economic relations with diverse producers and ensure their loyalty within networks focused on the rulers. On balance, the latter efforts may have posed the slighter risk to domination strategies than did the more efficient but politically dangerous option of aggregating artisans in one social group.

Power, therefore, was exercised indirectly through elites' manipulation of social networks in which they played crucial but distant roles. The wide dissemination of obsidian blades was essential to the success of these strategies because it was through the distribution of this valued item that debts were incurred, debts that ultimately redounded to the advantage of local rulers. The greater the number of consumers involved in such transactions, the wider the webs leaders could draw on for support through the mediation of knappers. In this way, numerous heterarchically structured webs could ultimately, if implicitly, be made to serve the purposes of hierarchy building. The very subtlety of this approach, requiring as it did the cooperation and coordinated action of numerous artisans who resided in diverse house groups, would have restricted the magnates' ability to exert power. The resulting hierarchy required constant negotiation and renegotiation among the participants to sustain. Absolute power was therefore beyond the reach of the Naco valley's Roble phase rulers.

Ritual, Ideology, and Power

The assets involved in power struggles range from tangible items employed in the quest for survival to those concepts and symbols used to create and convey a sense of the world and a person's place in it (Giddens 1984: 38, 258–261). In chapter 7 we considered how resources ranged toward the material end of that continuum, specifically craft products, might have figured in processes of hierarchy building and political centralization. Here we turn to the ways abstract premises and their means of expression in physical forms were employed in political contests. Specifically, we argue that those seeking power face several problems: the creation of a network that transcends preexisting loyalties to extant webs and links their members within a single affiliation, a way of expressing that identity in emotionally compelling ways, and the provision of common projects through which the web is enacted and enlivened—all while ensuring that discourses of identity and network are firmly centered on, and privilege, the rulers. Failure to accomplish the first three objectives results in a realm divided among factions whose primary loyalties to specific domestic nets undermine any sense of unity. Further, unless elites can define for themselves exalted positions within this newly defined network, their claims on power are open to question regardless of whatever physical assets they might control (Giddens 1984: 38, 258–261). Naco valley magnates during the Roble phase, like their brethren elsewhere in other times, had to create the entity they sought to lead and make that creation believable to its members (Brumfiel 1992, 2000a: 133; Preucel 2000; Van Buren and Richards 2000). Success in this endeavor required manipulating symbols that conveyed novel affiliations in ways that resonated with past understandings.

The localized networks that had to be encompassed within the new web consisted of house groups and households. The common projects by which these domestic nets were enacted included, among others, food sharing and participation in religious devotions. Commensality expressed more than intra-web generosity; it also stood for those processes of food production and distribution so essential to the materialization of network membership as well as to the participants' physical survival. Any effort by Roble phase Naco valley leaders to co-opt these nets within a wider affiliation would have had to accommodate and transform these networks and the processes by which they were embodied.

We will focus on two aspects of this process: how the feelings of common purpose and affiliation underlying inter-house/household webs were instantiated, and the steps local notables took to ensconce themselves at the center of such nets. The first process involved the manipulation of designs painted on ceramic vessels. These motifs, it is argued, helped reinforce feelings of intra-site cooperation while linking the residents of Sites PVN 144, PVN 306, and Naco to each other. They may also have tied, albeit indirectly, the valley's inhabitants to people who lived considerable distances from them.

Meeting the second objective involved the strategic deployment of concepts expressed through the form, decoration, and placement of special-purpose ritual architecture in Site PVN 306's western principal plaza (WPP) and Naco's southwest principal plaza. Here, the goal was not to create a body of styles widely shared across the settlement and region. Instead, these architectural symbols are limited to one portion of each center. Their close juxtaposition with elite households suggests that the buildings in question were commissioned by the center's rulers as part of their efforts to gain and secure power. The use of the WPP and the southwest principal plaza for large-scale public gatherings may have supported, and complicated, these efforts.

CREATING UNITY WITH STYLE

The Naco Viejo Ceramic Complex is dominated by unslipped and red-slipped jars and bowls (chapter 1; see also Urban 1993a; Wonderley 1981, 1986, 1987). Fabrics are characterized by large numbers of often sizable aplastic inclusions that comprise 40–50 percent of paste volume, and decoration of any sort is

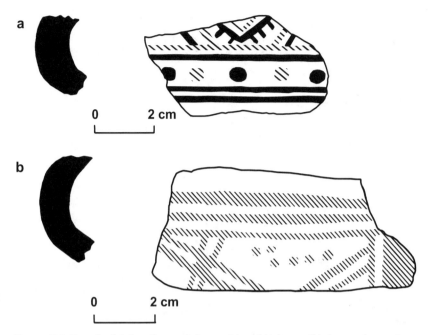

FIGURE 8.1 *Sample of designs from polychrome (a) and bichrome (b) decorated ceramic vessels diagnostic of Roble phase Naco valley collections*

generally rare. The principal exceptions to this pattern are the Nolasco and La Victoria Bichromes (figures 8.1 and 8.2). Members of this class are generally open bowls, usually with out-curving or out-slanting walls and pronounced basal breaks. Surfaces are slipped white and decorated on their exteriors and interiors with red-painted geometric and zoomorphic designs. The bowls are commonly supported by three hollow feet that usually make reference to birds; some are identified as stylized bird feet, while others appear to be abstract renditions of avian heads, the beaks of which point downward (Urban 1993a: 58; Wonderley 1981, 1986). This taxon was originally designated as Nolasco Bichrome by Anthony Wonderley (1981), who defined it based on the Naco assemblage (where it comprises 18% of the Roble phase collection; Urban 1993a: 57; Wonderley 1985; this figure includes incense burners decorated in the characteristic red-on-white style). At Sites PVN 306 and PVN 144 a distinction was made between two wares that appeared in the same forms and with very similar decorative motifs; Nolasco Bichrome has a paste character-ized by high quantities of quartz temper, while La Victoria Bichrome fabrics are finer textured and dominated by very small inclusions of gold and silver mica (Urban 1993a). This division implies that at least two major workshops,

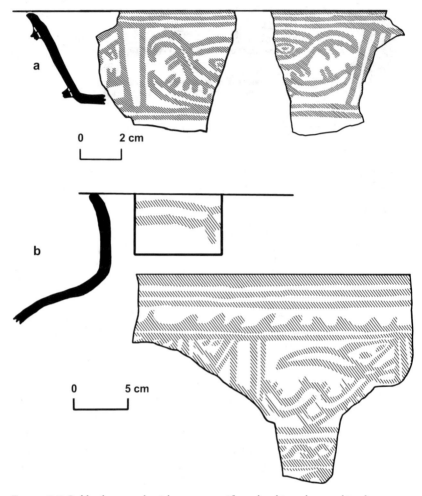

0   2 cm

0   5 cm

FIGURE **8.2** *Roble phase vessels with serpent motifs rendered in red on a white slip*

employing different paste recipes, were involved in fabricating vessels that, on the surface, are essentially identical.

Together, the Nolasco and La Victoria Bichromes make up 5 percent of the combined Site PVN 144 and PVN 306 Roble phase collections. As noted in chapter 6, these painted wares are found in domestic contexts at all three sites, ranging from elite households to trash deposits associated with humble residences. There are few other decorated ceramics of any sort in the assemblages. Wonderley (1981) reports four other white-slipped taxa decorated with designs painted in black (Forastero Bichrome) and red and black (Posas Polychrome, Cortes Polychrome, and Vagabundo Polychrome) that make up less than 0.001

to 0.6 percent of the Naco assemblage; examples of Forastero, Cortes, and Vagabundo together comprise 0.002 percent of the analyzed Roble phase ceramics from Sites PVN 144 and PVN 306. These latter bichromes and polychromes are sufficiently rare that a study of their distribution within the last two sites is meaningless. They likely represent the remains of a few imported vessels, and their sociopolitical significance to the basin's population is unclear. The much greater prevalence and wider distribution of red-on-white–painted bowls, however, indicates that they were fabricated locally. Their manufacture, distribution, and uses, therefore, were determined at least in part by the needs and objectives of the valley's varied inhabitants.

The open bowls in which Nolasco and La Victoria Bichromes most commonly appear suggest that they were used primarily to serve food (Wonderley 1986). The tripod supports attested to in numerous cases indicate that the comestibles were often elevated above the serving surface by 0.03–0.08 m, possibly as part of a display. The significance of the vessels' contents is further heightened by the locally unusual decorations that adorn them. Within the generally monochrome pottery assemblage of the Roble phase Naco valley, Nolasco and La Victoria Bichromes stand out. These decorated containers, therefore, were parts of the food-sharing activities through which house, household, and settlement-wide networks were materialized and enlivened.

Interpreting the red-painted designs poses certain problems. Primary among these is the fragmentary nature of most of the finds. It is difficult to extrapolate from these small pieces to the motifs that once covered complete vessels. Interpreting the Site PVN 306 and PVN 144 designs depends heavily on comparing them with larger, more complete Naco examples. To date, we have not identified any motifs that are unique to any one of these three settlements, although such distinctions cannot be precluded. Only a larger sample with clearer designs from areas outside the Naco site will help clarify the situation. At present, however, it seems reasonable to extrapolate with care from better-known Naco fragments to the general Nolasco–La Victoria design repertoire.

By and large, the motifs attested to on Nolasco and La Victoria bowls occur within a single design band that runs horizontally along the vessel's interior and exterior and is divided into panels. Motifs include crossed diagonal lines making an X, the background filled in with dots; a guilloche appearing between two horizontal lines; an elongated triangle or ellipse; concentric semicircles; and some less common elements, including S curves, balls, and step-frets (Urban 1993a: 58; Wonderley 1981, 1986). Wonderley, among others (Rice 1983: 868, 871; 1987: 101, 238), sees in the combination of these features the rendering of reptilian figures with long, sinuous bodies, most likely snakes (figure 8.2). The creature is often decorated with what appear to be feathers (the elongated triangle or ellipse alluded to earlier).

185

One obvious feature of these designs is their dramatic quality. The red paint stands out starkly against the white background, making the motifs difficult, if not impossible, to ignore. The contrasting colors catch the eye and direct attention to the design field. By raising the container on three legs, the creators enhanced the legibility of these painted symbols while adding yet another decorative element to the picture. By placing the decorations on the bowl's exterior, they also guaranteed that the motifs could be seen even when the vessel was full. The intention seems to have been to draw an unambiguous, explicit connection between those contents and the meanings conveyed by the designs.

As several authors have noted (Rice 1983: 868, 871; Wonderley 1981, 1986), the general form of Nolasco Bichrome vessels and the decorations that adorn them resemble examples from the contemporary highlands of Guatemala and the Peten Lakes area of the Maya lowlands. Wonderley has identified examples of this type in the nearby Sula Plain (1985), where it comprises about 4 percent of the Late Postclassic assemblages at two small domestic sites. Overall, Nolasco and La Victoria motifs are part of a general symbolic system widely spread throughout large parts of late prehistoric southern Mesoamerica. The feathered serpent design in particular has been singled out as an expression of a belief system tied to the "Quetzalcoatl cult," which originated during the Terminal Classic in northern Yucatan (Ringle, Gallareta Negron, and Bey 1998; Rice 1983: 875–876; Wonderley 1981).

Even though their decorations were inspired by foreign motifs, Nolasco and La Victoria were very likely made in or near the Naco valley (a point made originally in Wonderley 1986). Their general prevalence in local collections supports this view, as does the existence of undecorated ceramics in the same wares as the bichromes. In addition, the drop in the frequency of red-on-white–painted ceramics outside the basin (see the discussion of chronology in chapter 1) implies that these vessels were fashioned in the Naco valley, from which a few were exported to neighboring peoples.

Although the mechanisms of distribution are unclear, there is little doubt that these ceramic containers were widely used by all segments of the population, as Wonderley first suggested (1986). They comprise 1–14 percent of the midden assemblages outside Site PVN 306's main plazas, 1 percent of the analyzed eastern principal plaza (EPP) collections from terminal debris contexts, and 4 percent of the studied materials from the WPP, including the Str. 306-83 trash deposit. Seven of the middens unassociated with the Site PVN 306 plazas yielded proportions of bichromes between 5 and 9 percent. At Site PVN 144, Nolasco and La Victoria together make up 2–8 percent of the five analyzed midden collections from outside the principal plaza and 4 percent of the assemblage from the plaza. At Naco the proportions are even higher, ranging from 7 to 21 percent across excavated middens beyond the architectural core. The ubiquity of these sherds points to the central importance of red-and-white–painted bowls in activities pursued by members of house and household networks, regardless of their location or size. Everyone needed these containers, and no one seems to have lacked for them. Recovery of red-on-white–painted vessel fragments in fairly high proportions among debris associated with public gatherings at Sites PVN 306 (Str. 306-83) and PVN 144 (Str. 144-19) also indicates that these serving vessels figured in celebrations that encompassed sizable proportions of the populations residing at both settlements. The figures for bichromes in Naco's southwest principal plaza (47% from Str. 4F-14) are unusually high and most likely reflect the inclusion of large numbers of decorated incense burners in the total. In all cases, however, it appears that Nolasco and La Victoria Bichromes were called for wherever food was served, at scales ranging from the house to the site.

Through their common use, a set of distinctive, dramatically rendered symbols was consistently associated with socially significant processes of food presentation and consumption at varying scales of inclusivity. We may never know the full array of meanings those red-painted designs had for the people who engaged with them in the Roble phase Naco valley. In general, however, they were almost certainly infused with whatever significance was attached to the consumption and sharing of food among network participants in both intimate and public settings (Bartlett and McAnany 2000; Dietler 1996; Dietler and Hayden 2001; LeCount 2001; Vaughn 2004). Insofar as the comestibles themselves were symbols of network unity, they would have reflexively acted back on, and enriched the meanings of, the red-painted designs that adorned the serving vessels. Both sets of symbols, in short, were powerfully fused, forging in that synthesis a complex set of emotions viscerally linked to network identities embodied in part through food sharing (Schortman, Urban, and Ausec 2001; Van Buren and Richards 2000; Yaeger 2000). The widespread distribution of these bowls strongly suggests that this sense of affiliation permeated entire sites. In fact, the pervasiveness of this symbol system at all three investigated Roble phase Naco valley settlements implies that the designs and the activities in which they figured united the basin's populations in a sub-regional network associated with a distinctive identity.

The symbols used in fashioning this affiliation are of both foreign and local derivation. Strictly speaking, the serpent has no known precedent in Naco valley design traditions stretching back to the Middle Preclassic (1200–400 BC; see Urban 1993a; Urban and Schortman 2002). In the same vein, although white slipping very occasionally appears as a surface treatment at several points in the valley's prehistoric sequence, it is never common; nor was it often used as a background for red-painted designs (Urban 1993a). In these ways, Nolasco and La Victoria Bichromes represent a marked change from past practices. The general resemblance of the motifs to those attested to in the Maya lowlands and highlands further points to populations in these areas as sources of inspiration for the distinctive Naco bichromes.

On the other hand, Nolasco and La Victoria evince continuities with the past. The elements that comprise and bound the serpent form, for example, resemble curvilinear rope or braid designs painted in red on the unslipped light tan surfaces of jars during the Late and Terminal Classic (Ausec 2001; Wonderley 1986; figures 8.3 and 8.4). Bird images are drawn in black and red on the orange-slipped interiors of open bowls during the latter intervals (figure 8.5). We have argued elsewhere that these avians may have been defining symbols of an identity that encompassed the domain ruled from the Late Classic Naco valley center La Sierra (Schortman, Urban, and Ausec 2001). These Late and Terminal Classic birds are rendered very differently from their Roble phase counterparts, appear almost always on the interiors of bowls, and are never used as supports. Avian representations may therefore have continued from the Late Classic but with a twist, appearing now as legs and mixed with other elements to render "feathered serpents" (Ausec 2001). At least some of the geometric forms that adorn Nolasco and La Victoria bowls also have deep roots in the Naco valley. Painted Xs, step-frets, and the use of dots as "filler" find analogs in the red-painted designs that appear on the vertical necks and shoulders of large, unslipped jars commonly found in Late and Terminal Classic valley assemblages (Ausec 2001; Wonderley 1986).

The Nolasco and La Victoria symbol set, therefore, couches the foreign and strange within the local and familiar (Wonderley 1986; see also Rice and Cecil 2009 for a parallel case). The dramatically rendered designs would have been recognizable to both visitors conversant with the general themes conveyed by serpent imagery and those who had never left the valley and could see in the birds sinuous lines, Xs, and step-frets motifs that harkened back to earlier periods in the basin's history (see also Wonderley 1986). By uniting the parochial and the exotic, the Naco valley's Roble phase occupants linked notions of commensality to broad-ranging and highly localized symbolic systems. Immediate concerns of house and household converged with whatever universal themes were conveyed through serpents rendered in the starkly contrasting colors of red and white. In this way, even a meal celebrating the unity of an individual house was contextualized within a set of understandings simultaneously tied to a specific past and untethered to any particular place or time.

Until the workshops in which the red-on-white–painted bowls were fabricated are found, we cannot say who sponsored this design program. One way to begin addressing the problem is to ask who would have significantly benefited from the successful dissemination and adoption of these motifs. The

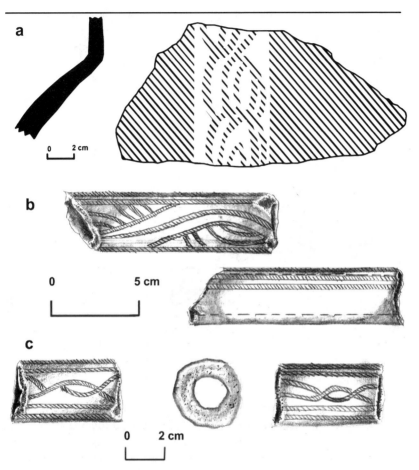

FIGURE 8.3 *Examples of the "braid motif" from red-on-natural and red-on-white deco-rated vessels dating to the Late/Terminal Classic (a) and Roble phase (b, c), respectively, in the Naco valley*

most likely candidates are the local elites (see also Wonderley 1986). There are several reasons to infer that these notables were instrumental in promoting the syncretic symbol system outlined earlier. First, this segment of the population is the one most likely to have been in contact with representatives of foreign realms where symbolic systems expressed through serpent motifs and red-on-white painting were found. Naco valley elites were therefore in the best position to appropriate the relevant symbols and ensure their execution on locally made bowls. Second, elites had the most to gain from promoting feelings of unity among their subjects. The domain they sought to rule, as is the case in

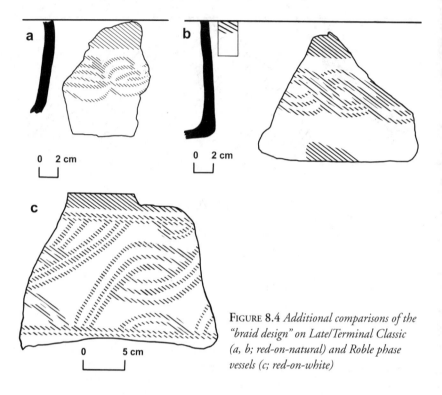

FIGURE 8.4 *Additional comparisons of the "braid design" on Late/Terminal Classic (a, b; red-on-natural) and Roble phase vessels (c; red-on-white)*

most hierarchically structured realms, encompassed networks that linked individuals to specific places and the people who occupied them (Brumfiel and Fox 1994; Schortman, Urban, and Ausec 2001). Fashioning an identity that transcends these local differences and forges a sense of commonality where none existed before is crucial to the creation of unified polities. This does not mean earlier loyalties must be replaced or eradicated. Rather, a commitment to the realm and to those who rule it must be added to the set of affiliations each person who lives in the domain at least occasionally actualizes.

Promotion of a network that encompassed a wide array of adherents, therefore, was central to the project of notables seeking to fashion a unified polity out of people with diverse, localized affiliations (Pugh and Rice 2009: 142). This web could not simply be imposed from above. Rather, its nature and meanings had to be negotiated with the members of the numerous localized webs that comprised it (Brumfiel 2000a; Yaeger 2000). Every participant would have to feel some solidarity with his or her compatriots in the network. Part of the solution in this particular case involved linking a distinctive set of painted motifs representative of the novel, inter-house affiliation with food sharing and displays conducted in every house and household. In this way,

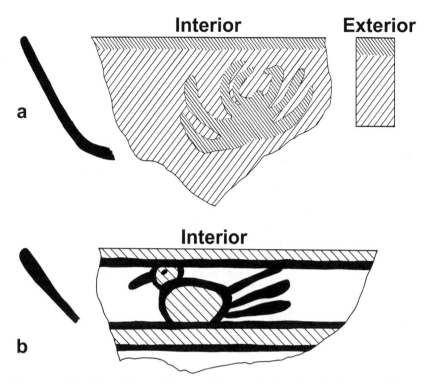

FIGURE 8.5 *Examples of Late and Terminal Classic bichromes (a) and polychromes (b) from the Naco valley*

the new identity was infused with powerful emotions tied to the immediate domestic unit that was itself created and re-created each day through recurring interactions that included commensality (Dietler 1996; Dietler and Hayden 2001; LeCount 2001; Vaughn 2004; Wonderley 1986). The new affiliation's power to unite members of different houses, therefore, depended on the continuing vitality of the domestic webs to which it made reference. Thus preexisting ties to house, household, and place were not eradicated but instead were deployed in the service of fashioning an identity that encompassed them and situated these nets within a broader context. Certainly, there was more to the creation of an extensive network than the promotion of new ceramic designs. Still, we argue that these motifs played important roles in forging a novel identity that brought together those who heretofore had not explicitly expressed enduring connections to each other.

The resulting web did not overtly privilege the political aspirations of any one faction. Everyone, to some extent, partook in the shared affiliation regardless of rank. Ensuring that this network was organized hierarchically required the manipulation of another set of symbols expressed through special-purpose buildings associated with large-scale rituals.

BUILDING EXPRESSIONS OF UNITY AND DISTINCTION

Structures 306-17, 306-19, and 306-174 in the WPP and Str. 4F-1 in Naco's southwest principal plaza constitute marked breaks in the valley's architectural tradition. Specifically, these edifices' round forms; the extensive use of plaster on Strs. 306-19 and 4F-1; the latter two's cogwheel shapes; the lower sloping zones that bordered Strs. 306-17, 306-19, and 4F-1 late in their use-lives; and the inferred presence of monuments atop the first two buildings singly and in combination set these constructions apart from their predecessors.

There is no good reason to believe these special-purpose constructions were inspired by local prototypes. Rather, they appear to have been salient architectural symbols that figured within the Quetzalcoatl cult (Demarest, Rice, and Rice 2004: 552; Freidel and Sabloff 1984: 33; Milbrath and Peraza Lope 2003: 23; Pollock 1936; Pugh 2001: 251; Ringle, Gallareta Negron, and Bey 1998: 186, 203, 222; Rosenswig and Masson 2002: 217; Sidrys and Andersen 1978: 648). Prominent among the symbols related to this movement are round and C-shaped buildings, the former similar to those seen in the WPP and the southwest principal plaza of Naco (Chase and Chase 1988: 43–44; Milbrath and Peraza Lope 2003: 4, 23; Ringle, Gallareta Negron, and Bey 1998). Who instigated these architectural changes, and what might their objectives have been? We argue here that it was members of the paramount households at Naco and Site PVN 306 who were largely responsible for the erection of Strs. 306-17, 306-19, 306-174, and 4F-1. The buildings are located adjoining these elite households. Those who lived in the neighboring plazas had a sufficient command over labor to raise substantial platforms for their own uses. They would therefore have been able to marshal the productive efforts of their supporters to fashion the circular buildings listed here. In addition, as noted in the previous section, notables who resided at Site PVN 306 and Naco also likely enjoyed privileged access to representatives of distant realms from whom they could obtain information about other religions and the symbols through which their precepts were materialized (Ringle, Gallareta Negron, and Bey 1998). In short, magnates at these two centers had the opportunity to learn about foreign belief systems and the means to put that knowledge into practice.

We suggest that the motivations underlying the observed architectural shifts were complex, born out of a tension between conflicting aims that were essential to elite political projects (Brumfiel 1992, 2000a: 133). On the one hand, as argued previously, would-be leaders had to define a network coterminous with the group of adherents they sought to rule. Preexisting allegiances were supplemented with a new affiliation that transcended their parochial boundaries. Such novel webs required a new identity enacted through unprecedented forms of cooperative behaviors and conveyed through symbols that, regardless of their sources, were charged with new meanings. At the same time, these magnates had to distinguish themselves from those they would lead (Brumfiel 2000a: 133; Preucel 2000: 73). Insofar as their preeminence relied on securing goods from afar, elites also had to forge alliances with interaction partners capable of supplying those items. Even if imports were not crucial to their political aims, rulers could benefit from associations with distant lords who might provide support against local uprisings and attacks from beyond the valley, as well as some of the charisma associated with physically distant realms (Freidel and Sabloff 1984: 192; Helms 1979, 1988, 1992; Masson 2001: 164; Renfrew 1982; Renfrew and Cherry 1986; Rice 1983: 876). Naco valley leaders were thus faced with a conundrum all elites must confront: to be simultaneously part of and above those they rule, equally linked to far-off domains and local adherents (Brumfiel 2000a; Pauketat and Emerson 1999; Schortman, Urban, and Ausec 2001). Associating themselves with a foreign religion was one means of resolving this tension.

By selectively adopting elements of the Quetzalcoatl cult, notables at Naco and Site PVN 306 insinuated themselves within a network that crossed multiple societies located at varying distances from the valley (Boone and Smith 2003; Masson 2000b: 249–263, 2001: 164, 2003a: 200; Pohl 2003a: 62–63; Smith 2003b). This web was apparently enacted in part through its members' occasional participation in religious practices that involved the manipulation of a shared symbol set freed from associations with a particular place and time (Berdan 2003c; Pohl 2003b). The "universal" quality of the Quetzalcoatl cult enabled its members to forge an "imagined community" that spanned territorially distinct realms (Canuto and Yaeger 2000; Isbell 2000; Preucel 2000). The bonds of trust and mutual understanding that linked participants would thus have enabled the exchange of ideas, personnel, and goods over potentially great territorial expanses (Braswell 2003c; Cohen 1969; Curtin 1984; Smith 2003b). Such inter-societal transfers may have been crucial to secure the imports, support, and charisma needed to maintain and reproduce hierarchical relations at home.

Interactions among members of this "universal" religion were apparently conducted on an equal footing. Although the "cult" may have originated at Chichen Itza and later been associated with Mayapan, the rulers of these northern Yucatan capitals did not exercise political hegemony among all their coreligionists by the Late Postclassic (Masson 2000b: 249–263; Pollock et al. 1962; Pugh 2003). This is certainly the case for the Naco valley, which shows no sign of ever having been incorporated within a foreign domain. The web enlivened through participation in the Quetzalcoatl cult thus spread beyond the political boundaries, and outside the control of, any one state. Rulers at Site PVN 306 and Naco were among the participants in this net.

How was this foreign religion integrated within Naco valley networks? On the one hand, there is good reason to believe the Quetzalcoatl cult was modified in the course of its incorporation into Naco valley beliefs and practices. As noted in the discussion of Nolasco and La Victoria Bichromes, representations of serpents linked to the "cult" were merged with local symbols to fashion what was likely a synthesis of the foreign and the familiar. Similarly, while circular buildings with no clear local precedents were raised, other aspects of the religion, such as the elaborately modeled and hourglass-shaped spiked incensarios associated with the Quetzalcoatl cult at Mayapan and elsewhere in Yucatan, are rarely found in the Naco valley (Masson 2000b: 265; Milbrath and Peraza Lope 2003: 7, 25; 2009; Pugh 2001, 2002–2004; Ringle, Gallareta Negron, and Bey 1998; see also Rice 1987: 181–184). Modeled censers, possibly associated with ancestor worship (Masson 2000a), are completely absent from our collections, while two fragments of spiked incense burners were found (one each at Sites PVN 144 and PVN 306), along with a single complete example. The latter is a small bowl with a restricted orifice unearthed near Str. 306-86, well away from the WPP. Those incense burners used in the valley now are overwhelmingly ladle censers, whose shallow open bowls are attached to long, hollow tube handles. Although this form is widespread throughout southern Mesoamerica, it has a long history within the Naco valley, where it dates back to at least the Late Classic. It appears, therefore, that while some architectural symbols of the "cult" were accepted and displayed prominently in the WPP and Naco's southwest principal plaza, the paraphernalia used in rites conducted in these locales had largely local inspirations. Whatever rituals the basin's magnates engaged in when they traveled to other centers, in their own realm they seemingly modified the observances by eschewing some aspects of the rites and their distinctive symbols.

The other step taken was to insinuate the performance of rites explicitly linked to the Quetzalcoatl cult into gatherings that occurred within the WPP and Naco's southwest principal plaza. As noted previously, these convocations, which combined feasting and religious observances, were among the primary cooperative activities that defined and reproduced webs encompassing members of numerous house groups (see also Joyce and Hendon 2000; Masson 2000b; Preucel 2000; Yaeger 2000). The orchestration of such convocations did not require the intervention of elites. They were, in essence, domestic ceremonies writ large, involving the same sorts of ritual and food-serving gear found throughout house groups of all social stations. To be indispensable to these rites of intensification and to the network they embodied, elites had to introduce some set of practices they alone could perform. The Quetzalcoatl cult filled that need.

By commissioning the erection of physically salient elements of this symbol set in the heart of the center, notables at Naco and Site PVN 306 explicitly linked a universal religion to a body of deep-seated local beliefs and practices. Appreciation for the foreign religion was enhanced by infusing it with the emotional power of values rooted in feasting and religious observances conducted within house groups and households. At the same time, traditional rites and feasts were imbued with the charisma of a cult derived from distant, high-prestige lands (Helms 1979, 1988, 1992, 1993; LeCount 2001; Vaughn 2004; Yaeger 2000). In the process, the elites found their indispensable role in forging an inter-house network (see also Masson 2000b: 463). They could monopolize the knowledge needed to conduct religious observances on and about Strs. 306-17, 306-19, 306-174, and 4F-1. Insofar as these performances were perceived as central to the observances conducted in the WPP and Naco's southwest principal plaza and to defining the sense of self celebrated there, then local rulers had established a route to power. Through cooperation within a network of the high-born abroad, these rulers controlled ideological resources useful in securing and sustaining their preeminence within their home domain.

The presence of roughly comparable, and sizable, symbols of this religious system at both Naco and Site PVN 306 implies that their leaders exercised comparable power and influence within the Roble phase basin. They were certainly able to establish membership in the same interregional network and employ its symbols to accomplish their own goals without undue interference from each other. There are no comparable symbols of this "cult" at Site PVN 144.

Site PVN 144's inhabitants did, however, construct a striking set of architectural symbols that have no parallels at their larger neighbors. These are the three large stucco masks that flank the western staircases on Strs. 144-8 and 144-18 along the western edge of the principal plaza. These features have been tentatively identified as representations of God M, a patron of Maya merchants, who is frequently rendered with a large bulbous nose (Douglass and Mooney 2001). Whatever specific meanings the masks were designed to convey, their general form and locations have no local precedents. They were, rather, inspired by foreign models, almost certainly those provided by agents who lived in the Maya lowlands. There is no compelling reason to think they were closely tied to the Quetzalcoatl cult. Construction of the masks implies participation by those who commissioned them in yet another extensive network through which ideas and goods moved and alliances were established. In this case, the web may have been explicitly tied to traders, although we cannot rule out the possibility that these foreign symbols were reinterpreted within the Naco valley.

The location of these exotic symbols at Site PVN 144 suggests that they figured differently in the creation of social networks than was the case for foreign-inspired architectural forms at Site PVN 306 and Naco. The stucco images border entrances to two buildings that likely housed gatherings of influential community members (see chapters 4 and 6). Such meeting houses date back in the Naco valley to at least the Terminal Classic (Schortman and Urban 2004b). The erection of venues to host social leaders was not new, therefore, although the decorations employed in this case were fairly novel.

In addition to the stucco images, Strs. PVN 144-8-2nd and 144-8-1st were adorned with a basal sloping zone, similar to those seen on Strs. 306-17, 306-19, and 4F-1. Both of the iterations of Str. 144-8's summit were also floored with plaster, part of which, at least in the penultimate version, was painted red. Such decoration of superstructure surfaces is attested to on buildings surrounding Naco's principal plazas but not at Site PVN 306. These decorative embellishments further distinguished this community house from its neighbors, although Str. 144-18, immediately north of Str. 144-8, may have been decorated in a similar fashion.

As discussed in chapter 6, these features may have been integral to the roles Strs. 144-8 and 144-18 played in negotiations among power holders within the Naco settlement cluster. These interactions, probably accompanied by communal feasts and rituals, might have been carried out under the aegis of different supernatural entities than those associated with the paramount households at Naco and Site PVN 306. Hence, the absence of direct references to symbols of the Quetzalcoatl cult on and around Site PVN 144's main plaza may have conveyed the intervention of different supernaturals appropriate to this very different context of inter-elite interaction. Even here, however, the same sorts of decorated food-serving bowls and ritual equipment found in public and private contexts were employed in celebrations conducted within the main plaza. Evocations of solidarity at all levels, from the smallest domestic webs to the network that embraced the entire settlement cluster, apparently employed much the same symbols that fused foreign and local concepts. Only the ways in which these enactments of local affiliations were tied to broader associations that privileged elite actors changed.

The final example of distinctive, foreign-inspired architecture known from the Roble phase basin is Naco's ballcourt (Str. 4F-15). Wonderley (1981) sees the distinctive I-shaped form as inspired by highland Maya prototypes, as is the arrangement of the court and the neighboring "temple" (Str. 4F-1). In particular, he argues that the east-west arrangement of Strs. 4F-1 and 4F-15, with the ballcourt on the west, mimics organizational schemes seen as early as the Terminal Classic at Chichen Itza and which continued during the Late Postclassic among "Mexicanized" cultures throughout the Maya highlands and lowlands (1981). Ballcourts are recorded during earlier periods in Naco valley prehistory. A particularly large example was erected at the Late Classic valley capital La Sierra, and a smaller court has been identified at Site PVN 110, where it dates to the Terminal Classic (Urban 1986). In both instances a lack of local prototypes strongly indicates that this architectural form, and the rites associated with it, were derived from areas outside the valley. In the case of Str. 4F-15 the fountainhead of inspiration lies to the west and north, from which the conceptual systems embodied in Site PVN 144's stucco masks and the circular buildings at Site PVN 306 and Naco were derived.

Within Sites PVN 144, PVN 306, and Naco, alien architectonic symbols were grafted onto traditional practices and, presumably, integrated with the beliefs and values underlying those actions. In all three cases, exotic images were directly tied to gathering places of importance to the community in which they functioned. The primary distinction is that the Site PVN 144 examples do not appear as freestanding edifices. Rather, here the symbols are attached to a form of construction that served a function—hosting meetings of elites—with local precedents. Embellishing Strs. 144-8 and 144-18 in this way certainly transformed them, linking the notables who met within the aforementioned constructions and the actions in which they engaged during such gatherings with supernatural forces distinct from those materialized in the open plazas adjoining the two paramount households.

In all of the cases outlined here, architectural symbols of foreign religions were not explicitly tied to specific individuals or even domestic units. Expressions of the Quetzalcoatl cult at Naco and Site PVN 306 are adjacent to, but not incorporated within, their respective elite households. So, too, the masks at Site PVN 144 adorn community structures, not the residences of local luminaries. This may have been part of a policy that cast exotic faiths and their symbols as properties of entire communities, even if elites played crucial roles in enacting rites within them. In this way, relations between exotic and parochial beliefs could be portrayed as mediated by local lords who were simultaneously part of and distinct from the populations they sought to lead.

Leaders of Sites PVN 144, PVN 306, and Naco also apparently concurred that symbols associated with the foreign and sacred were to be located west of their residences. Structures 306-17, 306-19, 306-174, 4F-1, and 4F-15 lie in this direction from the paramount households at Site PVN 306 and Naco. Even within that sacred space, debris from religious devotions was concentrated on the plaza's west margin (Strs. 306-182 and 4F-14). The same relations hold at Site PVN 144: buildings decorated with elements inspired by alien models are on the west side of the principal plaza; the clearest expressions of those distant contacts—the stucco masks—are affixed to the west sides of these edifices; and detritus associated with rites conducted in the plaza was collected on its west side (Str. 306-19, Unit 1). This patterning may signify an underlying principle of behavioral organization that linked the west with concepts of foreignness and any supernatural powers derived from distant domains.

SUMMARY

We hypothesize that the Naco valley's Roble phase elites effectively manipulated symbolic assets of both foreign and local origins to unite the realm they sought to rule, achieve prominence within that domain, and establish regular and sustained contact with their counterparts in other realms from whom they could secure the goods, ideas, and alliances needed to reproduce hierarchical relations at home. These objectives were accomplished by setting the parochial practices of food sharing and ritual by which house and household networks were enacted within the context of a universal religion, whose dominant symbols and rites were understood and enacted primarily by local notables (Baines and Yoffee 2000; Van Buren and Richards 2000).

Elites, working together within their own webs, used ideological resources in several ways to advance their political agenda. Social unity focused on paramount lords was achieved by associating symbols of the Quetzalcoatl cult directly with practices of food display and serving enacted in all houses and households at Sites PVN 306, PVN 144, and Naco (Dietler 1996; Dietler and Hayden 2001; LeCount 2001; Vaughn 2004). This linkage was achieved in part by promotion of a distinctive tripod bowl, the white-slipped exterior surfaces of which bore dramatic representations of serpents painted in red. As these reptiles were closely linked to the Quetzalcoatl cult, people looking at and eating from the red-painted containers would have been constantly reminded of the connections among food; the domestic webs in which it was produced, shared, and consumed; and the precepts of a religion unconnected to any particular place or time. Local events, such as house and household feasts, were thus contextualized within sacred premises that were universal in their scope and applicability. Every time house and household unity was enacted in food sharing, the participants' ties to a broader congregation of believers were highlighted. Similarly, the public rites and feasts through which this broader congregation instantiated its shared affiliation and solidarity were infused with the emotional power of practices conducted regularly within the smallest domestic webs.

The conversion of generalized inter-house unity into a hierarchically structured web was accomplished by the creation of physically salient architectural symbols explicitly tied to specific prominent households (Moore 1996, 2003). At Site PVN 306 and Naco, these symbols were platforms whose circular forms linked them directly to the Quetzalcoatl cult. The construction of a ballcourt at Naco adjoining the circular platform may have enhanced the power of the message the platform conveyed. The locations of all these buildings, immediately west of the settlements' primary elite households, unambiguously tied social leaders with prominent expressions of the new religion while still distancing the former from the latter (see also Masson 2000b: 197). The staging of large-scale feasts and rites on and around these edifices brought most, perhaps all, of a web's members in direct contact with the platforms and the concepts they embodied. By so doing, rulers encouraged their followers to experience celebrations of inter-house solidarity as expanded versions of those cooperative acts of sharing and ritual conducted in houses and households (Van Buren 2000). There is little doubt, however, that these gatherings were conducted under the aegis of local notables, structured according to principles that enhanced their preeminence within the community of worshippers. These magnates originally embraced the Quetzalcoatl cult, commissioned venues for its conduct, and tied those arenas closely to their residences. Whatever forms the original rites took, they almost certainly highlighted the importance of the center's rulers in the observances. Thus local relations of power could be elevated to universal hierarchical premises, just as feelings of house and household unity were enhanced by setting them within a sacred realm of broad temporal and territorial scope.

Site PVN 144, in turn, hosted large-scale feasts and rituals in its plaza and smaller gatherings of elites in two prominent community buildings (Strs. 144-8 and 144-18) adorned with yet another set of distinctive, foreign-derived symbols. These edifices were part of an elite household complex but were also gathering places for influential members of the entire settlement cluster. Structures 144-8 and 144-18, therefore, were analogous to the WPP and southwest plazas at Site PVN 306 and Naco but on a smaller scale; all were venues where community members confronted symbols expressive of foreign religions while engaging in activities that embodied network affiliations that transcended house and household ties. The goal in each case was the same—that is, to situate novel loyalties to supra-house/household entities within the context of sacred principles unfettered by ties to specific places and times. Leaders took pains to link these alien symbols with the polities they ruled and not exclusively to their own households. Nevertheless, elites abrogated to themselves crucial roles in mediating linkages among house, household, site, settlement cluster, and the cosmos in which these nets operated. By controlling this negotiation, a few gained power over many.

On a broader territorial scale, elite participation in foreign faiths such as the Quetzalcoatl cult gave them access to a network whose members consisted of notables and, likely, merchants from different realms who communicated using a common symbolic vocabulary (Masson 2000b: 41; Smith and Berdan

2003). At the very least, adherence to such belief systems provided a set of shared principles that facilitated forging the bonds of trust and mutual understanding crucial to establish enduring cooperative relations. It is by means of the network enacted through participation in common rites using shared symbols that goods, such as polyhedral obsidian cores, and ideas crucial to maintaining hierarchical relations at home spread. Restricting participation in this spatially extensive web to those who could decode and manipulate the relevant symbols would have helped its participants maintain exclusive control over politically potent valuables. Subordinates, therefore, could not challenge hierarchical relations by establishing independent access to these crucial items and concepts (Kipp and Schortman 1989).

In the course of synthesizing local and foreign practices and concepts, Naco valley magnates fashioned an extensive identity network that drew emotional power from the house and household webs it embraced, placed themselves at the center of this expansive net, and established long-term relations with high-status allies in other domains on whom they could rely for the political currency needed to sustain intra-societal hierarchies. There is no way of knowing to what extent, if at all, those who lived at Sites PVN 144, PVN 306, and Naco, as well as throughout the valley, accepted the precepts of these foreign religions (Alcock 2000: 119). Rituals continued to be conducted within houses and households in the investigated settlements using such traditional items as ladle incensarios. In addition, ceramic figurines, likely used in house group rites, are found exclusively in domestic contests outside Site PVN 306's paramount household (Brumfiel 2000b: 472–473; figure 8.6). These images are hand-modeled representations of sexless people, arms held across the chest and with simplified faces and no legs. The figurines have no known connection to exotic faiths and seem to represent items used solely in local religious devotions. Members of each house and household, therefore, likely conducted their own rites for their own needs using materials with exclusively local significance. They were not completely dependent on elites to meet their spiritual requirements and thus maintained at least a modicum of autonomy.

The combination of symbols that had great time depth with those of the new religion on Nolasco and La Victoria Bichromes further implies that foreign precepts were adapted to mesh with local understandings and beliefs. In addition, the absence of such late diagnostics of the Quetzalcoatl cult as modeled and hourglass-shaped spiked incense burners in valley collections indicates that the ritual system was not adopted wholesale at any of the investigated centers. Rather, its premises and symbols were modified for local consumption. Nevertheless, the ubiquity of red-on-white–painted bowls in domestic contexts throughout the investigated sites points to a general acceptance of at least some aspects of the foreign symbol system and their association with house and

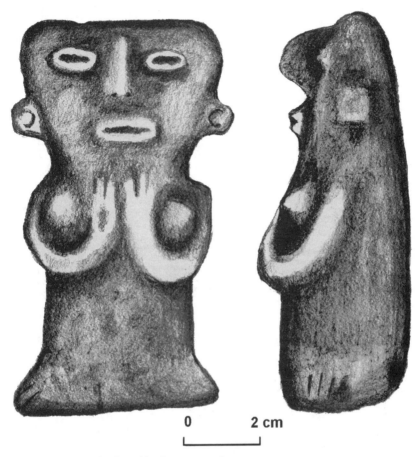

0   2 cm

FIGURE 8.6 *Example of a Roble phase ceramic figurine*

household feasts. The multiple renovations attested to on architectural symbols of the "cult" at Site PVN 306 (Strs. 306-17 and 306-19) and on the masks on Str. 144-8, as well as the latter building's multiple construction stages, hint at the protracted survival of these constructions and their continued use as public foci. Foreign religious precepts may not have been equally embraced by all valley inhabitants, and their significance may have been interpreted variably by those who held different structural positions defined by age, gender, rank, occupation, and place of residence. There is no denying, however, that foreign-inspired symbols spread widely across the basin and permeated even the most intimate recesses of daily life. Few of the valley's residents were untouched by them. Elite manipulation of exotic and traditional symbols and practices, therefore, contributed to the forging of new webs organized along hierarchical lines.

NINE

Networks and Social Memory

Chapters 7 and 8 outline the tangible and conceptual resources deployed by those who sought power at Roble phase Sites PVN 144, PVN 306, and Naco. The networks created in part through the strategic use of those assets linked contemporaries of different political ranks. Preeminence is greatly strengthened, however, if power differences are rooted in the past (Alcock 2000; Bloch 1977a, 1977b; Casey 1987; Hendon 2000; Schank and Abelson 1995). Insofar as rulers can fashion credible narratives linking their present prerogatives to ancient precedents, they can clothe dynamic and contingent power relations within timeless schemes that encourage acceptance of that which cannot be changed. Magnates therefore generally contend for control over social memory, the widely accepted recollection of earlier events, and the perceived relevance of those events for present circumstances (Van Dyke and Alcock 2003: 2). Such efforts take many forms. In some cases the current significance of real or imagined past actions and personages may be stressed (Casey 1987: 206; DeMarrais, Castillo, and Earle 1996; Huyssen 2003: 101; Meskell 2003; Schank and Abelson 1995). Monuments may therefore be raised to commemorate a ruler's ancestors, or specific locales may be singled out for special treatment. In this way, physically salient constructions help "anchor the past in the present" (Meskell 2003: 36). Alternatively, inconvenient "truths" may be purposefully forgotten by hiding signs of them from general view. Thus memorials to earlier leaders can be buried and sites tied up with specific memories reinterpreted or ignored (Casey 1987: 186–189; Joyce 2003: 116–120; Schreiber 2005: 250–251; Van Dyke and Alcock 2003: 3).

Would-be leaders, therefore, must not only forge ties with those with whom they live but also create believable connections with antecedents who populate a remembered past (Beaudry, Cook, and Mrozowski 1991; Casey 1987: 216–230). Successful co-optation of power requires, in other words, that elites place themselves at the nexus of webs that extend out horizontally in the present and back, vertically, into history. Failure to accomplish these twin goals weakens leaders' claims to power and their ability to transmit those privileges into the future.

REACHING INTO THE PAST THROUGH ARCHITECTURE

The clearest sign that Site PVN 306's rulers made direct claims on the past is evidenced by their preservation of architecture associated with what had been a Terminal Classic center located 3 m east of the eastern principal plaza (EPP) (see also Rice 2009 for a comparable example from the Maya lowlands). The focal point of the earlier occupation is Str. 306-105 (see figure 3.2). This stone-faced platform stood 1.9 m high during its final construction stage, measured 12.34 m north-south, and supported an extensive earthen-floored summit that covered 7.2 m north-south (the building's east-west dimensions were not revealed). Structure 306-105 is near the exact center of a group of twenty-one surface-visible structures that together cover 7,300 m². Plazas are not obvious within most of this densely nucleated cluster; the only two such patios pivot on Str. 306-105, extending east and south of that building. Excavations in this portion of the settlement uncovered all or most of six edifices, including Str. 306-105. Four of these buildings are low platforms 0.23–0.66 m high, and one is a surface-level construction whose perimeter was defined by substantial stone foundations. All five of these edifices apparently served as residences, whereas Str. 306-105's considerable size and lack of such built-in furniture as benches in its final version indicate that it was a focal point for community gatherings and possibly worship.

A second nucleus of Terminal Classic occupation lies 260 m west of the eastern cluster. Here, four substantial platforms (Strs. 306-1/4) bound a patio on all sides. Limited excavations on Strs. 306-1 and 306-4 revealed that they were stone-faced, earth-filled platforms standing 0.5–0.74 m high. Based on their forms and associated artifacts, these edifices were likely residences. Structure 306-54, a 0.12-m-high stone-faced terrace situated 36 m southwest and downslope from this plaza group, was apparently raised to slow erosion below the patio's southwest flank.

It is not clear what, if any, Terminal Classic construction existed between these two foci. An extensive, minimally 0.46-m-thick midden deposit dating to this interval was encountered beneath Str. 306-128 on the east edge of the EPP. This and scattered finds of diagnostic Terminal Classic remains in tests dug into the EPP indicate that trash relating to the period spread over a considerable area west of the eastern architectural nucleus. Settlement was not apparently continuous, however, between the east and west structure aggregates.

Site PVN 306's Terminal Classic occupation was substantial. The presence of the monumental Str. 306-105 here sets it apart from most of the relatively small settlements dating to this span. Instead, Terminal Classic Site PVN 306 was among thirteen contemporary settlements that contained 1–13 platforms standing at least 1.5 m tall (figure 9.1). These sizable constructions imply that the sites in question were foci of political power; at least some of their residents could command the labor to raise monumental platforms (Schortman and Urban 2004b). Site PVN 306 falls toward the small end of that range, suggesting that its leaders were less powerful than some of their contemporaries in the Naco valley.

There are several striking features about the way Site PVN 306's Terminal Classic constructions were treated during the Roble phase. First, they were left standing throughout the late prehistoric occupation of the center. There is little evidence that stones were recycled from these earlier edifices into their successors' facades and foundations. In fact, all of the investigated buildings, save Str. 306-105, were very well preserved when excavated; Str. 306-105 had been heavily looted in recent times. Site PVN 306's late prehistoric inhabitants, therefore, did not take advantage of the readily available supplies of building materials presented by the Terminal Classic edifices but left them largely untouched, albeit in ruined states.

Second, there are only slight hints that any of the studied buildings were used during the Roble phase. Artifacts dating to this span were rarely identified in assemblages associated with or overlying Terminal Classic architecture. This absence is all the more striking given the EPP's proximity to ruins of the earlier occupation; a scant 3 m separates Strs. 306-123 and 306-121, which were built roughly 400 years apart. Not only were Roble phase occupants of the settlement refraining from robbing stones associated with earlier edifices, they were also not jettisoning their trash onto these buildings.

Third, seven burials were found on and around three structures dating to the Terminal Classic in the eastern cluster. The locations of these interments, resting above the bases of platform facings, strongly indicate that they were introduced well after the buildings were abandoned. Unfortunately, none of

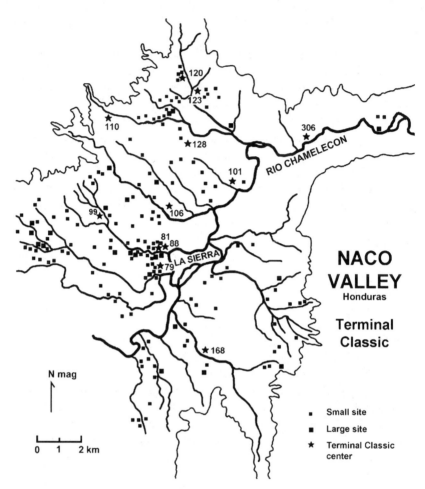

FIGURE 9.1 *Map of settlement distribution within the Late and Terminal Classic Naco valley. Note the juxtaposition of Sites PVN 99 and Naco, on the one hand, and Sites PVN 144 and PVN 128, on the other.*

these burials included any temporally diagnostic grave goods; nor were clear pit lines associated with them. Their high stratigraphic positions in relation to Terminal Classic architecture, however, point to interment having taken place well after the buildings were abandoned and earth had begun to accumulate around them. Given the absence of clear markers relating the remains to the post-Conquest period, these individuals were very likely buried during the Roble phase. The last prehistoric denizens of the settlement, therefore, apparently treated at least parts of the Terminal Classic settlement as a necropolis. There were no signs of late burials in the western patio group.

Finally, the very close juxtaposition of the EPP and the largest concentration of Terminal Classic architecture at Site PVN 306 is striking. Surface evidence and excavations elsewhere at the center indicate that Site PVN 306's main plazas could have been erected on many other portions of this relatively flat terrace. Location of the EPP directly adjoining Str. 306-105 and its surrounding aggregate was therefore not dictated by any obvious practical necessity. Rather, there was something about the eastern Terminal Classic architectural cluster that attracted the premier Roble phase household to build next to it.

A similar situation may also pertain at Site PVN 144. Here, the Terminal Classic remains are much more substantial, represented by the six monumental constructions and twenty-two smaller platforms that comprise Site PVN 128, 0.25 km to the northeast (Schortman and Urban 2004b; figures 9.1, 9.2). The latter settlement was one of the largest Terminal Classic centers in the Naco valley as measured by the sizes and numbers of its component buildings. Excavations conducted at Site PVN 128 uncovered 936 m^2 in the course of clearing fourteen buildings, three of which were sizable platforms 1.4–2.6 m high (Schortman and Urban 2004b). These investigations revealed that, like Site PVN 306's eastern cluster, Site PVN 128 was a focal point for hierarchically organized networks centered on a cadre of elite residents at the settlement (Schortman and Urban 2004b). Based on differences in the scale and number of their constructions, Site PVN 128's rulers apparently exercised more power, possibly over a larger population, than did their contemporaries at Site PVN 306.

These differences aside, the Terminal Classic buildings at Sites PVN 128 and PVN 306 were treated in much the same ways. Specifically, platforms at the former settlement evinced little evidence of damage from ancient stone robbing. They were apparently left relatively untouched until recent times, when looting and road construction took their toll on the edifices. Further, despite the short distance separating Sites PVN 128 and PVN 144, very little Roble phase material is found on or around the earlier buildings. Unlike the case at Site PVN 306, however, there were no late burials associated with Site PVN 128's Terminal Classic constructions. Whatever connections might have been made between Site PVN 144's occupants and the ruins lying 250 m away, they did not apparently involve treating the latter as final resting places for the former.

Naco's architectural core was also situated near major construction dating to the Terminal Classic. The extensive modifications made to Naco and its environs by colonial and later occupation stretching into the present make it difficult to ascertain the nature and scale of architecture here dating to any prehistoric span. At least one center composed of seven edifices up to 2.5 m

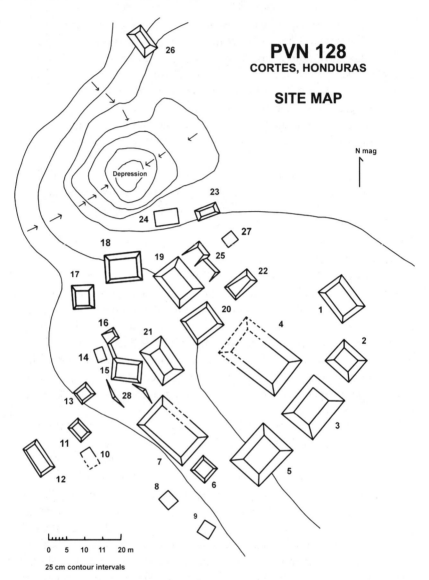

PVN 128
CORTES, HONDURAS

SITE MAP

N mag

Depression

26
23
24
27
18
19
25
17
22
16
21
20
1
14
15
4
2
13
28
11
10
3
12
7
5
8
6
9

0   5   10   11   20 m

25 cm contour intervals

FIGURE 9.2 *Map of Site PVN 128, a Terminal Classic center in the Naco valley*

tall and grouped around two plazas, however, lies on the west border of the Roble phase center and seems to have survived the last prehistoric centuries intact (Site PVN 99; figure 9.1). Limited test excavations on two of the monumental platforms at Site PVN 99, however, revealed no burials dating to any span.

Such juxtapositions between late and earlier political centers could, of course, be fortuitous. The physical criteria that must have been met to support moderately large settlements in both the Terminal Classic and the Roble phase were much the same, for example easy access to flat, fertile land and a year-round supply of water. It is not surprising, therefore, that populations continued to cluster in the same spots throughout the Naco valley's long prehistory; in fact, evidence of occupation at Sites PVN 306, PVN 128, PVN 99, and Naco reaches well back into the Preclassic and continues without apparent break through at least the Terminal Classic. What is surprising is that later occupants did not directly reoccupy or do noticeable damage to structures raised by their predecessors. It is as though Terminal Classic edifices were preserved, unmodified, as monuments to a past deemed important by at least some Late Postclasssic population segments. How widespread this reverence was among the occupants of Sites PVN 306, PVN 144, and Naco is not clear. Elites very likely numbered themselves among those who respected their predecessors, as they would have had the power to either raze earlier buildings or restrain their followers from pillaging these ruins.

It is also noteworthy that this apparent celebration of the past was highly selective. Roble phase people consciously chose to erect their centers near certain, but not all, sizable Terminal Classic settlements. They apparently avoided the largest of the earlier centers, La Sierra, which had been the valley's capital during the Late Classic and remained a major political and population center into the Terminal Classic (Schortman and Urban 2004b). Linkages were made between specific sets of Roble phase magnates and what was recalled about particular Terminal Classic political foci and, presumably, their leaders.

The lines of evidence outlined here imply that Terminal Classic constructions at Sites PVN 306, PVN 144, and possibly Naco were held in some regard by these settlements' late prehistoric inhabitants. At the very least, they did not pillage them or treat the buildings as trash receptacles. In fact, the ruined edifices of this earlier period were sufficiently important that Roble phase centers were raised near but not over large-scale Terminal Classic platforms. This relationship is clearest at Site PVN 306, where the preeminent household established its residences and seat of power adjoining a concentration of Terminal Classic buildings. The burial of some members of the Site PVN 306's Roble phase population around Terminal Classic platforms provides even stronger evidence that connections between the past and the present were explicitly drawn. The same direct linkages to antecedent events and personages were made less explicitly, or at least not in quite the same ways, at Site PVN 144 and Naco. Still, in all cases the decision to raise Roble phase political capitals near prominent monuments to Terminal Classic leadership and to preserve those expressions of power intact strongly implies that late prehistoric elites were drawing their predecessors into a network focused on themselves. We are not certain how this connection was imagined by rulers and ruled. The fact that it existed and was important to substantiate the former's claims to preeminence in the fourteenth through early sixteenth centuries seems clear, however.

REACHING INTO THE PAST WITH STYLE

Analysis of 14,018 Naco Viejo Ceramic Complex pottery sherds from Sites PVN 306 and PVN 144 revealed an assemblage marked by considerable cultural continuity with the basin's ceramic tradition reaching back into the Middle Preclassic. Changes in pottery forms and designs, as well as in other categories of material culture, certainly occurred, but the shifts do not constitute dramatic disjunctions. Instead, the sequence is characterized by a gradual unfolding of stylistic, formal, and technological themes likely reflecting stable populations and evolving cultural understandings and practices. The most dramatic shifts in ceramic decoration and form are represented by the red-on-white–painted bichromes discussed in chapters 1 and 8. Even in this case, however, designs of clear foreign inspiration were synthesized with locally derived motifs to create symbols that couched foreign concepts in familiar terms. This incorporation of exotic motifs within a local decorative repertoire was fairly common in the Naco valley ceramic sequence. The red-on-white–painted bichromes, therefore, do not necessarily constitute a disjunction in local populations or in basic principles of pottery decoration but instead are part of a venerable tradition of design syncretism within the Naco valley (Wonderley 1986).

What is striking about the Naco valley's Roble phase ceramics are the assemblage's relative simplicity and its harkening back to surface treatments that had not been common in the basin since the Late Preclassic. Red slipping, a prevalent form of decoration during the Middle and Late Preclassic, had all but disappeared during the Classic period but was once again frequently attested to in Roble phase collections (Urban 1993a). A comparable shift is recorded in the Maya lowlands, where red slipping follows a similar temporal trajectory (Masson 2001; Rice 1983). Vertical-neck jars with direct rims that had been relatively common during the Preclassic also underwent a resurgence in the Late Postclassic. This form is exceedingly rare in Classic period Naco valley assemblages, where jars tend to have either flaring necks or vertical necks with pronounced everted rims. Restricted orifice jars (tecomates) are relatively common in Preclassic Naco deposits but do not reappear in later collections. Somewhat smaller bowls with in-curving walls resemble these tecomates and do constitute a significant proportion of Roble phase forms in several taxa. Once again, such neckless forms characterized by restricted orifices are rarely attested to in Classic period assemblages.

This is not to say that Roble phase ceramics are indistinguishable from their Late Preclassic counterparts. Decorative treatments such as brushing and red painting on white-slipped surfaces are distinctive of pottery vessels made in the basin during the last two prehistoric centuries. In addition, such append-ages as hollow supports in the form of bird feet or heads are diagnostic of the Roble phase. Nevertheless, the similarities between Preclassic and Roble phase ceramics are remarkable, especially given the more than 1,000 years separating the two periods. The significance of these commonalities to those who made and used the vessels is unclear. It is hard to imagine that Roble phase potters recalled traditions dating back to before AD 200 and consciously revived them. Such attributes as red slipping may have been adopted from lowland Maya populations involved in their own program of reviving Late Preclassic decora-tive modes (Masson 2000b: 44–45, 47; 2001; Rice 1983). If so, what seems to have been a reversion to earlier decorative attributes was merely the adoption of treatments from neighboring populations, with similarities to earlier Naco valley treatments simply fortuitous. Such an explanation still begs the question of why these innovations would have been so readily and widely accepted. Whether autochthonously developed or borrowed from afar, the widespread use of such attributes as red slips implies that they resonated positively with all segments of the Naco valley's Roble phase population. This resonance was almost certainly rooted in memories associated with certain ceramic designs. It may be, however, that the primary factors motivating changes in ceramic forms and treatments had less to do with what was recalled fondly concerning Preclassic pottery and more to do with negative associations linked to Classic period ceramic designs and treatments.

On a general level, it seems that the Naco valley's Roble phase inhabitants were eschewing certain prominent ceramic modes associated with the Late and Terminal Classic. Specifically, orange slipping of open bowls, the painting of those vessels in red and red-and-black designs, and the fashioning of large jars whose shoulders and vertical necks were adorned with red-painted designs of avian and geometric forms are characteristic of the earlier periods but com-pletely absent from the Roble phase ceramic repertoire (Urban 1993a). We are confronted, therefore, with a seeming contradiction. On the one hand, prominent members of Roble phase populations in the Naco valley were asso-ciating themselves with the remains of Terminal Classic political leaders. At the same time, however, any such connections were actively denied in the ceramic containers used by all of the basin's late prehistoric occupants. The distinctive symbols painted on jars and bowls by those who lived in Terminal Classic polities were replaced by a novel set of images that, while drawing inspiration from past examples, still diverged from their predecessors in form and manner of execution. This disjunction in the way architecture and ceramics dating to the Terminal Classic were treated strongly indicates that the views of the past entertained by Roble phase peoples in the Naco valley were conflicted.

What these conflicts might have entailed depends on what the symbols emblazoned on Late and Terminal Classic vessels meant to the basin's Roble phase denizens. We have argued elsewhere that during the Late Classic, one particularly salient component of that earlier design repertoire, the bird, was closely linked with a hierarchically structured network that tied together all residents of the valley and was focused on elites who ruled from the site of La Sierra (Schortman, Urban, and Ausec 2001). During the succeeding Terminal Classic, the same bird continues to appear on pottery as well as, much more rarely, in stone sculpture. The Late Classic was a period of locally unprecedented political centralization in which those who resided in La Sierra's site core concentrated power over populations within and immediately outside the valley in their own hands. During the Terminal Classic, power fragmented. While La Sierra remained an important political and population center, its magnates now shared the stage with numerous elites who could also commission large-scale constructions. The occupants of Sites PVN 99, PVN 128, and PVN 306 were among those whose usurpation of power contributed to the decentralization of the Late Classic La Sierra realm. The continued importance of the same avian imagery during these political transformations implies that the significance attributed to this motif changed. The bird may have originally symbolized a unified domain and the elites who ruled it. As this imagery survived the balkanization of that polity, new power holders likely strove to preserve some sense of valley-wide unity, even if it was no longer focused on a specific ruling house.

However these relations may have played out, it is clear that increasing diversity and elaboration of ceramic designs in the Late and Terminal Classic Naco valley correlated closely with major political shifts (see also Masson 2001: 161–162). Significant transformations within network structures were involved in these changes, but throughout the seventh through tenth centuries, ceramic designs were implicated in the creation of hierarchically organized webs that encompassed the entire basin and its environs. By the eleventh century, clear signs of such hierarchical formations had disappeared from the Naco valley; monumental constructions were not erected during the Early Postclassic, nor is there any evidence of population nucleation. The Early Postclassic pottery assemblage underwent dramatic simplification; its vessels were virtually undecorated, although there is strong continuity in forms (Urban 1993a). As hierarchical nets were reestablished in the Roble phase, older designs were not resurrected to express inequality. Something about the messages conveyed through Late and Terminal Classic symbols emblazoned on ceramics was no longer considered appropriate. As noted in chapter 8, references were still made to birds in the Nolasco/La Victoria Bichromes, but the form of the bird had changed, as had its location on the outside of bowls and as supports for those containers. These oblique references to avian images may have safely recalled links to past concepts without conjuring up meanings tied to specific Late and Terminal Classic rulers or forms of governance.

The shift to earlier forms of pottery decoration, therefore, might not represent a conscious evocation of clearly remembered Late Preclassic lifestyles and organizational forms. It may instead express a disavowal of political concepts and arrangements explicitly embodied in Late and Terminal Classic ceramic designs. As Roble phase rulers refashioned a polity-wide identity (see chapter 8), they cautiously revived avian imagery but transformed it sufficiently so as to recall a general sense of past affiliations shorn of their associations with older ruling houses. Distinctive vessel forms, such as the high vertical-necked jars with everted rims, that had been canvases for so many Late and Terminal Classic design displays, along with other motifs tied to the earlier bird images, were dropped from the Roble phase repertoire. They may have been too closely associated with the political messages conveyed in avian form to survive in the new contexts. The decision to revert to red slipping as the primary means of decoration could therefore simply reflect a desire to avoid any overt reference to symbols that evoked memories of particular forms of hierarchy and power. The similarity between Roble phase and Preclassic assemblages would, in this view, result from an accidental convergence of approaches to vessel treatments based largely on the limited array of materials available in the valley for fashioning and decorating pottery containers.

The changes in ceramic assemblages outlined here are matched by comparable shifts in most aspects of material culture. Mold-made, fired clay whistles, figurines, and ocarinas that assumed a variety of anthropomorphic and zoomorphic forms were commonplace throughout the Naco valley during the Late and Terminal Classic (figure 9.3). These effigies disappear completely from the archaeological record by the Early Postclassic. When figurines reappeared in the Roble phase, they assumed radically different forms and were not explicitly associated with musical instruments (see figure 8.6). Incense burners also underwent drastic transformations. The variety of three-prong, modeled, ladle, and complex incensarios that characterized the basin's Late and Terminal Classic collections was reduced by the Roble phase to tube-handled ladle censers and, very rarely, spiked bowls (figures 9.3 and 9.4). *Candeleros,* flat-topped ceramic forms with one to more than twenty-four conical holes punched into their tops, also disappeared after the end of the Terminal Classic, as did ceramic stamps used for decorating cloth and human skin and such jewelry as clay pendants and ear spools. These shifts bespeak profound transformations in a variety of behavioral arenas, from personal adornment to ritual. The refusal to

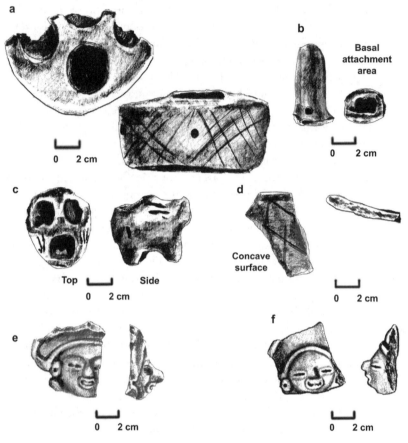

FIGURE 9.3 *Examples of candeleros (a, c), incensarios (b, d), and figurines (e, f) dating to the Late and Terminal Classic in the Naco valley*

revive these artifact forms during the fourteenth through early sixteenth centuries also indicates that the basin's denizens were uninterested in re-engaging in the activities in which these objects had played integral parts. It is as if most of Terminal Classic Naco valley life was blotted out from memory even as hierarchically structured social forms were reconstituted in the Roble phase.

SUMMARY

The Naco valley's Roble phase rulers confronted the same problem all would-be leaders face; that is, how to make their pretensions to power seem like parts of a timeless and unchanging universe rather than the machinations of en-

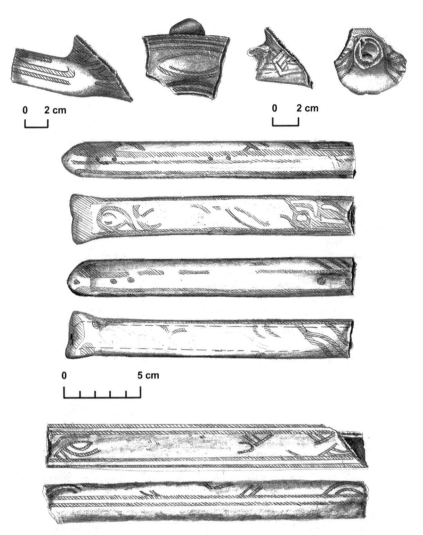

0   2 cm

0   2 cm

0   5 cm

FIGURE 9.4 *Examples of Roble phase tube-handle ladle incensarios from test excavations conducted in Naco*

terprising agents taking advantage of opportunities offered by particular moments in time. To achieve this objective, these rulers had to build networks that connected them to previous notables and notable events. By their very nature, the recollections on which those webs were founded would have been partial and selective. Operating outside even the flexible constraints of written documents concerning the past, what any occupant of the Roble phase Naco valley remembered about his or her history was likely heavily influenced by current

215

concerns and understandings. Elites, however, layered onto the various factors that condition recall their own conscious desires to privilege themselves within novel political relations. Building networks into the past, therefore, very much required shaping social memory (Alcock 2000, 2005; Bloch 1977a, 1977b; Casey 1987; Schank and Abelson 1995).

To say the least, this is not an easy job. Earlier events and personages can be deeply problematic for those seeking to restructure sociopolitical relations in the present. Whereas some figures and happenings can provide powerful rationalizations for hierarchical political structures, others may evoke negative associations that could lead to questions about the wisdom of such arrange-ments and the motivations and fitness to rule of those promoting them. Thus highlighting certain features of history and ensuring particular interpretations of those features require simultaneously forgetting other aspects and repressing alternative views.

Both processes can be glimpsed in operation within the Roble phase Naco valley. On the one hand, elites strove to link themselves with aspects of Terminal Classic rulership. This interval was, from the perspective of the basin's fourteenth-century inhabitants, the most recent period in which there were moderately well-defined hierarchical social formations. By raising their paramount households close to the ruins of Terminal Classic power centers, leaders at Naco and Sites PVN 306 and PVN 144 were apparently making claims to some association with the hierarchical formations those settlements represented. The care taken to leave the earlier sites intact and unencumbered by late prehistoric occupation further testifies to the regard in which Terminal Classic monumental buildings were held by elites at least. The ties thus forged are clearest at Site PVN 306, where not only was the paramount elite house-hold established only 3 m west of the settlement's Terminal Classic eastern fo-cus but some members of the Roble phase population were buried around these earlier edifices. It is not at all clear that those interred in the eastern Terminal Classic aggregate were members of the social group that resided in the EPP. The simple form of the uncovered burials would, in fact, argue against such a view. While we do not know who was laid to rest in the environs of Site PVN 306's Terminal Classic buildings, this burial practice strongly implies a close connection between at least some segment(s) of the settlement's Roble phase population and whatever was represented by Terminal Classic architecture.

At the same time selected features of the Terminal Classic were remem-bered positively, at least by late prehistoric elites, others were clearly not viewed in such a manner. Specifically, Roble phase potters assiduously avoided dis-tinctive symbols emblazoned on pottery vessels and tied to aspects of Late and Terminal Classic rule. So complete was this disavowal of decorative mo-tifs and their referents that certain vessel forms, such as vertical, high-necked jars with everted rims, prominently associated with the earlier symbol system, disappeared altogether. Decorated types, specifically red-on-white–painted bichromes, did constitute a consistent minority of Roble phase assemblages. The forms in which they most commonly appeared (tripod bowls), the serpent motifs that adorned them, and the mode of rendering these designs together constitute a marked departure from Late and Terminal Classic precedents. Even as late prehistoric magnates sought to use ceramics to forge polity-wide identities, they avoided explicit references to symbols employed in similar efforts four centuries and more before. Despite the fact that we lack a clear idea of what the motifs involved meant to those who used them, it is obvious that Terminal Classic designs were anathema to Roble phase rulers and, presumably, their supporters.

We cannot say at this point what Terminal Classic figures and events were incorporated in the nets constructed by Roble phase elites. From their selective use of architecture and aspects of pottery design, however, we can infer that the process of casting history in the service of present concerns was a creative one. Certain aspects of the relatively recent past were embraced, while others were hidden firmly from view. In the process much was forgotten, and that which was recalled was almost certainly reinterpreted in ways that made sense in, and served the interests of, networks operating in the Naco valley during the fourteenth through early sixteenth centuries. Such selectivity implies that a tension ran beneath these uses of the past, a tension that may not have been fully resolved when the Spanish first brought these "people without history" into the European orbit (Wolf 1982).

TEN

Conclusions

NETWORKS AND SOCIETY

A society, as defined here (see chapter 2), is a territorially bounded network of networks. Members of a society together, if variably, participate in a common web that has distinguishable, if ever mutable and porous, physical limits (Wolf 1982: 18, 2001). A society incorporates and subsumes localized nets, such as house groups and households. Its borders are also transcended by networks that link some of its members with compatriots living in other societies. The important point is that residents of a specific area participate in a web that subsumes smaller domestic nets and define themselves in part through participation in this overarching network. Societies, like all nets, are products of purposeful human choices to associate with some and not with others. One of the primary projects around which a society crystallizes is the exercise of power. Societies are in part outcomes of efforts by elites to distinguish their clients from those beholden to other magnates, thus staking claims to the goods and services of a specific population (Schortman, Urban, and Ausec 2001). The drawing of borders is a step toward establishing privileged demands on the labor and loyalty of a certain population.

We have argued at several points that small-scale domestic networks within the late prehistoric Naco valley were arranged within distinct webs focused on elite households at Sites PVN 144, PVN 306, and Naco. This position is based on the proposition that members of these households exercised some power over their compatriots who lived in smaller, more isolated houses. Each such household, therefore, comprised a central node within hierarchically structured networks that encompassed varying numbers of adherents. The comparable sizes and decorative elaboration seen in the constructions surrounding Naco's northeast principal plaza and Site PVN 306's eastern principal plaza (EPP) imply that the residents of these architectural groups enjoyed roughly equivalent prominence within the valley. Site PVN 144's household was able to command smaller labor forces in erecting its domiciles and so was probably ranked lower in the valley-wide political hierarchy. Nevertheless, that site's unique configuration and combination of functions suggest that it played a central role in muting inter-household competition and encouraging feelings of solidarity throughout the Naco valley settlement cluster.

Neither of the Naco valley's paramount households was able to claim absolute dominion over the basin's population. Rather, elites who lived at Naco seem to have reached an impasse with those who resided at Site PVN 306. As discussed in chapter 6, these notables may have anchored two ends of a single, extensive settlement that stretched an estimated 5 km southwest-northeast. It is this population cluster that the Spanish likely glossed as "Naco."

In many ways, the settlement aggregate made up of Sites PVN 306, PVN 144, and Naco qualifies as a society. Close and regular interactions among its participants are signaled by the precise and numerous material and behavioral similarities found throughout its extent. These commonalities reach down to the level of individual houses, where nearly identical paraphernalia was used in such essential tasks as food preparation and serving as well as in religious devotions. Public gatherings were also apparently organized in similar ways, combining feasting with religious observances conducted around comparable ritual foci established with the same concern for directionality. As noted repeatedly throughout this volume, populations in the late prehistoric Naco valley were not homogeneous with respect to practice or belief. There were differences in the scales and intensities at which ubiquitous activities were pursued at different locales within and between sites. Similarly, some behaviors, such as those associated with the ball game, were restricted to unique locales within the valley. Nonetheless, as important as it is to bear these differences in mind, they appear as variations on cultural themes that were widespread across known portions of the basin.

Too little is known about behavior and material patterns in neighboring areas to delimit the borders of this society with any certainty. Anthony Wonderley's work in the Sula Plain hints at the existence of other networks in this nearby basin, related to, but possibly distinguishable from, those defined for the Naco valley (1985). As noted in chapter 1, materials from the contemporary middle Ulua drainage 40 km to the south do not closely resemble those discussed here. Such distinctions do not preclude the existence of webs that connected residents of these zones. They do, however, suggest that such connections were neither intense nor regular enough to define a distinct society. More work is required to limn the outlines of webs that might have tied residents of the Naco settlement cluster to those who lived in nearby areas and to assess the intensity and nature of these linkages.

Whatever its boundaries may have been, the Naco settlement cluster likely served as the core of a society that flourished during the fourteenth through early sixteenth centuries. Rather than comprising a network of networks orchestrated from above, this particular configuration took shape in a context of unresolved competitions for preeminence among its most powerful members. How this society operated in such an unstable political environment will be considered in the next section.

SUMMARY OF POWER AND
NETWORKS IN THE ROBLE PHASE NACO VALLEY

Our investigations of Roble phase Naco valley material and social forms yield a very basic outline of the networks within which the basin's population was organized. They also provide suggestions as to how these webs were implicated in power contests and in the creation of the society outlined earlier in this chapter. As incomplete as this overview is, it highlights the complexity of late prehistoric political structures in the Naco valley and the manifold ways these fragile and volatile arrangements were implicated within far-reaching processes through the actions of network members.

Houses and Households

The most basic social web identified at all three investigated sites consists of those individuals of different genders and varying ages who resided in a single house. Here, web membership was enacted by daily participation in common projects of production, reproduction, and devotion. These tasks included producing, preparing, and sharing food, as well as engaging in religious rites that employed ceramic ladle incense burners and, in some cases, pottery figurines. House nets were therefore constantly being defined in the processes of daily interactions that gave rise to a common sense of self and shared purpose. Although not defined primarily by their roles in political struggles, house groups posed essential problems to those seeking power. These challenges included (1) redirecting their members' productive efforts into projects that advanced elite goals, (2) supplementing loyalties to houses with affiliations that transcended those narrow boundaries, and (3) focusing allegiances on a small body of leaders acknowledged as having legitimate claims to the support of the majority. Building hierarchies and centralizing power required that house groups be subsumed within larger nets, their members' sense of themselves contextualized within frameworks of production and meaning that privileged would-be rulers.

These goals were partially achieved through several related steps. The first involved the formation of a network within Sites PVN 144, PVN 306, and Naco through which elites could coordinate their efforts to achieve domination. The mechanism employed in each case was the creation of a single household whose members resided in relatively substantial constructions surrounding a sizable plaza. Solidarity within this net was enacted by common participation in a range of economic, social, and ideological tasks that replicated those attested to in individual houses. In one sense, therefore, the household was a house writ large.

Households were not, however, simply amplified versions of smaller domestic units. The fact that they were organized according to somewhat different principles is suggested by the presence of special-purpose constructions, such as Strs. 306-124, 306-125, and 306-22 in the EPP. As we argued in chapter 3, these buildings likely played key roles in integrating household members within a single, relatively unified web. It was probably through activities conducted within these venues that any pressures that encouraged the fissioning of domestic nets into individual houses were addressed and overcome.

Difficulties in identifying individual residences, especially those not built atop surface-visible platforms, mean we cannot preclude the possibility that households were more widespread in the Roble phase Naco valley than it now appears. What is clear, however, is that webs incorporating several house groups within one residential net were only prominently expressed in a few cases, one each of which is found at Naco and Sites PVN 306 and PVN 144. If other households existed, they were not as forcefully materialized on the landscape.

The formation of a household, therefore, apparently required overcoming strong tendencies that favored the autonomy of individual houses. The significant effort invested in creating the domiciles that comprise plaza groups implies that one reward for frustrating domestic divisions was privileged control over relatively sizable amounts of labor. Households, in sum, appear as the self-conscious creations of people who ostentatiously joined together in the pursuit of common domestic, ritual, and political projects. Their regular and sustained cooperation would certainly have given them an advantage in dealing with the smaller, scattered domestic groups in which their subordinates were organized.

It would probably be a mistake to attribute too much unity to these paramount households. Variations in the sizes and degrees of decorative elaboration among their component residences, especially evident at Site PVN 306, imply that different people within one household enjoyed variable success in their efforts to control labor. What the bases for such intra-household political discrepancies might have been is unknown. Still, the fact that they existed tentatively points to some tension born of competitions over power within elite residential webs.

However successful households were in coordinating the actions of their members in pursuit of shared objectives, they apparently had not divined a means of forging inter-household cooperation for political projects conducted on a grander scale. The location of the two largest known plaza groups at opposite ends of the Naco settlement cluster, in fact, implies the operation of centripetal forces driving them apart. Most likely their participants were competing for control over networks of supporters. The comparable sizes and decorative embellishments evidenced in each household plaza indicate that neither set of contestants had achieved a lasting advantage in this struggle by the early sixteenth century. Rather, members of each household were using much the same sets of tangible and conceptual assets to seize leadership of webs of comparable extent and size. The failure of one network to gain exclusive control over the distribution of these resources resulted in the inferred stalemate.

Power and the Manipulation of Tangible Resources

The clearest example of the way relations of inequality were tangibly enacted in the late prehistoric basin involves the fashioning and exchange of obsidian blades. These distinctive implements were fabricated by a few part-time specialists who lived in modest accommodations at Naco and Site PVN 306, well outside elite households. The widespread distribution of blades across both settlements and Site PVN 144, where there is no good evidence for their production, indicates that this commodity passed freely and in considerable volumes among all known valley residents. The mechanisms by which such transfers were effected remain unknown. However the transactions were arranged, the movement of obsidian blades linked consumers and producers of equivalent rank in relatively stable social and economic relations. Operating largely outside direct elite supervision, these nets were shaped primarily by choices artisans and consumers made concerning those with whom they wished to affiliate within and across site boundaries. Exchanges involving obsidian blades were thus one way among presumably many by which the denizens of Sites PVN 306, PVN 144, and Naco palpably established, expressed, and extended connections among members of different houses. These sorts of heterarchically structured ties, cross-cutting localized domestic webs, promoted the regular, close, and stable interactions materialized in the archaeological record.

The challenge for would-be leaders was to turn these interactions among equals into a hierarchically structured web focused explicitly on elites. This, we argue, was attempted through centralized monopolies over the local distribution of polyhedral obsidian cores essential to blade knapping. Converting this crucial raw material into political capital required that elites alone negotiate relations between two networks, one extending beyond the valley to the distant sources from which the cores were derived and the other providing artisans within the basin with this indispensable component of their trade.

The former web depended on cooperation among rulers of different domains and traders who enacted their ties through the exchange of what were likely many tangible and intangible prestations, including polyhedral obsidian cores. There is little to suggest that such links were hierarchically structured. Instead, it is more likely that this territorially extensive web united merchants and political elites who interacted as equals and were mutually dependent on each other for the support and goods needed to sustain their preeminence at home. The crucial point is that these magnates policed participation in the web, ensuring that only the high-born had access to the symbols that defined net membership. We will return to the issue of how such boundaries were drawn later in this chapter.

Once obsidian nuclei entered the Naco valley, we hypothesize that they were used to forge bonds of inequality between giver and receiver. Elites, as the sole sources of cores, monopolized their intra-basin distribution and were thus in an excellent position to dictate the terms of their exchange. Unable to circumvent these noble entrepreneurs, blade knappers would have surrendered labor and loyalty in return for the basic materials from which they fashioned their own economic and social networks.

Such control over a handful of artisans would not, by itself, yield political preeminence. The key to transforming the indebtedness of a few into dominion over many, we believe, lies in the elites' ability to enhance and exploit the centrality of blade knappers within larger social and economic nets. By favoring select house groups with the knowledge and raw materials needed to fabricate blades, magnates gave these artisans decided advantages in the creation of social networks vis-à-vis other house groups. They alone could have fabricated the much-desired tools whose exchange helped define these webs. The alliances forged through the exchange of blades and the goods and services received in return for these tools would have flowed toward, and centered on, knappers. Artisans were ndebted to elites for the cores that made their centrality in socioeconomic nets possible, and at least some of those obligations and items would have flowed up the hierarchy from artisans to their high-born patrons. In this way elites ultimately, if indirectly, controlled a wide array of networks that cross-cut individual houses, entrapping entire populations in webs of obligation and debt.

Engagement by these nodal house groups in other crafts, including pottery making, fashioning flake tools from perlite and chert, and spinning/weaving, would only have enhanced their importance in Roble phase socioeconomic webs. Whether the latter occupations were encouraged by local rulers or resulted from the initiatives of specific house groups is unknown. Whatever their inspiration, the proliferation of specialized manufacturing within certain houses redounded to the benefit of elites.

A monopoly over the parochial distribution of obsidian cores is a slender thread with which to weave a unified realm. Elite prominence depended on maintaining good relations with foreign suppliers of this commodity and frustrating efforts by others to circumvent their exclusive control over the dissemination of blade cores within the valley (Kipp and Schortman 1989). Further, insofar as craft workers were free to build their own networks, they could establish strong foundations from which to challenge the pretensions of their social betters. At the very least, artisans and their house groups were in a position to negotiate for concessions from the elites they served, thus yielding a fragile political structure. Such potential threats to elite dominance may have encouraged the distribution of cores to several house groups. In this way, no one set of artisans could use a monopoly over blade fabrication to establish its preeminence in multiple webs.

The strategy was successful up to a point. The distribution of blade cores suggests that the residents of prominent households who lived at Naco and Site PVN 306 moved effectively to control exclusively the distribution of these nuclei to their immediate supporters. In fact, "gifts" of cores were probably one way of attracting and tying clients to these elite-led webs. The prospect of securing blades from knappers may, in turn, have lured additional supporters to these nets, resulting in the concentration of people observed around Naco's northeast principal plaza and Site PVN 306's EPP. Such triumphs were tempered by the failure of either household to exclude the other from the networks through which polyhedral cores were obtained. Consequently, no one set of contestants could use the local distribution of this essential resource to gain lasting political advantages over the other.

Reordering the Conceptual Realm

Bolstering support for paramount households required the creation of other networks that were more firmly and directly under centralized control. Leaders of prominent households at Naco and Site PVN 306 in particular pursued this strategy through the promotion of ideologies that simultaneously stressed intra-web solidarity and inequality. The former was encouraged by the promotion of novel symbols that adorned food-serving bowls used by all segments of the valley's population. These motifs synthesized local elements with long histories in Naco valley design traditions with exotic features emblematic of the Quetzalcoatl cult then widespread throughout southern Mesoamerica. In this way, new network-wide affiliations were simultaneously linked to parochial beliefs deeply rooted in the basin's past and to conceptual structures untethered to particular places and times. Valley residents were thus encouraged to contextualize their historical connections to antecedent local populations within broader identities that encompassed the entire Naco valley and ultimately may have extended beyond its borders.

The emotional attraction of these new networks was enhanced by linking them closely to food sharing within the house group. Commensality embodied essential projects of food production, distribution, and consumption that together defined the house as an enduring social entity. By emblazoning symbols of a network-encompassing affiliation on ceramic bowls used to serve food within these domestic webs, the novel linkages were infused with the deeply felt positive emotions engendered in ceremonies of house group solidarity. The enactment of large-scale feasts using the same sorts of containers, possibly including all members of the webs centered on elite households, would have reinforced the ties between house and network in ways that were hard to ignore (Chase and Chase 1988). Such appeals to unity would have countered tendencies toward fissioning based on loyalties to specific houses.

The engendering of feelings of network unity facilitated centralized control but did not by itself ensure who would exercise that power. To turn supra-house affiliations to their own purposes, would-be leaders had to place themselves at the center of these extensive networks. They did so in this case by monopolizing the performance of certain rites that were integral to the functioning of the new webs. The observances in question were centered on circular structures erected within the open western plazas of Naco (Str. 4F-1) and Site PVN 306 (Strs. 306-17, 306-19, and 306-174). These buildings are virtually unprecedented in the Naco valley architectural corpus and were clearly inspired by foreign models, once again closely linked to the Quetzalcoatl cult.

The relatively large amounts of skilled and unskilled labor invested in three of these four constructions suggest that they were commissioned by local notables who lived in the households adjoining Strs. 4F-1, 306-17, 306-19, and 306-174. The juxtaposition of elite households and ritual foci also points to control of the latter by members of the former. The conduct of rites involving round structures was thus emphatically not open to all but only to those with the means to erect these essential ritual foci. Further, use of the platforms required knowledge of the conceptual structures embodied in the form and organization of these buildings. Insofar as such knowledge was derived from foreign sources, it could be monopolized by those who participated in the extra-valley webs through which the relevant information flowed (Boone and Smith 2003; Masson 2003b; Smith 2003b). The most likely occupants of the basin to have been familiar with this information were the elites who lived in the paramount households of Naco and Site PVN 306.

The relationship between elite ritual and broad network affiliations is suggested by the events that occurred within the open western plazas that contained Strs. 4F-1, 306-17, 306-19, and 306-174. In both Naco and Site PVN 306, these extensive spaces were venues for rituals and feasts that involved large segments, perhaps all, of the entire populations of both settlements. These celebrations employed many of the same serving and storage vessels, as well as ladle incense burners, used in similar events conducted within house groups. Hence, public activities in the western plazas were analogs, on a much larger scale, of the ritual and food-sharing projects that defined membership in house groups throughout the late prehistoric Naco valley. One major difference is that at the centers of these general gatherings were dramatically distinctive architectural forms with no known counterparts outside the western plazas. The conjunction of foreign-inspired building forms with food sharing and rites tied to local domestic webs strongly suggests that elements of an alien faith were incorporated with local practices and beliefs. Insofar as elites alone performed rituals linked to the exotic religion, they exercised exclusive control over aspects of the syncretized observances enacted in conjunction with large numbers of their followers. Members of the Naco and Site PVN 306 paramount households, in short, had developed a project through which their multiple webs were united and in which they occupied privileged positions.

We cannot know the precise manner by which foreign and local beliefs and actions were fused. Similarly, the extent to which different segments of ancient Naco valley populations believed in the elite-sponsored religion's precepts cannot be discerned. All we can say is that food was shared and religious observances were conducted within the Naco and Site PVN 306 western plazas. Whether all of the participants came with enthusiasm or not, large numbers of people did gather in these areas, and their views of themselves and those around them were likely shaped in the course of interactions conducted within these architecturally bounded spaces (Goffman 1974). The multiple resurfacings of Str. 306-19's plaster surfaces, the several stages of construction seen on that building and on Str. 4F-1, and the renovations made to Str. 306-17 indicate that these symbols endured for a protracted span. Both lines of evidence imply that the effort to imbue local practice with alien conceptions was at least partially successful in attracting and holding the attention of the populations that resided near each plaza group. By extension, we surmise that elites benefited from this success in that they were able to create a novel political order of which they were generally acknowledged as the legitimate leaders (Van Buren and Richards 2000).

As was the case with households, it would be a mistake to attribute too much homogeneity in belief and action to elite-sponsored rites. The ballcourt erected off the south edge of Naco's southwest principal plaza has no known counterpart anywhere in the contemporary valley. Rites associated with the ball game, therefore, were probably limited to elites who lived at this center. These distinctive religious practices suggest that Naco's magnates embraced elements of foreign religions that were not accepted elsewhere within the Roble phase valley. The stucco masks unearthed at Site PVN 144 also find no analogs in the basin. These locally unique architectural decorations are once again inspired by foreign concepts but are not clearly tied to faiths expressed through ballcourts or circular platforms. These varied symbols may have been tied in different ways to the interactions among elite factions within the Late Postclassic Naco valley. The replication of the distinctive architectural forms seen in Strs. 4F-1, 306-17, 306-19, and, to a more limited extent, 306-174 points to some overlap in these exotic religious systems even as the erection of unique architectural forms speaks to distinctions within inter-elite webs.

Importantly, the emotional power of elite-sponsored religions and the affiliations they enacted originated in part in their association with practices that were ultimately derived from those conducted within small-scale domestic webs. The successful creation of hierarchically structured multi-house networks, therefore, did not require the obliteration of smaller-scale, presumably earlier, localized webs. In fact, promotion of the novel, extensive affiliation could not have succeeded without linking it clearly and explicitly to feelings engendered within house groups that continued to engage in common economic, social, and ritual projects.

The political strategies outlined here were only partially successful in that claims to power among leading factions were never prioritized. Members of the two prominent households participated in much the same extra-valley nets by which foreign religious symbols and practices were acquired. They deployed these exotic constructs in very similar manners, thus ensconcing themselves at the centers of two equivalent, hierarchically structured networks. As neither set of contestants could exclude the other from the knowledge needed to imagine, rationalize, and materialize these conceptual systems, they remained at an impasse. In the process of promoting very similar religious practices in search of adherents, the competing factions encouraged the widespread acceptance of a syncretized faith that combined local and foreign elements in nearly identical ways.

Histories of Power

Power in the Roble phase basin also depended on elite manipulation of networks that extended back in time. Those who seek to rule need to cast their claims to power not just in terms of present realities but also as natural outgrowths of processes that stretch into the past. In this way, a volatile field of negotiated political relations was transformed into an enduring structure, the inevitable outcome of events initiated by previous actors. Contests for pre-eminence, therefore, involved efforts to shape a consensus on social memory (Van Dyke and Alcock 2003: 2). As in all aspects of life, people rarely achieve their goals on their own. In this case, however, allies were sought from among historical personages whose significance was largely determined by the strategic calculations of later actors.

There is some evidence that Roble phase Naco valley elites were actively claiming ties to earlier political leaders. This effort is clearest at Site PVN 306, where the paramount household established its residences a scant 3 m west of the Terminal Classic center located on the settlement's east margin. The latter was left largely intact, and its buildings were apparently used as sepulchers for at least some members of the Roble phase population. This close juxtaposition of monuments to past and present power, the preservation of those earlier expressions of preeminence, and their use as burial locations strongly imply that later rulers were explicitly linking themselves to some version of previous political actors and events.

Connections spanning different eras are less clearly expressed at Naco and Site PVN 144. The latter is 250 m southwest of Site PVN 128, one of the largest Terminal Classic political capitals in the valley, and Naco is bordered on the west by another focus of political power during this interval (Site PVN 99). In neither case, however, were Roble phase individuals interred on or around earlier edifices; nor is the connection between Terminal Classic monumental platforms and their Roble phase successors as clear as it is at Site PVN 306. The same basic political strategy may have been employed throughout the late prehistoric Naco valley, but with different degrees of emphasis. At Site PVN 306, ties to earlier leaders were unambiguously drawn, whereas at the other two settlements a greater physical and social distance was maintained between antecedents and successors. The reasons for such differences are unclear.

The memories promoted by Roble phase magnates were selective. Determining what was recalled and how it was remembered depended to a considerable extent on the exigencies of current political struggles (Alcock 2000; Van Dyke and Alcock, eds., 2003). Thus Terminal Classic monuments to power were preserved and, at Site PVN 306 at least, venerated, whereas ceramic designs associated with those earlier regimes were not replicated on Roble phase vessels. As argued in chapter 9, at least some of these earlier motifs probably materialized membership in political networks dominated by elites who re-sided in such centers as Sites PVN 99, PVN 128, and the eastern cluster at Site PVN 306. Primary among these distinctive symbols were birds that, when they did appear in the fourteenth through sixteenth centuries, were radically transformed so as to bear only a slight resemblance to their earlier prototypes. Avians were sustained as a prominent theme in Naco valley symbol systems even as the birds themselves took different forms and were found on different parts of pottery containers.

Dramatic simplifications in the design repertoire of the basin's potters, and changes in the nature of the symbols with which they adorned ceramic vessels, suggest that some aspects of past political forms were purged from memory even while those embodied in monumental platforms were highlighted. As in all cases of network building, some people, or features of their identities, are excluded while others are welcomed. This is apparently the case whether webs link living people at one moment in time or extend back to include progenitors who have little voice in the matter. The process of acceptance and rejection is always a creative one, limited in part by the claims others organized along simi-lar lines in different webs make on the same resources, in this case the symbols by which memory is expressed.

Just as palpable and conceptual assets in the late prehistoric valley could not be monopolized by one set of elites, so, too, connections to the past were open to manipulation by multiple households. At least thirteen decaying mon-uments to Terminal Classic glory were dotted around the valley, each one of which could have been a touchstone for assertions of power. Given the appar-ent inability of one household to establish preeminent claims to whatever pres-tige was tied to these Terminal Classic capitals, the road was open for various contestants to stake their own connections to history.

Limits on Power and Hierarchy

Efforts to forge hierarchies and concentrate power enjoyed very limited success. Each of the paramount households commanded sufficient labor to erect locally impressive residences. They did, in this particular sense, prevail in capturing the labor of others and turning it to their own purposes. Even at Naco and Site PVN 306, however, the resulting monuments to elite power were modest in scale and adornment. The largest domiciles would have required only limited amounts of labor to erect and maintain. Further, materials recov-ered from paramount households do not indicate that their members success-fully accumulated considerable quantities of valuables. Their roles as mediators within extensive trade networks may have precluded keeping much of what they exchanged (Freidel and Sabloff 1984; Wonderley 1981). Nevertheless, it is difficult to escape the notion that valuables used exclusive by notables to distinguish themselves from subordinates were conspicuous by their paucity at Sites PVN 144, PVN 306, and Naco.

The truncated hierarchy seen at the three studied settlements, and the relative poverty of the material assemblages associated with paramount households, may both arise from the strategies elites used to claim preeminence within their respective nets. Notables advanced their political agendas within a field of pre-existing social webs composed largely of individual house groups. Successful construction of a unified, hierarchically structured network required motivating members of these localized domestic units to acquiesce in giving up some of their autonomy in decision-making along with the fruits of their labor. All of the evidence in hand indicates that magnates were not in a position to impose a new political order on the valley's majority. Instead, they had to create a consensus on what that new order would look like and who might legitimately lead it (Van Buren and Richards 2000). Reaching such an agreement required expending considerable political capital, including valuables such as obsidian and elaborately decorated pottery vessels.

The hoarding of blades might have made local notables "rich" but would not have bound supporters to them. Instead, elites entered into special relationships with artisans in several houses, providing them with cores in return for the ability to tap into the networks enacted through the exchange of the blades made from those nuclei. The more blades that were in circulation, the wider the spread of these webs and the more people who were enmeshed within nets of dependence that ultimately, if circuitously, tied them to elite entrepreneurs. That obliqueness was part of the problem from the rulers' perspective. Unable to control the flow of blades directly, they had to rely on maintaining the goodwill and cooperation of knappers who employed considerable skill in transforming raw material into political capital. By spreading cores out among several houses, leaders at Naco and Site PVN 306 ensured that no one set of craft workers could turn a monopoly over blade production to its exclusive political advantage. This practice, however, also meant that members of the paramount household had to negotiate with, and coordinate the actions of, numerous blade producers. We can only imagine that this process introduced a significant element of contingency into power relations that would have been obviated by centralized control over obsidian working. For whatever reasons, such a solution was not pursued.

Similarly, concentration of the most complexly decorated ceramics within paramount households could have distinguished their members clearly from those they led. Such stockpiling, however, would have stymied elite efforts to incorporate members of distinct house groups within broader affiliations. It was through the widespread distribution of these vessels that symbols that materialized inter-house affiliations penetrated each domestic web. Easing access to these containers was therefore essential to forge a unified affiliation and infuse that identity with the emotional power born of daily interactions among intimates. Once again, negotiating the terms of the new order required distributing wealth in the interest of sustaining power (Baines and Yoffee 2000).

We do not mean to imply that Roble phase elites lived an impoverished existence within their respective plaza groups. The few pieces of copper recovered in excavations within Site PV 306's EPP, together with the more numerous whole artifacts of this material looted from Naco (Wonderley 1981), point to just some of the valuables local rulers could collect and over which they probably exercised exclusive control. The point is, however, that convincing the majority to enter into new hierarchical relations and surrender some power to leaders required achieving a consensus on the rightness of these new arrangements. Reaching that agreement meant expending considerable amounts of valuables as incentives to those who would be part of these new arrangements. While they did not strip social leaders of all their wealth, these processes still countered the large-scale accumulation of preciosities in relatively few hands.

The practices of negotiation and consensus building outlined here resulted in a fragile political structure. The assets controlled by Roble phase Naco valley paramount households were comparatively few, and their deployment in political projects required the cooperation of people from different ranks. Obsidian nuclei had to be secured from peers abroad and transformed into finished tools through the actions of non-elite artisans. Rites celebrated on and around special-purpose buildings drew their power from religious observances conducted outside elite control, within house groups. Exacerbating the structure's instability was the failure of any one elite faction to create and dominate a single, society-wide web. Unable to control the local use of key conceptual and physical assets exclusively, the two prominent households were locked in an unresolved competition over adherents. This contest required the expenditure of considerable political capital in the form of feasts, obsidian cores, and decorated ceramics. Such siphoning off of energy and resources in constant negotiations for supporters meant these assets were not available to sustain projects aimed at creating a single hierarchical structure that encompassed the entire basin. Consequently, power relations were fragmented by the early sixteenth century, and the political situation was probably volatile.

Sustaining such a tense political order within one society over any length of time would have been difficult. We argued in chapter 2 that all networks are enacted and defined by their members' participation in common projects. What shared activities might have been used to diffuse some of the tension among competing elites and their webs of adherents and to forge some sense of unity among them? One possibility is that events that transpired in and around the community buildings, Strs. 144-8 and 144-18, served this purpose. Site PVN 144 is located between Site PVN 306 and Naco. It is also the only known household to include sizable constructions that might have served as gathering places for leading members of the settlement cluster. This impression could, of course, result from incomplete and incommensurate excavation samples. Nevertheless, the large, open, elaborately outfitted rooms that cap Str. 144-8 and probably its northern neighbor are unusual among known late prehistoric Naco valley constructions, as are the masks that flank their western entryways. These two constructions stand out markedly from all other examples of contemporary architecture in the basin.

The other buildings comprising the Site PVN 144 main plaza are also notably different from those recorded at Naco and Site PVN 306. In no other case did we locate constructions dedicated to food processing (Str. 144-11), the storage and cooking of comestibles (Str. 144-5-2nd), and possibly food serving (Str. 144-5-1st). The gatherings of influential individuals atop the two western edifices may have been accompanied by large-scale feasting conducted within the neighboring patio. The high density of incense burners found in the Str. 144-19, Unit 1 trash deposit and the deities depicted on the stucco masks imply that these convocations were carried out within a sacred context. That context, however, was likely associated with supernatural forces distinct to some extent from those that presided over local performances of the Quetzalcoatl cult at Naco and Site PVN 306. The masks adorning Strs. 144-8 and 144-18 are not replicated elsewhere in the valley and may represent deities different from those evoked in the western plazas of Naco and Site PVN 306. Insofar as opposing households in the Naco settlement cluster employed symbols of the Quetzalcoatl cult in contests over adherents, the invocation of other supernatural forces on Strs. 144-8 and 144-18 may have created a neutral space in which erstwhile competitors could gather and cooperate, at least in some situations.

If this was the case, then Site PVN 144 was both a place of residence for those of intermediate status (in Strs. 144-1 and 144-2) and a locale where at least some segments of the broader society gathered periodically to resolve conflicts and reinforce the unity of the settlement-wide net of which they were parts. By dividing participation in these rites of intensification between those meeting in Strs. 144-8 and 144-18 and others gathered in the plaza, distinctions of rank were maintained even in the course of reproducing network solidarity. Site PVN 144's main plaza and community structures were, in short, loci for enacting projects that defined a hierarchically structured network that encompassed the entire settlement cluster. This remained a web, however, in which power contests might be muted but were not fully resolved.

This reconstruction generally parallels forms of "multepal," or corporate, leadership attested to throughout the late prehistoric Maya lowlands (e.g., Freidel and Sabloff 1984: 182; Kepecs and Masson 2003; Masson 2003b; Pugh 2003; see also Blanton, Feinman, and Peregrine 1996; Renfrew 1974). There is no reason to think that this mode of political organization was imported from distant locales. Rather, rule by council seems to have been a solution to resolving power contests within weakly centralized polities that was adopted in numerous locales across southern Mesoamerica. Apparently, residents of the Naco valley were among the participants in this widespread political experiment.

It would be a mistake to exaggerate non-elites' capacity simply to ignore their rulers as they saw fit. Clearly, relatively large numbers of people were attracted to live near households established at Sites PVN 144, PVN 306, and Naco and, once there, to contribute to the construction of elite residences. They also attended public gatherings in designated plazas and committed themselves to the regular upkeep of symbols integral to the performance of rites conducted by local notables. The majority was part of the order that privileged some at the expense of many. These individuals, organized within their own domestic webs, did exact some benefit from these unequal relations, however. Through their bargaining with elites, obsidian blades were made widely available, and celebrations of house group unity were not only permitted but encouraged. Elites could rule, but only with the consent of the governed, and that consent did not come cheap. The result was a hierarchical structure in which power differences were muted.

NACO AND INTER-SOCIETAL INTERACTION

It has long been acknowledged that Naco, however it is defined, occupied a central role in exchange networks stretching from Mesoamerica deep into lower Central America (Chamberlain 1966; Strong, Kidder, and Paul 1938; Wonderley 1981). It is more than a little ironic, therefore, that Wonderley and we have unearthed so little evidence in support of this interpretation. There is no reason to doubt the veracity of Conquest period accounts or to speculate on other possible locations for Naco. A sizable settlement, or collection of settlements, certainly existed at the appropriate place and for the expected period of time. In fact, taken together, Naco and Sites PVN 144 and PVN 306 comprise one of the largest late prehistoric aggregations of people archaeologically attested to in Southeast Mesoamerica. The size of the Naco settlement cluster, at least, warrants acceptance of its prehispanic significance.

The rarity of trade goods is likely the result of a host of factors. A similar dearth of foreign commodities at the well-known entrepôt of Cozumel, off Yucatan's east coast, was explained by the perishable nature of many of the items exchanged (e.g., Berdan et al. 2003: 100). Further, commercial transactions wherein the value of goods lies in their utility in acquiring other commodities are not conducive to accumulating valuables at trading centers (Freidel and Sabloff 1984; Rathje and Sabloff 1973; Sabloff and Freidel 1975).

At the same time, looting has taken a toll on the artifact inventories of all three studied settlements. Wonderley recorded the presence of copper axes and bells, reported to have come from Naco, in a private collection (1981). No such preciosities are known from the other two centers, although we cannot rule out their existence. Sites PVN 306 and PVN 144 were being transformed by farming and modern settlement when first examined, and any marketable items likely did not remain on-site for long once uncovered.

The absence of evidence for trade can therefore be explained. These accounts of what might have been are at best plausible but unsatisfying. They do not contradict the scant ethnohistoric chronicles of Naco's socioeconomic importance even as they do not support them. What is much clearer from the materials in hand is the extent to which the valley's population was implicated in networks that extended well outside the basin. The symbols emblazoned on red-on-white–painted ceramic containers are, as has been noted, inspired in part by foreign models, especially those provided by the Quetzalcoatl cult. Even more emblematic of that faith are the circular constructions that occupy prominent positions in Naco's and Site PVN 306's western public plazas.

To be sure, the nature and degree of participation in this "cult" were variable. Elites were more fully versed in foreign theologies than were their subordinates. The latter experienced exotic ideas and practices as mediated by notables who lived in the predominant households. Still, even where religions inspired by distant models are fused with parochial worldviews and icons, their adoption affects the course of local developments, if for no other reason than those developments, and understandings of them, are now couched in broader contexts. By linking local practices, such as food consumption, to concepts of broad application, the significance of comestibles and the networks through which they were shared must have changed. This was, after all, what we posited elites were trying to accomplish: forging new affiliations that transcended immediate domestic ties. The enactment of these expanded relations and identities in public gatherings suggests that the strategy was at least partially successful. What we cannot determine is the extent to which participants in such convocations used these novel ideas to imagine ties with people and supernatural figures beyond the valley's confines. At least there was an opportunity to make such connections, which had not existed during the preceding Early Postclassic.

The extent to which foreign concepts spurred the Naco valley's residents to reconceptualize their world may never be known. Similarly, whatever behavioral consequences such shifts might have had for local political contests in the long run went unrealized when Spanish invaders truncated the basin's autochthonous historical trajectory. What is clear is that the ideas and symbols that defined the Mesoamerican world, such as feathered serpents and circular ritual constructions, were creatively reconstituted in the daily practices of numerous agents acting within conditions that pertained in specific places at particular moments in time. To understand how seemingly "universal" symbols figured in parochial political and cultural processes, we must investigate the manner in which they were employed in the goal-seeking actions of people working in webs of varying spatial extents. The Naco valley represents one of what were likely many ways of synthesizing the local and the interregional.

THE ROBLE PHASE'S PLACE WITHIN THE NACO VALLEY'S DEVELOPMENTAL TRAJECTORY

When we consider the broad sweep of Naco valley prehistory, the Roble phase marks one of several periods of increased political centralization and hierarchy building. Each of these spikes in complexity is separated by intervals in which unified realms fragmented and inequalities were suppressed. Centralization and hierarchy were most pronounced during the Terminal Preclassic (200 BC–AD 200) and the Late Classic, when Site PVN 123 and La Sierra, respectively, were the sole primate centers in the basin. The Roble phase represents a final resurgence of powerful indigenous elites. Once more, notables were seeking to enmesh small domestic groups within larger, hierarchically ordered political structures.

There is no reason to believe this process had come to an end by the time the Spanish arrived. As noted earlier, hierarchies were still relatively rudimentary, and two major power centers coexisted within the same overarching society. How extant networks might have been reformulated in a future unencumbered by Spanish colonialism will remain forever unknown. It is possible, however, to look back from the edge of history to see how the machinations of the Naco valley's last rulers compare with strategies implemented by their precursors. Attention here focuses specifically on the Late Classic, the period of political centralization for which we have the most detailed information.

Acquisition of power in the Late Classic and Roble phase was pursued through parallel strategies. In both cases, elites sought to create bounded societies in which they held sway. This objective was achieved through the imposition of centralized control over the intra-valley acquisition, fabrication, and distribution of certain tangible and conceptual assets that were valued widely within the realm but could only be obtained from polity leaders. Such monopolies enabled notables in each instance to subvert the autonomy of localized domestic webs and enforce participation in a hierarchically structured network directed by paramount lords. Success in these efforts depended in both intervals on the participation of Naco valley magnates in webs that linked them with their counterparts in other realms, from whom at least some of these essential resources and ideas were regularly and predictably secured. The extra-valley nets in question were constructed around shared understandings and practices expressed through a limited array of physical symbols that materialized network membership. In the Late Classic and Roble phase, the conceptual frameworks that guided inter-elite transactions were derived from lowland Maya notables at Copan and the Quetzalcoatl cult, respectively. Nevertheless, interactions conducted across borders were apparently pursued among equals in both cases. All participants in the transactions were thus free to reinterpret, up to a point, the unifying symbol system to fit their own understandings and circumstances.

In essence, therefore, Roble phase political processes were instigated by strategies that mirrored those pursued approximately five centuries earlier within the basin. The primary differences involve the greater degree to which La Sierra's magnates meddled with the means of production, the form of rulership Late Classic elites sought to impose, and the ways paramount lords employed foreign symbols to delimit and unify their realm.

Unlike Roble phase notables, who indirectly supervised the distribution of obsidian blades through the strategic distribution of cores, La Sierra's paramount lords organized production in a variety of media on relatively large scales. These notables oversaw workshops located at their capital, where artisans fabricated obsidian blades, ceramic vessels in at least two large stone-lined kilns, artifact blanks from marine shell, and the production of ceramic figurines, whistles, and ocarinas. Data in hand suggest that very few residents of rural areas engaged in crafts and were largely dependent on artisans working at the center for such widely used items as pottery vessels, obsidian blades, and ritual paraphernalia (figurines, whistles, ocarinas, and probably ceramic incense burners); marine shell blanks were exported and not apparently turned into finished goods for local consumption. These crafts involved imported obsidian and shell as well as high-quality clays that were especially plentiful in La Sierra's immediate environs. Local rulers, therefore, successfully managed to procure raw materials on a large scale and supervise the conversion of these assets into finished goods. There is no sign of such extensive interference by elites in the relations of production during the Roble phase.

Late Classic Naco lords, like their Roble phase counterparts, also organized themselves into a household, with their residences arranged around a central plaza (figure 10.1). The Late Classic paramount plaza group, however, is far larger than those raised at Sites PVN 306, PVN 144, and Naco. In addition,

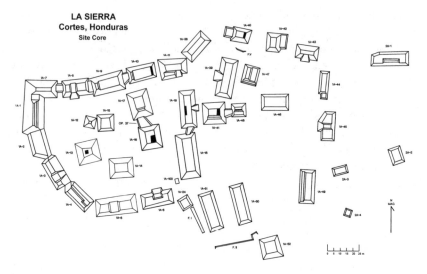

FIGURE 10.1 *Map of the La Sierra site core*

no other Late Classic Naco valley domestic compound compares in size to the La Sierra example. Thus there was only one Late Classic paramount household whose members exercised privileged control over large amounts of labor. This situation contrasts with the more modest constructions seen in the Roble phase basin, as well as with the dual, roughly equivalent power centers housed at Naco and Site PVN 306. Hierarchy during the Late Classic was therefore more pronounced and clearly focused on a specific household than in later periods of valley prehistory.

The nature of rulership also differed. Late Classic lords participated in lowland Maya-inspired rites that stressed the potency of individual rulers and their connections with deified ancestors (Freidel, Schele, and Parker 1995; Schele and Freidel 1990; Schele and Miller 1986). Paraphernalia associated with this conceptual scheme was found almost exclusively within the plaza of the La Sierra paramount household and included modeled incense burners, *Spondylus* sp. shells, and a carved stone tenoned head adorned with a simplified version of the turban that distinguished Maya rulers at contemporary Copan. Artifacts in the first two classes were used by lowland Maya aristocrats in rites that evoked and celebrated deities, especially royal ancestors (Schele and Freidel 1990; Schele and Miller 1986). These objects were likely employed in much the same way by rulers at La Sierra, one of whom was commemorated on the aforementioned tenoned sculpture, the only portrait recovered from any time period in the valley. Late Classic leadership, in short, was apparently vested in the hands of charismatic individuals and presumably their families. This is in sharp contrast to the faceless, more corporate forms of political structures that characterized the basin in the Roble phase and during all other known intervals (see also Blanton, Feinman, and Peregrine 1996; Renfrew 1974).

The affiliation that spanned the Late Classic valley was conveyed through symbols unique to that realm (Schortman, Urban, and Ausec 2001). As in the Roble phase, these emblems appeared prominently on ceramic containers used by all valley residents to store and serve comestibles (see figure 8.5). Once again, therefore, elites seeking to forge bonds among distinct domestic webs linked expressions of a novel affiliation with processes of food sharing through which relations within these intimate groups were regularly enacted. The power of polity-wide networks and their identities were infused with the potent and positive feelings generated during celebrations of domestic unity.

Unlike the Roble phase instance, however, signifiers of the Late Classic polity-wide net did not incorporate foreign motifs. All residents of the basin had access to imported polychrome vessels, mostly cylinders emblazoned with symbols that expressed exotic concepts. These containers were not, in any obvious way, used to define membership in the La Sierra domain, and their styles were not incorporated in local products. Such a division suggests that vessels bearing foreign and parochially inspired designs conveyed very different meanings possibly tied to equally divergent networks in which all of the basin's inhabitants took part to varying degrees. No comparable pattern was recorded in the Roble phase valley, where imported ceramics were extremely rare.

Along similar lines, whereas architectural emblems of participation in the Quetzalcoatl cult were prominently displayed in public arenas, their Late Classic counterparts were hidden away within the plaza of the paramount household. The latter were apparently temples used in the performance of rites led by elites who resided on the surrounding platforms. By locating these ritual foci away from public view, La Sierra's lords maintained a strict separation between parochial and foreign conceptual structures tied to rulership. The latter were seemingly the unique provenance of rulers unsullied, from the elite perspective, by local associations. The one exception to this trend was the La Sierra ballcourt, which was situated southeast of the primary household compound and could easily have been reached by large numbers of people. There is no evidence, however, that foreign and autochthonous symbols were synthesized in the practice of public rites during the Late Classic, as they were in the Roble phase.

Late Classic and Roble phase lords, therefore, promoted novel political orders by strategically deploying tangible and conceptual resources. People were motivated to participate in these hierarchically structured networks by centralized control over widely needed goods and the promotion of beliefs that stressed the essential unity of valley populations. La Sierra's magnates emphasized their privileged position within this newly imagined realm by linking themselves exclusively to supernatural forces, possibly including their own deified ancestors. These magnates even went so far as to single out in a durable material form a specific member of the ruling cadre as a paramount ruler, a step no known Naco valley monarch had dared to make before or would advance later.

Ultimately, even the striking success of La Sierra's potentates rested on the same sorts of negotiations with elite peers, artisans, and their subordinates in general in which Roble phase leaders had engaged. Insofar as power at home depended on acquiring goods from afar, the political preeminence of Late Classic and Roble phase lords hung by the slender threads that connected them to all other members of their inter-elite network. Disruptions at any point in the web that interfered with the movement of goods and ideas across it could seriously undermine the political aspirations of all participants. The collapse of the Copanec dynasty in the early ninth century may have been particularly ominous for all those who patterned their interactions on symbolic structures inspired by that center's monarchs (Andrews and Fash, eds. 2005; Fash 2001; see also Renfrew 1982). It is not surprising, therefore, that the La Sierra rulers fell from power sometime during that same century, with their household abandoned and its temples dismantled and buried along with the vast majority of their distinctive ritual gear.

Similarly, once artisans were established at the Late Classic capital under elite patronage, they comprised another interest group whose needs had to be satisfied to ensure their cooperation in elite political projects. In fact, potters, blade knappers, and the like were sufficiently numerous that they could have formed their own networks based on the shared experiences of their crafts and their positions within the realm. The fact that they lived close together at La Sierra would have facilitated the creation of such webs. There is good evidence that Late Classic craft workers not only survived the fall of their erstwhile patrons but actually flourished during the prolonged period of political fragmentation that characterized the Terminal Classic. Freed of centralized control, artisans not only continued to pursue their specialties at the capital but were now found in nearly every domestic group scattered in all parts of the valley. Attempts to create a centrally administered economy of craft specialists may have ultimately contributed to the creation of powerful interest groups who, when they united, posed a serious threat to those they were intended to serve.

Whatever role(s) craft workers played in the demise of centralized rule at La Sierra, it is clear that the political preeminence of paramount elites in the Late Classic and Roble phase was always fragile and relied on maintaining the goodwill of the governed. Efforts to create a ruling class dramatically separated from its subordinates, on the model of lowland Maya potentates, did not succeed. Leaders and followers were forever linked in negotiations over the terms of inequality, the degree to which power could be stripped from the many and vested in the hands of a few, and the creation of identities linking localized domestic webs within broader affiliations. Such contests consistently employed both abstract and palpable assets derived from local and foreign sources. Elites, however, never reached the point where they could determine absolutely how these resources would be deployed in creating debt and redefining the conceptual realm. Their subordinates always maintained a say in the matter. Political formations during the Roble phase can therefore be understood as outgrowths of earlier developments and political experiments that unfolded under historical conditions specific to the last Precolumbian centuries.

IMPLICATIONS

The value of any perspective lies to a great extent in its ability to raise new questions that lead to productive insights. We argue that concentrating on networks, as opposed to spatially bounded societies and realms, accomplishes this goal by recasting processes of political centralization and hierarchy building in helpful ways.

It does so because a network perspective focuses attention firmly on how political processes operate close to the ground. By examining how people organized themselves to employ resources in pursuit of common political projects, we are forced to consider how claims to power are advanced, defended, and challenged through the actions of self-reflexive, variably well-informed, goal-driven actors. This has at least the salutary effect of delaying efforts to identify causative structural variables before fully understanding what it is we are trying to explain. By identifying the crucial and shifting nexus among networks, assets, and projects, we can make a good start in describing political processes and specifying what has to be accounted for in understanding these relations.

The use of networks as basic units of analysis also yields a more fluid and, we would argue, more realistic picture of interpersonal relations than do approaches that treat bounded societies as starting points for study. Rather than beginning by trying to identify territorially distinct units, we are encouraged to reimagine such entities as the outcomes of decisions people made to affiliate with some and distance themselves from others in pursuit of certain aims under ever-shifting circumstances. The resulting linkages are never fixed and are subject to reevaluation as conditions change. These connections also differ considerably in their spatial extents, tying people directly and indirectly to small-scale domestic webs as well as to their counterparts who reside over considerable distances. Societies, in short, are seen as networks of networks,

241

the relations and movements among which are negotiated by their members. Different materials, in this view, are integral to the enactment of variably evanescent webs, and their patterning must be described and explained in relation to the operation of these nets and the goals of those allied within them.

Finally, as outlined in chapter 2, a network perspective is beneficial in that it encourages a reconsideration of the venerable divide in social theory between structure and agency (Bourdieu 1977; Giddens 1984; Mauss 2007). A network approach is founded on the notion that political structure does not exist independent of the events through which power relations are enacted (Mauss 2007; Schortman 2008). Structure and action are inextricably intertwined because all initiatives, political and otherwise, are enabled through the mobilization of conceptual and physical resources derived from structure. Marshaling such assets, in turn, requires cooperation among actors organized within networks to accomplish shared goals. Webs are therefore simultaneously parts of, and the means for changing, structure.

All interactions, within and outside the political sphere, are thus constrained and enabled by the resources people secure through participation in established nets into which they are born (Giddens 1984; Goffman 1974; Mann 1986; Sewell 1992). Such assets and webs may seem to exist apart from, and to be causally prior to, action. This is true insofar as structural relations among networks and resources constitute blueprints for behavior. Nevertheless, these models for action must be actualized through the deeds of agents to have social significance. Crucial to the conversion of potential into behavior are the willingness, creativity, enthusiasm, or lack of same that people bring to their use of extant nets and how they manipulate resources in pursuit of the projects through which structure lives.

Political structure, therefore, is only relevant insofar as its precepts are acted upon and is always subject to change as people renegotiate their membership in, and relations among, different networks, contend for assets through those webs, and (re)define the projects they pursue with their confederates. Decisions on how to proceed in all these endeavors are determined by the structured relations among the webs to which individuals are heir, the changing circumstances in which these relations are enacted, and the capacity of people to perceive and seize the opportunities to modify the structure these shifting conditions provide.

The political formations we have described were therefore products of history and of what the Naco valley's Roble phase denizens made of those traditions. When the first Spanish conquistadors arrived on the scene, power relations were still in flux. People organized within different networks that extended over varying distances were staking claims to preeminence and resisting those pretensions through the strategic manipulation of key conceptual and material resources. Some had gained advantages in these contests, but their ability to distinguish themselves from the rest of the population in both power and position remained limited. The capacity of people organized within houses to mobilize basic physical and ideological resources meant they could enact projects that ensured the vitality of these numerous small webs. Control over such resources provided a foundation from which elite pretensions could be challenged and their claims on labor and support curbed. No house group was autonomous, however. Their participants needed access to items and symbols that local lords alone provided. Such key assets could therefore be used to reward engagement in projects through which new, hierarchically structured webs were constituted and reproduced.

The result was a society with variably porous boundaries in which ideas, symbols, and objects that were derived from varied distances and spanned centuries figured in competitions for political advantage among members of different domestic webs. How this emerging society was bounded and understood by its members is an important question. It is not, however, the most fruitful point from which to begin to understand the dynamic interplay among the factions from which that society arose. It is far more productive, we contend, to begin such analyses with concepts that more directly address how social interactions were structured rather than with the outcomes of those transactions in the form of a society. That is what we have attempted here.

Reference List

Abercrombie, N., S. Hill, and B. Turner
1980   *The Dominant Ideology Thesis.* London: George Allen and Unwin.

Abrams, E.
1994   *How the Maya Built Their World: Energetics and Ancient Architecture.* Austin: University of Texas Press.

Adams, R. McC.
1992   Ideologies: Unity and Diversity. In *Ideology and Pre-Columbian Civilization,* A. Demarest and G. Conrad, eds., 205–221. Seattle: University of Washington Press.

Alcock, S.
2000   Classical Order, Alternative Orders, and the Uses of Nostalgia. In *Order, Legitimacy, and Wealth in Ancient States,* J. Richards and M. Van Buren, eds., 110–119. Cambridge: Cambridge University Press.

2005   Roman Colonies in the Eastern Empire: A Tale of Four Cities. In *The Archaeology of Colonial Encounters: Comparative Perspectives,* G. Stein, ed., 297–329. Santa Fe: School of American Research.

Alexander, R., and S. Kepecs
2005   The Postclassic to Spanish-Era Transition in Mesoamerica: An Introduction. In *The Postclassic to Spanish-Era Transition in Mesoamerica: Archaeological*

Perspectives, S. Kepecs and R. Alexander, eds., 1–12. Albuquerque: University of New Mexico Press.

Anderson, D.
1978   Monuments. In *The Prehistory of Chalchuapa, El Salvador,* vol. 1: *Introduction, Surface Surveys, Excavations, Monuments, and Special Deposits,* R. Sharer, ed., 155–180. Philadelphia: University of Pennsylvania Press.

Anderson, K.
1994   Geoarchaeological Investigations. In *Sociopolitical Hierarchy and Craft Production: The Economic Bases of Elite Power in a Southeast Mesoamerican Polity,* part 3: *The 1992 Season of the Naco Valley Archaeological Project,* E. Schortman and P. Urban, eds., 85–125. Gambier, OH: Anthropology Department, Kenyon College, and Tegucigalpa, Honduras: Instituto Hondureno de Antropologia e Historia.

Andres, C., and K. A. Pyburn
2004   Out of Sight: The Postclassic to Early Colonial Periods at Chau Hiix, Belize. In *The Terminal Classic in the Maya Lowlands: Collapse, Transition, and Transformation,* A. Demarest, P. Rice, and D. Rice, eds., 402–423. Boulder: University Press of Colorado.

Andrews, E. W., and W. Fash, eds.
2005   *Copan: The History of an Ancient Maya Kingdom.* Santa Fe: School of American Research.

Arnold, J.
1995   Social Inequality, Marginalization, and Economic Processes. In *Foundations of Social Inequality,* T. D. Price and G. Feinman, eds., 87–103. New York: Plenum.

Ashmore, W., and R. Wilk
1988   Household and Community in the Mesoamerican Past. In *Household and Community in the Mesoamerican Past,* R. Wilk and W. Ashmore, eds., 1–27. Albuquerque: University of New Mexico Press.

Ausec, M.
2001   Getting out of Style? Symbolic Continuity in the Naco Valley Ceramic Assemblage. Paper presented at the sixty-sixth Society for American Archaeology meeting, New Orleans, LA.

Baines, J., and N. Yoffee
2000   Order, Legitimacy, and Wealth: Setting the Terms. In *Order, Legitimacy, and Wealth in Ancient States,* J. Richards and M. Van Buren, eds., 13–17. Cambridge: Cambridge University Press.

Bancroft, H.
1886   *The Work of Hubert Howe Bancroft,* vol. 7: *History of Central America,* vol. 2: *1530–1800.* New York: McGraw-Hill.

Barth, F.
1969   Introduction. In *Ethnic Groups and Boundaries: The Social Organization of Culture Difference*, F. Barth, ed., 9–38. Boston: Little, Brown.

Bartlett, M., and P. McAnanay
2000   "Crafting" Communities: The Materialization of Formative Maya Identities. In *The Archaeology of Communities: A New World Perspective*, M. Canuto and J. Yaeger, eds., 102–122. New York: Routledge.

Baudez, C., and P. Becquelin
1973   *Archeologie de los Naranjos, Honduras.* Études Mésoamericaines 2. Mexico City: Mission Archéologique et Ethnologique Française au Mexique.

Beaudry, M., L. Cook, and S. Mrozowski
1991   Artifacts and Active Voices: Material Culture as Social Discourse. In *The Archaeology of Inequality*, R. McGuire and R. Paynter, eds., 150–191. Oxford: Blackwell.

Beck, R., Jr., D. Bolender, J. Brown, and T. Earle
2007   Eventful Archaeology: The Place of Space in Structural Transformation. *Current Anthropology* 48(6):833–860.

Berdan, F.
2003a   Borders in the Eastern Aztec Empire. In *The Postclassic Mesoamerican World*, M. Smith and F. Berdan, eds., 73–77. Salt Lake City: University of Utah Press.
2003b   The Economy of Postclassic Mesoamerica. In *The Postclassic Mesoamerican World*, M. Smith and F. Berdan, eds., 93–95. Salt Lake City: University of Utah Press.
2003c   Themes in World Systems Regions. In *The Postclassic Mesoamerican World*, M. Smith and F. Berdan, eds., 225–226. Salt Lake City: University of Utah Press.

Berdan, F., S. Kepecs, and M. Smith
2003   A Perspective on Late Postclassic Mesoamerica. In *The Postclassic Mesoamerican World*, M. Smith and F. Berdan, eds., 313–317. Salt Lake City: University of Utah Press.

Berdan, F., M. Masson, J. Gasco, and M. Smith
2003   An International Economy. In *The Postclassic Mesoamerican World*, M. Smith and F. Berdan, eds., 96–108. Salt Lake City: University of Utah Press.

Black, N.
1995   *The Frontier Mission and Social Transformation in Western Honduras: The Order of Our Lady of Mercy 1525–1773.* Boston: Brill Academic.

Blanton, R.
1994   *Houses and Households: A Comparative Study.* New York: Plenum.

Blanton, R., G. Feinman, and P. Peregrine
   1996   A Dual-Processual Theory for the Evolution of Mesoamerican Civilization. *Current Anthropology* 37:1–14.

Bloch, M.
   1977a   The Disconnection between Power and Rank as a Process. *Archives Européene de Sociologie* 18:107–148.
   1977b   The Past and the Present in the Present. *Man* (n.s.) 12:278–292.

Boone, E.
   2003   A Web of Understanding: Pictorial Codices and the Shared Intellectual Culture of Late Postclassic Mesoamerica. In *The Postclassic Mesoamerican World*, M. Smith and F. Berdan, eds., 207–221. Salt Lake City: University of Utah Press.

Boone, E., and M. Smith
   2003   Postclassic International Styles and Symbol Sets. In *The Postclassic Mesoamerican World*, M. Smith and F. Berdan, eds., 186–193. Salt Lake City: University of Utah Press.

Bordieu, P.
   1977   *Outline of a Theory of Practice*. R. Nice, transl. Cambridge: Cambridge University Press.
   1979   Symbolic Power. *Critique of Anthropology* 4:77–86.
   1989   Social Space and Symbolic Power. *Sociological Theory* 7:14–25.

Bowser, B.
   2000   From Pottery to Politics: An Ethnoarchaeological Study of Political Factionalism, Ethnicity, and Domestic Pottery Style in the Ecuadorian Amazon. *Journal of Archaeological Method and Theory* 7:219–248.

Braswell, G.
   2003a   Highland Maya Polities. In *The Postclassic Mesoamerican World*, M. Smith and F. Berdan, eds., 45–49. Salt Lake City: University of Utah Press.
   2003b   Obsidian Exchange Spheres. In *The Postclassic Mesoamerican World*, M. Smith and F. Berdan, eds., 131–158. Salt Lake City: University of Utah Press.
   2003c   K'iche'an Origins, Symbolic Emulation, and Ethnogenesis in the Maya Highlands. In *The Postclassic Mesoamerican World*, M. Smith and F. Berdan, eds., 297–303. Salt Lake City: University of Utah Press.

Brumfiel, E.
   1992   Breaking and Entering the Ecosystem: Gender, Class, and Faction Steal the Show. *American Anthropologist* 94:551–567.
   1994   Factional Competition and Political Development in the New World: An Introduction. In *Factional Competition and Development in the New World*, E. Brumfiel and J. Fox, eds., 3–13. Cambridge: Cambridge University Press.
   1996   Comment on Agency, Ideology, and Power in Archaeological Theory, a Special Section of *Current Anthropology* 37:48–50.

2000a   The Politics of High Culture: Issues of Worth and Rank. In *Order, Legitimacy, and Wealth in Ancient States*, J. Richards and M. Van Buren, eds., 131–139. Cambridge: Cambridge University Press.

2000b   Figurines of the Aztec State: Testing the Effectiveness of Ideological Domi-
[1994]   nation. In *The Ancient Civilizations of Mesoamerica: A Reader*, M. Smith and M. Masson, eds., 468–482. Oxford: Blackwell.

Brumfiel, E., and J. Fox, eds.

1994   *Factional Competition and Development in the New World*. Cambridge: Cambridge University Press.

Caldwell, J.

1964   Interaction Spheres in Prehistory. In *Hopewellian Studies*, J. Caldwell and R. Hall, eds., 134–143. Scientific Papers 12. Springfield: Illinois State Museum.

Campbell, R.

2009   Toward a Networks and Boundaries Approach to Early Complex Polities. *Current Anthropology* 50:821–848.

Canby, J.

1949   Excavations at Yarumela, Spanish Honduras. Unpublished PhD dissertation, Department of Anthropology, Harvard University, Cambridge, MA.

1951   Possible Chronological Implications of the Long Ceramic Sequence Uncovered at Yarumela, Spanish Honduras. In *The Civilization of Ancient America*, S. Tax, ed., 79–85. Chicago: University of Chicago Press.

Canuto, M., and J. Yaeger

2000   Introducing an Archaeology of Communities. In *The Archaeology of Communities: A New World Perspective*, M. Canuto and J. Yaeger, eds., 1–15. New York: Routledge.

Carmack, R.

1981   *The Quiche Mayas of Utatlan: The Evolution of a Highland Mayan Kingdom*. Norman: University of Oklahoma Press.

Carr, C.

1995   A Unified Middle-Range Theory of Artifact Design. In *Style, Society, and Person*, C. Carr and J. Neitzel, eds., 171–258. New York: Plenum.

Casey, E.

1987   *Remembering: A Phenomenological Study*. Bloomington: Indiana University Press.

Certeau, M. de.

1984   *The Practice of Everyday Life*. S. Rendall, transl. Berkeley: University of California Press.

Chamberlain, R.

1966   *The Conquest and Colonization of Honduras: 1502–1550*. New York: Octagon Books.

Chase, D., and A. Chase
1988   *A Postclassic Perspective: Excavations at the Maya Site of Santa Rita Corozal, Belize.* San Francisco: Pre-Columbian Art Research Institute.

Clark, J.
1987   Politics, Prismatic Blades, and Mesoamerican Civilization. In *The Organization of Core Technology*, J. Johnson and C. Morrow, eds., 259–284. Boulder: Westview.

Clark, J., and W. Parry
1990   Craft Specialization and Cultural Complexity. *Research in Economic Anthropology* 12:289–346.

Cohen, A.
1969   *Custom and Politics in Urban Africa: A Study of Hausa Migrants in Yoruba Towns.* Berkeley: University of California Press.
1979   Political Symbolism. *Annual Review of Anthropology* 8:87–113.
1981   *The Politics of Elite Culture: Explorations in the Dramaturgy of Power in a Modern African Nation.* Berkeley: University of California Press.

Cohen, R.
1978   Ethnicity: Problem and Focus in Anthropology. *Annual Review of Anthropology* 7:379–403.

Conlee, C.
2003   Local Elites and the Reformation of Late Intermediate Period Sociopolitical and Economic Organization in Nasca, Peru. *Latin American Antiquity* 14:47–65.

Costin, C.
1991   Craft Specialization: Issues in Defining, Documenting, and Explaining the Organization of Production. In *Archaeological Method and Theory*, vol. 3, M. Schiffer, ed., 1–56. Tucson: University of Arizona Press.
2001   Craft Production Systems. In *Archaeology at the Millennium: A Sourcebook*, G. Feinman and T. D. Price, eds., 273–327. New York: Kluwer Academic and Plenum.

Crumley, C.
1979   Three Locational Models: An Epistemological Assessment for Anthropology and Archaeology. In *Advances in Archaeological Method and Theory*, vol. 2, M. Schiffer, ed., 141–173. New York: Academic Press.

Curet, L.
1996   Ideology, Chiefly Power, and Material Culture: An Example from the Greater Antilles. *Latin American Antiquity* 7:114–131.

Curtin, P.
1984   *Cross-Cultural Trade in World History.* Cambridge: Cambridge University Press.

Dahlin, B., C. Jensen, R. Terry, D. Wright, and T. Beach
  2007   In Search of an Ancient Maya Market. *Latin American Antiquity* 18:363–384.

Demarest, A., P. Rice, and D. Rice
  2004   The Terminal Classic in the Maya Lowlands: Assessing Collapses, Terminations, and Transformations. In *The Terminal Classic in the Maya Lowlands: Collapse, Transition, and Transformation,* A. Demarest, P. Rice, and D. Rice, eds., 545–572. Boulder: University Press of Colorado.

DeMarrais, E., L. Castillo, and T. Earle
  1996   Ideology, Materialization, and Power Strategies. *Current Anthropology* 37:15–31.

de Montmollin, O.
  1989   *The Archaeology of Political Structure.* Cambridge: Cambridge University Press.

Diaz del Castillo, B.
  1916   *The True History of the Conquest of New Spain.* A. P. Maudslay, transl. London: Hakluyt Society.

Dietler, M.
  1996   Feasts and Commensal Politics in the Political Economy. In *Food and the Status Quest: An Interdisciplinary Perspective,* P. Wiessner and W. Schiefenhovel, eds., 87–125. Providence, RI: Berghahn Books.

Dietler, M., and B. Hayden
  2001   Digesting the Feast: Good to Eat, Good to Drink, Good to Think. In *Feasts: Archaeological and Ethnographic Perspectives on Food, Politics, and Power,* M. Dietler and B. Hayden, eds., 1–20. Washington, DC: Smithsonian Institution Press.

Dixon, B.
  1989   A Preliminary Settlement Pattern Study of a Prehistoric Cultural Corridor: The Comayagua Valley, Honduras. *Journal of Field Archaeology* 16:257–271.

Donley, L.
  1982   House Power: Swahili Space and Symbolic Markers. In *Symbolic and Structural Archaeology,* I. Hodder, ed., 63–73. Cambridge: Cambridge University Press.

Douglas, M., and B. Isherwood
  1979   *The World of Things.* New York: Basic Books.

Douglass, J.
  2002   *Hinterland Households: Rural Agrarian Household Diversity in Northwest Honduras.* Boulder: University Press of Colorado.

Douglass, J., and J. Mooney
  2001   Changes in Household Residence and Settlement between the Classic and Postclassic Periods in the Naco Valley, Northwest Honduras. Paper presented

at the fifteenth Simposio de Investigaciones Arqueologicas en Guatemala, Museo Nacional de Arqueologia y Etnologia, Guatemala.

Durkheim, E.
1984   *The Division of Labor in Society*. W. D. Halls, transl. Glencoe, IL: Free
[1893]   Press.

Earle, T.
1997   *How Chiefs Come to Power: The Political Economy in Prehistory*. Stanford:
        Stanford University Press.

Earle, T., and J. Ericson, eds.
1977   *Exchange Systems in Prehistory*. New York: Academic Press.

Ekholm, K.
1972   *Power and Prestige: The Rise and Fall of the Kongo Kingdom*. Uppsala: SKRIV
        Service AB.

Euraque, D.
2004   Antropologos, arqueologos, imperialismo, y la Mayanizacion de Hondu-
        ras: 1890–1940. In *Conversaciones históricas con el mestizaje y su identidad
        nacional en Honduras*, D. Euraque, ed., 37–68. San Pedro Sula, Honduras:
        Centro Editorial srl.

Fash, W.
2001   *Scribes, Warriors, and Kings: The City of Copan and the Ancient Maya*. Lon-
        don: Thames and Hudson.

Feinman, G., S. Upham, and K. Lightfoot
1981   The Production Step-Measure: An Ordinal Index of Labor Input in Ce-
        ramic Manufacture. *American Antiquity* 46:871–884.

Ferguson, Y., and R. Mansbach
1996   *Polities: Authority, Identities, and Change*. Columbia: University of South
        Carolina Press.

Flannery, K.
1972   The Origins of the Village as a Settlement Type in Mesoamerica and the
        Near East: A Comparative Study. In *Man, Settlement, and Urbanism*, P. Ucko,
        R. Tringham, and G. Dimbleby, eds., 25–53. London: Gerald Duckworth.
1976   The Early Mesoamerican House. In *The Early Mesoamerican Village*, K.
        Flannery, ed., 16–24. New York: Academic Press.

Foucault, M.
1995   *Discipline and Punish: The Birth of the Prison*. New York: Vintage.

Fowler, W.
1989   *The Cultural Evolution of Ancient Nahua Civilizations: The Pipil-Nicarao of
        Central America*. Norman: University of Oklahoma Press.

Freidel, D.
1985   New Light on the Dark Age: A Summary of Major Themes. In *The Low-
        land Maya Postclassic*, A. Chase and P. Rice, eds., 285–309. Austin: Univer-
        sity of Texas Press.

Freidel, D., and J. Sabloff
1984   *Cozumel: Late Maya Settlement Patterns*. Orlando: Academic Press.

Freidel, D., L. Schele, and J. Parker
1995   *Maya Cosmos: Three Thousand Years on the Shaman's Path*. New York: William Morrow.

Friedman, J.
1982   Catastrophe and Continuity in Social Evolution. In *Theory and Explanation in Archaeology: The Southampton Conference*, C. Renfrew, M. Rowlands, and B. Segraves, eds., 175–196. New York: Academic Press.

Friedman, J., and M. Rowlands
1977   Notes towards an Epigenetic Model of the Evolution of Civilization. In *The Evolution of Social Systems*, J. Friedman and M. Rowlands, eds., 201–276. Pittsburgh: University of Pittsburgh Press.

Gailey, C.
1987   Culture Wars: Resistance to State Formation. In *Power Relations and State Formation*, T. Patterson and C. Gailey, eds., 35–56. Washington, DC: American Anthropological Association.

Galaskiewicz, J., and S. Wasserman
1994   Introduction: Advances in the Social and Behavioral Sciences from Social Network Analysis. In *Advances in Social Network Analysis: Research in the Social and Behavioral Sciences*, S. Wasserman and J. Galaskiewicz, eds., xi–xvii. Thousand Oaks, CA: Sage.

Gasco, J., and F. Berdan
2003   International Trade Centers. In *The Postclassic Mesoamerican World*, M. Smith and F. Berdan, eds., 109–116. Salt Lake City: University of Utah Press.

Geertz, C.
1973   Thick Description: Toward an Interpretive Theory of Culture. In *The Interpretation of Cultures: Selected Essays of Clifford Geertz*, C. Geertz, ed., 3–30. New York: Basic Books.

Giddens, A.
1984   *The Constitution of Society: Outline of the Theory of Structuration*. Berkeley: University of California Press.

Gillespie, S.
2000   Beyond Kinship: An Introduction. In *Beyond Kinship: Social and Material Reproduction in House Societies*, R. Joyce and S. Gillespie, eds., 1–21. Philadelphia: University of Pennsylvania Press.

Glass, J.
1966   Archaeological Survey of Western Honduras. In *Handbook of Middle American Indians*, vol. 4: *Archaeological Frontiers and External Connections*, G. Ekholm and G. Willey, volume eds., R. Wauchope, general ed., 157–179. Austin: University of Texas Press.

Goffman, E.
 1974 *Frame Analysis: An Essay on the Organization of Experience.* Cambridge, MA: Harvard University Press.
 1997 *The Goffman Reader.* C. Lemert and A. Branaman, eds. Oxford: Blackwell.

Gordon, G.
 1896 *Prehistoric Ruins of Copan, Honduras: A Preliminary Report of the Explorations by the Museum, 1891–1895.* Memoirs of the Peabody Museum of Archaeology and Ethnology 1(1). Cambridge, MA: Harvard University.
 1898 *Researches in the Uloa Valley, Honduras.* Memoirs of the Peabody Museum of Archaeology and Ethnology 1(4). Cambridge, MA: Harvard University.

Hammond, N., and M. Bobo
 1994 Pilgrimage's Last Mile: Late Maya Monument Veneration at La Milpa, Belize. *World Archaeology* 26:19–34.

Hassig, R.
 1985 *Trade, Tribute, and Transportation: The Sixteenth Century Political Economy of the Valley of Mexico.* Norman: University of Oklahoma Press.

Hayden, B.
 1995 Pathways to Power: Principles for Creating Social Inequalities. In *Foundations of Social Inequality*, T. D. Price and G. Feinman, eds., 15–86. New York: Plenum.

Healy, P.
 1984 The Archaeology of Honduras. In *The Archaeology of Lower Central America*, F. Lange and D. Stone, eds., 113–164. Albuquerque: School of American Research, University of New Mexico Press.

Helms, M.
 1979 *Ancient Panama: Chiefs in Search of Power.* Austin: University of Texas Press.
 1988 *Ulyssey's Sail: An Ethnographic Odyssey of Power, Knowledge, and Social Distance.* Princeton: Princeton University Press.
 1992 Long-Distance Contacts, Elite Aspirations, and the Age of Discovery in Cosmological Context. In *Resources, Power, and Interregional Interaction*, E. Schortman and P. Urban, eds., 157–174. New York: Plenum.
 1993 *Craft and the Kingly Ideal: Art, Trade, and Power.* Austin: University of Texas Press.

Henderson, J.
 1979 The Valle de Naco: Ethnohistory and Archaeology in Northwestern Honduras. *Ethnohistory* 24:363–377.

Henderson, J., I. Sterns, A. Wonderley, and P. Urban
 1979 Archaeological Investigations in the Valle de Naco, Northwestern Honduras: A Preliminary Report. *Journal of Field Archaeology* 6:169–192.

Hendon, J.
 1996 Archaeological Approaches to the Organization of Domestic Labor: Household Practice and Domestic Relations. *Annual Review of Anthropology* 25: 45–61.

2000 Having and Holding: Storage, Memory, Knowledge, and Social Relations. *American Anthropologist* 102:42–53.

Hirth, J. K.

1993 Identifying Rank and Socioeconomic Status in Domestic Contexts: An Example from Central Mexico. In *Prehistoric Domestic Units in Western Mesoamerica*, R. Santley and J. K. Hirth, eds., 121–146. Boca Raton, FL: CRC Press.

1998 The Distributional Approach: A New Way to Identify Market Exchange in the Archaeological Record. *Current Anthropology* 39:451–476.

Hodder, I.

1979 Economic and Social Stress and Material Culture Patterning. *American Antiquity* 44:446–454.

Horning, A.

2000 Archaeological Considerations of "Appalachian" Identity: Community-Based Archaeology in the Blue Ridge Mountains. In *The Archaeology of Communities: A New World Perspective*, M. Canuto and J. Yaeger, eds., 210–230. New York: Routledge.

Huyssen, A.

2003 *Present Pasts: Urban Palimpsests and the Politics of Memory*. Stanford: Stanford University Press.

Isbell, W.

2000 What We Should Be Studying: The "Imagined Community" and the "National Community." In *The Archaeology of Communities: A New World Perspective*, M. Canuto and J. Yaeger, eds., 243–266. New York: Routledge.

Jackson, J., Jr.

2001 *Harlemworld: Doing Race and Class in Contemporary Black America*. Chicago: University of Chicago Press.

Jones, C.

1996 *Tikal Report No. 16: Excavations in the East Plaza of Tikal*, 2 vols. Philadelphia: University Museum, University of Pennsylvania.

Jones, S.

1997 *The Archaeology of Ethnicity: Constructing Identities in the Past and Present*. New York: Routledge.

Joyce, R.

2000 Heirlooms and Houses: Materiality and Memory. In *Beyond Kinship: Social and Material Reproduction in House Societies*, R. Joyce and S. Gillespie, eds., 189–212. Philadelphia: University of Pennsylvania Press.

2003 Concrete Memories: Fragments of the Past in the Classic Maya Present (500–1000 AD). In *Archaeologies of Memory*, R. Van Dyke and S. Alcock, eds., 104–125. London: Blackwell.

2004 Unintended Consequences? Monumentality as a Novel Experience in Formative Mesoamerica. *Journal of Archaeological Method and Theory* 11: 5–29.

Joyce, R., and J. Hendon
2000   Heterarchy, History, and Material Reality: "Communities" in Late Classic Honduras. In *The Archaeology of Communities: A New World Perspective*, M. Canuto and J. Yaeger, eds., 143–160. New York: Routledge.

Kenoyer, J.
2000   Wealth and Socioeconomic Hierarchies of the Indus Valley Civilization. In *Order, Legitimacy, and Wealth in Ancient States*, J. Richards and M. Van Buren, eds., 88–109. Cambridge: Cambridge University Press.

Kepecs, S.
2005   Mayas, Spaniards, and Salt: World Systems Shifts in Sixteenth-Century Yucatan. In *The Postclassic to Spanish-Era Transition in Mesoamerica: Archaeological Perspectives*, S. Kepecs and R. Alexander, eds., 117–137. Albuquerque: University of New Mexico Press.

Kepecs, S., and R. Alexander, eds.
2005   *The Postclassic to Spanish-Era Transition in Mesoamerica: Archaeological Perspectives*. Albuquerque: University of New Mexico Press.

Kepecs, S., and P. Kohl
2003   Conceptualizing Macroregional Interaction: World Systems Theory and the Archaeological Record. In *The Postclassic Mesoamerican World*, M. Smith and F. Berdan, eds., 14–19. Salt Lake City: University of Utah Press.

Kepecs, S., and M. Masson
2003   Political Organization in Yucatan and Belize. In *The Postclassic Mesoamerican World*, M. Smith and F. Berdan, eds., 40–44. Salt Lake City: University of Utah Press.

Kipp, R., and E. Schortman
1989   The Political Impact of Trade in Chiefdoms. *American Anthropologist* 91: 370–385.

Kirshen, P., and N. Sprang
2005   MBRS Watershed Hydrology: Rio Motagua, Rio Chamelecon, and Rio Ulua. www.mbrs.org.bz/dbdocs/proceedings/watersheds/BarriosNov05/hydro intro.pps. Accessed October 2009.

Knoke, D.
1994   Networks of Elite Structure and Decision Making. In *Advances in Social Network Analysis: Research in the Social and Behavioral Sciences*, S. Wasserman and J. Galaskiewicz, eds., 274–294. Thousand Oaks, CA: Sage.

Knox, H., M. Savage, and P. Harvey
2006   Social Networks and the Study of Relations: Networks as Method, Metaphor and Form. *Economy and Society* 35:113–140.

Kohl, P.
1987   The Use and Abuse of World Systems Theory: The Case of the Prehistoric West Asian State. In *Advances in Archaeological Method and Theory*, vol. 11, M. Schiffer, ed., 1–35. Orlando: Academic Press.

Kohl, P., and E. Chernykh
2003   Different Hemispheres, Different Worlds. In *The Postclassic Mesoamerican World*, M. Smith and F. Berdan, eds., 307–312. Salt Lake City: University of Utah Press.

LeCount, L.
2001   Like Water for Chocolate: Feasting and Political Ritual among the Late Classic Maya at Xunantunich, Belize. *American Anthropologist* 103:935–953.

Lightfoot, K., and A. Martinez
1995   Frontiers and Boundaries in Archaeological Perspective. *Annual Review of Anthropology* 24:471–492.

Lightfoot, K., A. Martinez, and A. Schiff
1998   Daily Practice and Material Culture in Pluralistic Social Settings: An Archaeological Study of Culture Change and Persistence from Fort Ross, California. *American Antiquity* 63:199–222.

Longyear, J., III
1944   *Archaeological Investigations in El Salvador*. Memoirs of the Peabody Museum of Archaeology and Ethnology 9(2). Cambridge, MA: Harvard University.
1947   Cultures and Peoples of the Southeastern Maya Frontier. *Theoretical Approaches to Problems* 3:1–12.
1952   *Copan Ceramics: A Study of Southeastern Maya Pottery*. Publication 597. Washington, DC: Carnegie Institution of Washington.
1966   Archaeological Survey of El Salvador. In *Handbook of Middle American Indians*, vol. 4: *Archaeological Frontiers and External Connections*, G. F. Ekholm and G. R. Willey, volume eds., R. Wauchope, series ed., 132–156. Austin: University of Texas Press.

Lothrop, S.
1925   The Museum Central American Expedition, 1924. *Indian Notes* 2:12–23.
1927   *Pottery Types and Sequences in El Salvador*. Indian Notes and Monographs 1(4). New York: Museum of the American Indian, Heye Foundation.
1939   The Southeastern Frontier of the Maya. *American Anthropologist* 41:42–54.

Lycett, M.
2005   On the Margins of Peripheries: The Consequences of Differential Incorporation in the Colonial Southwest. In *The Postclassic to Spanish-Era Transition in Mesoamerica: Archaeological Perspectives*, S. Kepecs and R. Alexander, eds., 97–115. Albuquerque: University of New Mexico Press.

Mann, M.
1986   *The Sources of Social Power*, vol. 1: *A History of Power from the Beginning to A.D. 1760*. Cambridge: Cambridge University Press.

Marcus, J.
1993   Ancient Maya Political Organization. In *Lowland Maya Civilization in the Eight Century A.D.*, J. Sabloff and J. Henderson, eds., 111–183. Washington, DC: Dumbarton Oaks.

2000   Toward an Archaeology of Communities. In *The Archaeology of Communities: A New World Perspective*, M. Canuto and J. Yaeger, eds., 231–242. New York: Routledge.

Masson, M.
1999   Postclassic Maya Communities at Progresso Lagoon and Laguna Seca, Northern Belize. *Journal of Field Archaeology* 26:285–306.
2000a   Postclassic Maya Ritual at Laguna de On Island, Belize. In *The Ancient*
[1994] *Civilizations of Mesoamerica: A Reader*, M. Smith and M. Masson, eds., 441–467. Oxford: Blackwell.
2000b   *In the Realm of Nachan Kan: Postclassic Maya Archaeology at Laguna de On, Belize*. Boulder: University Press of Colorado.
2001   Changing Patterns of Ceramic Stylistic Diversity in the Pre-Hispanic Maya Lowlands. *Acta Archaeologica* 72:159–188.
2003a   The Late Postclassic Symbol Set in the Maya Area. In *The Postclassic Mesoamerican World*, M. Smith and F. Berdan, eds., 194–200. Salt Lake City: University of Utah Press.
2003b   Economic Patterns in Northern Belize. In *The Postclassic Mesoamerican World*, M. Smith and F. Berdan, eds., 269–281. Salt Lake City: University of Utah Press.

Mauss, M.
2007   *Manual of Ethnography*. D. Lussier, transl., N. J. Allen, ed. New York: Durkheim and Berghahn Books.

McGuire, R.
1983   Breaking Down Cultural Complexity: Inequality and Heterogeneity. In *Advances in Archaeological Method and Theory*, vol. 6, M. Schiffer, ed., 91–142. New York: Academic Press.

McGuire, R., and R. Paynter, eds.
1991   *The Archaeology of Inequality*. Oxford: Blackwell.

McKillop, H.
1996   Ancient Maya Trading Ports and the Integration of Long-Distance and Regional Economies: Wild Cane Cay in South-Coastal Belize. *Ancient Mesoamerica* 7:49–62.

Meskell, L.
2003   Memory's Materiality: Ancestral Presence, Commemorative Practice and Disjunctive Locales. In *Archaeologies of Memory*, R. Van Dyke and S. Alcock, eds., 34–55. London: Blackwell.

Milbrath, S., and C. Peraza Lope
2003   Revisiting Mayapan: Mexico's Last Maya Capital. *Ancient Mesoamerica* 14: 1–46.
2009   Survival and Revival of Terminal Classic Traditions at Postclassic Mayapan. *Latin American Antiquity* 20:581–606.

Moholy-Nagy, H.
1990   The Misidentification of Lithic Workshops. *Latin American Antiquity* 3: 268–278.

Monaghan, J.
1995   *The Covenants with Earth and Rain: Exchange, Sacrifice, and Revelation in Mixtec Society*. Norman: University of Oklahoma Press.

Moore, J.
1996   *Architecture and Power in the Ancient Andes: The Archaeology of Public Buildings*. Cambridge: Cambridge University Press.
2003   Archaeology in Search of Architecture. In *Theory and Practice in Mediterranean Archaeology: Old World and New World Perspectives*, J. Papadopoulos and R. Leventhal, eds., 235–246. Los Angeles: Cotsen Institute of Archaeology, University of California.

Morley, S.
1920   *The Inscriptions at Copan*. Publication 219. Washington, DC: Carnegie Institution of Washington.

Neff, L. T.
1993   Non-Platform Occupation at Viejo Brisas del Valle, Northwest Honduras. MA thesis, Department of Anthropology, Rutgers, the State University of New Jersey, New Brunswick.

Ortner, S.
1995   Resistance and the Problem of Ethnographic Refusal. *Comparative Studies in Society and History* 37:173–193.

Pagden, A. R., transl.
1971   *Hernan Cortez—Letters from Mexico*. New York: Grossman.

Pauketat, T., and S. Alt
2003   Mounds, Memory, and Contested Mississippian History. In *Archaeologies of Memory*, R. Van Dyke and S. Alcock, eds., 151–179. London: Blackwell.

Pauketat, T., and T. Emerson
1999   Representations of Hegemony as Community at Cahokia. In *Material Symbols: Culture and Economy in Prehistory*, J. Robb, ed., 302–317. Occasional Papers 26. Carbondale: Center for Archaeological Investigations, Southern Illinois University.

Paynter, R.
1990   The Archaeology of Equality and Inequality. *Annual Review of Anthropology* 18:369–399.

Paynter, R., and R. McGuire
1991   The Archaeology of Inequality: Culture, Domination, and Resistance. In *The Archaeology of Inequality*, R. Paynter and R. McGuire, eds., 1–27. Oxford: Blackwell.

Peregrine, P.
1991   Prehistoric Chiefdoms on the American Midcontinent: A World System Based on Prestige Goods. In *Core/Periphery Relations in Precapitalist Worlds*, C. Chase-Dunn and T. Hall, eds., 193–211. San Francisco: Westview.

Pinto, G.
1991   Sociopolitical Organization in Central and Southwest Honduras at the Time of the Conquest: A Model for the Formation of Complex Society. In *The Formation of Complex Society in Southeastern Mesoamerica*, W. Fowler, ed., 215–235. Boca Raton, FL: CRC Press.

Pohl, J.
2003a   Creation Stories, Hero Cults, and Alliance Building: Confederations of Central and Southern Mexico. In *The Postclassic Mesoamerican World*, M. Smith and F. Berdan, eds., 61–66. Salt Lake City: University of Utah Press.
2003b   Ritual and Iconographic Variability in Mixteca-Puebla Polychrome Pottery. In *The Postclassic Mesoamerican World*, M. Smith and F. Berdan, eds., 201–206. Salt Lake City: University of Utah Press.

Pollard, H.
1993   Merchant Colonies, Semi-Mesoamericans, and the Study of Culture Contact: A Comment on Anwalt. *Latin American Antiquity* 4:383–385.

Pollock, H.
1936   *Round Structures of Aboriginal Middle America*. Publication 471. Washington, DC: Carnegie Institution of Washington.

Pollock, H., R. Roys, T. Proskouriakoff, and A. L. Smith
1962   *Mayapan, Yucatan, Mexico*. Publication 619. Washington, DC: Carnegie Institution of Washington.

Popenoe, D.
1934   Some Excavations at Playa de los Muertos, Ulua River, Honduras. *Maya Research* 1:61–85.

Preucel, R.
2000   Making Pueblo Communities: Architectural Discourse at Kotyiti, New Mexico. In *The Archaeology of Communities: A New World Perspective*, M. Canuto and J. Yaeger, eds., 58–77. New York: Routledge.

Pugh, T.
2001   Flood Reptiles, Serpent Temples, and the Quadripartite Universe: The *Imago Mundi* of Late Postclassic Mayapan. *Ancient Mesoamerica* 12:247–258.
2002–   Activity Areas, Form, and Social Inequality in Residences at Late Postclas-
2004   sic Zacpeten, Peten, Guatemala. *Journal of Field Archaeology* 29:351–367.
2003   A Cluster and Spatial Analysis of Ceremonial Architecture at Late Postclassic Mayapan. *Journal of Archaeological Science* 30:941–953.
2009   Residential and Domestic Contexts at Zacpeten. In *The Kowoj: Identity, Migration, and Geopolitics in Late Postclassic Peten, Guatemala*, P. Rice and D. Rice, eds., 173–191. Boulder: University Press of Colorado.

Pugh, T., and P. Rice
2009   Kowoj Ritual Performance and Societal Representations at Zacpeten. In *The Kowoj: Identity, Migration, and Geopolitics in Late Postclassic Peten, Guatemala*, P. Rice and D. Rice, eds., 141–172. Boulder: University Press of Colorado.

Rapoport, A.
1982   *The Meaning of the Built Environment: A Nonverbal Communication Approach.* Beverly Hills: Sage.

Rathje, W., and R. McGuire
1982   Rich Men . . . Poor Men. *American Behavioral Scientist* 25(6):705–716.

Rathje, W., and J. Sabloff
1973   Ancient Maya Commercial Systems: A Research Design for the Island of Cozumel, Mexico. *World Archaeology* 5:221–231.

Renfrew, C.
1974   Beyond a Subsistence Economy: The Evolution of Social Organization in Prehistoric Europe. In *Reconstructing Complex Societies*, C. Moore, ed., 69–85. Bulletin 20. Chicago: American School of Oriental Research.
1975   Trade as Action at a Distance: Questions of Integration and Communication. In *Ancient Civilization and Trade*, J. Sabloff and C. C. Lamberg-Karlovsky, eds., 3–59. Albuquerque: University of New Mexico Press.
1982   Polity and Power: Interaction, Intensification, and Exploitation. In *An Island Polity: The Archaeology of Exploitation in Melos*, C. Renfrew and M. Wagstaff, eds., 264–290. Cambridge: Cambridge University Press.

Renfrew, C., and J. Cherry, eds.
1986   *Peer Polity Interaction and Socio-Political Change.* Cambridge: Cambridge University Press.

Rice, D., and P. Rice
2005   Sixteenth- and Seventeenth-Century Maya Political Geography in Central Peten, Guatemala. In *The Postclassic to Spanish-Era Transition in Mesoamerica: Archaeological Perspectives*, S. Kepecs and R. Alexander, eds., 139–160. Albuquerque: University of New Mexico Press.

Rice, P.
1983   Serpents and Styles in Peten Postclassic Pottery. *American Anthropologist* 85:866–880.
1984   Obsidian Procurement in the Central Peten Lakes Region, Guatemala. *Journal of Field Archaeology* 11:181–194.
1987   *Macanche Island, El Peten, Guatemala: Excavations, Pottery, and Artifacts.* Gainesville: University of Florida Press.
2009   The Archaeology of the Kowoj: Settlement and Architecture at Zacpeten. In *The Kowoj: Identity, Migration, and Geopolitics in Late Postclassic Peten, Guatemala*, P. Rice and D. Rice, eds., 81–83. Boulder: University Press of Colorado.

Rice, P., and L. Cecil
    2009   The Iconography and Decorative Programs of Kowoj Pottery. In *The Ko-woj: Identity, Migration, and Geopolitics in Late Postclassic Peten, Guatemala*, P. Rice and D. Rice, eds., 238–275. Boulder: University Press of Colorado.

Ringle, W., T. Gallareta Negron, and G. Bey III
    1998   The Return of Quetzalcoatl: Evidence for the Spread of a World Religion during the Epiclassic Period. *Ancient Mesoamerica* 9:183–232.

Roscoe, P.
    1993   Practice and Political Centralisation. *Current Anthropology* 34:111–140.

Rosenswig, R., and M. Masson
    2002   Transformation of the Terminal Classic to Postclassic Architectural Land-scape at Caye Coco, Belize. *Ancient Mesoamerica* 13:213–235.

Royce, A.
    1982   *Ethnic Identity: Strategies of Diversity*. Bloomington: Indiana University Press.

Roys, R.
    1972   *The Indian Background of Colonial Yucatan*. Norman: University of Okla-homa Press.

Runciman, W.
    1982   Origins of States: The Case of Archaic Greece. *Comparative Studies in So-ciety and History* 24:351–377.

Sabloff, J., and D. Freidel
    1975   A Model of a Pre-Columbian Trading Center. In *Ancient Civilizations and Trade*, J. Sabloff and C. C. Lamberg-Karlovsky, eds., 369–408. Albuquer-que: University of New Mexico Press.

Sabloff, J., and R. Rathje, eds.
    1975   *A Study of Changing Pre-Columbian Commercial Systems: The 1972–1973 Seasons at Cozumel, Mexico; a Preliminary Report*. Peabody Museum of Ar-chaeology and Ethnology. Cambridge, MA: Harvard University.

Santley, R., and J. K. Hirth, eds.
    1993   *Prehispanic Domestic Units in Western Mesoamerica*. Boca Raton, FL: CRC Press.

Schank, R., and R. Abelson
    1995   *Knowledge and Memory*. Volume 8 of the series *Knowledge and Memory: The Real Story. Advances in Social Cognition*, R. Wyer Jr., ed. Hillsdale, NJ: Lawrence Erlbaum Associates.

Schele, L., and D. Freidel
    1990   *The Forest of Kings*. New York: William Morrow.

Schele, L., and M. Miller
    1986   *The Blood of Kings: Dynastic Ritual in Maya Art*. New York: George Bra-ziller, Inc., in association with the Kimbell Art Museum, Fort Worth, TX.

Scholes, F. V., and R. Roys
1948   *The Maya-Chontal Indians of Acalan-Tixchel.* Publication 560. Washington, DC: Carnegie Institution of Washington.

Schortman, E.
1989   Interregional Interaction in Prehistory: The Need for a New Perspective. *American Antiquity* 54(1):52–65.

Schortman, E., and S. Nakamura
1991   Crisis of Identity: Late Classic Competition and Interaction on the Southeast Maya Periphery. *Latin American Antiquity* 2:311–336.

Schortman, E., and P. Urban
1986   Introduction. In *The Southeast Maya Periphery*, P. Urban and E. Schortman, eds., 1–14. Austin: University of Texas Press.
1994   Living on the Edge: Core/Periphery Relations in Ancient Southeastern Mesoamerica. *Current Anthropology* 35:401–430.
2004a   Modeling the Roles of Craft Production in Ancient Political Economies. *Journal of Archaeological Research* 12:185–226.
2004b   Opportunities for Advancement: Intra-Community Power Contests in the Midst of Political Decentralization in Terminal Classic Southeastern Mesoamerica. *Latin American Antiquity* 15:251–272.

Schortman, E., P. Urban, W. Ashmore, and J. Benyo
1986   Interregional Interaction in the Southeast Maya Periphery: The Santa Barbara Archaeological Project 1983–1984 Seasons. *Journal of Field Archaeology* 13:259–272.

Schortman, E., P. Urban, and M. Ausec
2001   Politics with Style: Identity Formation in Prehispanic Southeastern Mesoamerica. *American Anthropologist* 103(2):1–19.

Schortman, H.
2008   Marcel Mauss: A Reconsideration. Senior honors thesis, Department of Sociology, Kenyon College, Gambier, OH.

Schreiber, K.
2005   Imperial Agendas and Local Agency: Wari Colonial Strategies. In *The Archaeology of Colonial Encounters: Comparative Perspectives*, G. Stein, ed., 237–262. Santa Fe: School of American Research.

Sewell, W.
1991   A Theory of Structure: Duality, Agency, and Transformation. *American Journal of Sociology* 98:1–29.

Sharer, R.
1978   The Type-Variety Descriptions. In *The Prehistory of Chalchuapa, El Salvador,* vol. 3: *Pottery and Conclusions*, R. Sharer, ed., 9–75. Philadelphia: University of Pennsylvania Press.

Sharer, R., ed.
1978   *The Prehistory of Chalchuapa, El Salvador,* 3 vols. Philadelphia: University of Pennsylvania Press.

Sharer, R., and D. Grove, eds.
1989   *Regional Perspectives on the Olmec.* School of American Research Advanced Seminar Series. Cambridge: Cambridge University Press.

Sharer, R., and L. Traxler
2006   *The Ancient Maya,* 6th ed. Stanford: Stanford University Press.

Sheets, P.
1984   The Prehistory of El Salvador: An Interpretive Summary. In *The Archaeology of Lower Central America,* F. Lange and D. Stone, eds., 85–112. Albuquerque: School of American Research, University of New Mexico Press.
1992   *The Ceren Site.* New York: Harcourt Brace Jovanovich College Publishers.

Sheets, P., ed.
2002   *Before the Volcano Erupted: The Ancient Ceren Village in Central America.* Austin: University of Texas Press.

Sherman, W.
1978   *Forced Native Labor in Sixteenth-Century Central America.* Lincoln: University of Nebraska Press.

Sidrys, R., and J. Andersen
1978   A Second Round Structure from Northern Belize, Central America. *Man* (new series) 13:638–650.

Smith, M.
1987   Household Possessions and Wealth in Agrarian States: Implications for Archaeology. *Journal of Anthropological Archaeology* 6:297–335.
1994   Social Complexity in the Aztec Countryside. In *Archaeological Views from the Countryside: Village Communities in Early Complex Societies,* G. Schwartz and S. Falconer, eds., 143–159. Washington, DC: Smithsonian Institution Press.
1997   Life in the Provinces of the Aztec Empire. *Scientific American* 277(3):76–83.
2003a   Key Commodities. In *The Postclassic Mesoamerican World,* M. Smith and F. Berdan, eds., 117–125. Salt Lake City: University of Utah Press.
2003b   Information Networks in Postclassic Mesoamerica. In *The Postclassic Mesoamerican World,* M. Smith and F. Berdan, eds., 181–185. Salt Lake City: University of Utah Press.
2007   Inconspicuous Consumption: Non-Display Goods and Identity Formation. *Journal of Archaeological Method and Theory* 14:412–438.

Smith, M., and F. Berdan
2000   The Postclassic Mesoamerican World System. *Current Anthropology* 41:283–286.

2003   Postclassic Mesoamerica. In *The Postclassic Mesoamerican World*, M. Smith and F. Berdan, eds., 3–13. Salt Lake City: University of Utah Press.

Smith, M., and F. Berdan, eds.
2003   The Spatial Structure of the Mesoamerican World System. In *The Postclassic Mesoamerican World*, M. Smith and F. Berdan, eds., 21–34. Salt Lake City: University of Utah Press.

Smith, M., and C. Heath-Smith
2000   Rural Economy in Late Postclassic Morelos: An Archaeological Study. In
[1994]   *The Ancient Civilizations of Mesoamerica: A Reader*, M. Smith and M. Masson, eds., 217–235. Oxford: Blackwell.

Smith, R.
1971   *The Pottery of Mayapan*. Papers of the Peabody Museum of Archaeology and Ethnology 66. Cambridge, MA: Harvard University.

Spence, M.
2005   A Zapotec Diaspora Network in Classic Period Central Mexico. In *The Archaeology of Colonial Encounters: Comparative Perspectives*, G. Stein, ed., 173–205. Santa Fe: School of American Research.

Spencer, C.
1982   *The Cuicatlan de Cañada and Monte Alban: A Study of Primary State Formation*. New York: Academic Press.

Stein, G.
1999   *Rethinking World Systems: Diasporas, Colonies, and Interactions in Uruk Mesopotamia*. Tucson: University of Arizona Press.

Stone, D.
1940   The Ulua Valley and Lake Yojoa. In *The Maya and Their Neighbors*, C. Hay, R. Linton, S. Lothrop, H. Shapiro, and G. Valiant, eds., 386–394. New York: Appleton Century.
1941   *Archaeology of the North Coast of Honduras*. Memoirs of the Peabody Museum of Archaeology and Ethnology 9. Cambridge, MA: Harvard University.
1942   A Delimitation of the Area and Some of the Archaeology of the Sula-Jicaque Indians of Honduras. *American Antiquity* 7:376–388.
1957   *The Archaeology of Central and Southern Honduras*. Papers of the Peabody Museum of Archaeology and Ethnology 49(3). Cambridge, MA: Harvard University.

Strong, W.
1935   *Archaeological Investigations in the Bay Islands, Spanish Honduras*. Miscellaneous Collections 92(14). Washington, DC: Smithsonian Institution.

Strong, W., A. Kidder II, and A. D. Paul Jr.
1938   *Preliminary Report on the Smithsonian–Harvard University Archaeological Expedition to Northwestern Honduras, 1936*. Miscellaneous Collections 97(1). Washington, DC: Smithsonian Institution.

Tourtellot, G.
  1988   Developmental Cycles of Households and Houses at Seibal. In *Household and Community in the Mesoamerican Past*, R. Wilk and W. Ashmore, eds., 97–120. Albuquerque: University of New Mexico Press.

Trigger, B.
  1984   Archaeology at the Crossroads: What's Next? *Annual Review of Anthropology* 13:275–300.
  1990   Monumental Architecture: A Thermodynamic Explanation of Symbolic Behavior. *World Archaeology* 22:119–132.

Turner, V.
  1964   Symbols in Ndembu Ritual. In *Closed Systems and Open Minds: The Limits of Naivety in Social Science*, M. Gluckman, ed., 20–51. Chicago: Aldine.

Urban, P.
  1986   Systems of Settlement in the Precolumbian Naco Valley, Northwestern Honduras. PhD dissertation, Department of Anthropology, University of Pennsylvania, Philadelphia. Ann Arbor, MI: University Microfilms.
  1993a   Naco Valley. In *Pottery of Prehistoric Honduras: Regional Classification and Analysis*, J. Henderson and M. Beaudry-Corbett, eds., 30–63. Institute of Archaeology Monograph 35. Los Angeles: University of California.
  1993b   Central Santa Barbara Region. In *Pottery of Prehistoric Honduras: Regional Classification and Analysis*, J. Henderson and M. Beaudry-Corbett, eds., 136–171. Institute of Archaeology Monograph 35. Los Angeles: University of California.

Urban, P., and E. Schortman
  2002   Power without Bounds? Middle Preclassic Political Developments in the Naco Valley, Honduras. *Latin American Antiquity* 13:131–152.

Urban, P., and E. Schortman, eds.
  1986   *The Southeast Maya Periphery*. Austin: University of Texas Press.

Van Buren, M.
  2000   Political Fragmentation and Ideological Continuity in the Andean Highlands. In *Order, Legitimacy, and Wealth in Ancient States*, J. Richards and M. Van Buren, eds., 77–87. Cambridge: Cambridge University Press.

Van Buren, M., and J. Richards
  2000   Introduction: Ideology, Wealth, and the Comparative Study of Civilizations. In *Order, Legitimacy, and Wealth in Ancient States*, J. Richards and M. Van Buren, eds., 3–12. Cambridge: Cambridge University Press.

Van Dyke, R., and S. Alcock
  2003   Archaeologies of Memory: Introduction. In *Archaeologies of Memory*, R. Van Dyke and S. Alcock, eds., 1–13. London: Blackwell.

Van Dyke, R., and S. Alcock, eds.
  2003   *Archaeologies of Memory*. London: Blackwell.

Vaughn, K.
2004   Households, Crafts, and Feasting in the Ancient Andes: The Village Context
        of Early Nasca Craft Consumption. *Latin American Antiquity* 15:61–88.

Vincent, J.
1974   The Structuring of Ethnicity. *Human Organization* 33:375–379.
1978   Political Anthropology: Manipulative Strategies. *Annual Review of Anthro-
        pology* 7:175–194.

Voorhies, B., and J. Gasco
2004   *Postclassic Soconusco Society: The Late Prehistory of the Coast of Chiapas,
        Mexico.* Monograph 14. Albany: Institute for Mesoamerican Studies, State
        University of New York. Distributed by University of Texas Press, Austin.

Wauchope, R.
1970   Protohistoric Pottery of the Guatemalan Highlands. In *Monographs and
        Papers in Maya Archaeology*, W. Bullard Jr., ed., 89–244. Papers of the Pea-
        body Museum of Archaeology and Ethnology 61. Cambridge, MA: Har-
        vard University.

Weeks, J., N. Black, and J. S. Speaker
1987   From Prehistory to History in Western Honduras: The Care Lenca in the
        Colonial Province of Tencoa. In *Interaction on the Southeast Mesoamerican
        Frontier: Prehistoric and Historic Honduras and El Salvador*, E. Robinson,
        ed., 65–94. Oxford: British Archaeological Reports Series.

Wells, E. C.
2003   Artisans, Chiefs, and Feasts: Classic Period Social Dynamics in Southeast-
        ern Mesoamerica. PhD dissertation, Department of Anthropology, Ari-
        zona State University, Tempe.

Wells, E. C., and B. Nelson
2007   Ritual Pilgrimage and Material Transfers in Prehispanic Northwest Mexico.
        In *Mesoamerican Ritual Economy: Archaeological and Ethnological Perspec-
        tives*, E. C. Wells and K. Davis-Salazar, eds., 137–166. Boulder: University
        Press of Colorado.

Wells, P.
1980   *Culture Contact and Culture Change.* Cambridge: Cambridge University
        Press.
1984   *Farms, Villages, and Cities: Commerce and Urban Origins in Late Prehistoric
        Europe.* Ithaca, NY: Cornell University Press.

Wheatley, P.
1975   Satyanita in Suvarmadvipa: From Reciprocity to Redistribution in Ancient
        Southeast Asia. In *Ancient Civilizations and Trade*, J. Sabloff and C. C.
        Lamberg-Karlovsky, eds., 227–283. Albuquerque: University of New Mex-
        ico Press.

Wiessner, P.
1983   Style and Social Interaction in Kalahari San Projectile Points. *American
        Antiquity* 48:253–276.

Wilk, R., and W. Ashmore, eds.
1988   *Household and Community in the Mesoamerican Past.* Albuquerque: University of New Mexico Press.

Wilk, R., and W. Rathje
1982   Household Archaeology. *American Behavioral Scientist* 25(6):617–639.

Wobst, H. M.
1977   Stylistic Behavior and Information Exchange. In *For the Director: Research Essays in Honor of James B. Griffin,* C. Cleland, ed., 317–342. Anthropological Papers 61. Ann Arbor: Museum of Anthropology, University of Michigan.
1999   Style in Archaeology or Archaeologists in Style. In *Material Meanings: Critical Approaches to the Interpretation of Material Culture,* E. Chilton, ed., 118–132. Salt Lake City: University of Utah Press.

Wolf, E.
1982   *Europe and the People without History.* Berkeley: University of California Press.
1990   Distinguished Lecture: Facing Power—Old Insights, New Questions. *American Anthropologist* 92:586–596.
2001   Inventing Society. In *Pathways of Power: Building an Anthropology of the*
[1988]   *Modern World,* E. Wolf, with S. Silverman, ed., 320–334. Berkeley: University of California Press.

Wonderley, A.
1981   Late Postclassic Excavations at Naco, Honduras. PhD dissertation, Department of Anthropology, Cornell University, Ithaca, NY. Ann Arbor, MI: UMI Dissertation Series.
1985   The Land of Ulua: Postclassic Research in the Naco and Sula Valleys, Honduras. In *The Lowland Maya Postclassic,* A. Chase and P. Rice, eds., 254–269. Austin: University of Texas Press.
1986   Material Symbolics in Pre-Columbian Households: The Painted Pottery of Naco, Honduras. *Journal of Anthropological Research* 42:497–534.
1987   Imagery in Household Pottery from "La Gran Provincia de Naco." In *Interaction on the Southeast Mesoamerican Frontier: Prehistoric and Historic Honduras and El Salvador,* E. Robinson, ed., 304–327. Oxford: British Archaeological Reports Series.

Wylie, A.
2002   *Thinking with Things: Essays in the Philosophy of Archaeology.* Berkeley: University of California Press.

Yaeger, J.
2000   The Social Construction of Communities in the Classic Maya Countryside. In *Archaeology of Communities in the Ancient Americas,* M. Canuto and J. Yaeger, eds., 123–142. London: Routledge.

Yde, J.
  1938   *An Archaeological Reconnaissance of Northwestern Honduras.* Publication 9. New Orleans: Middle American Research Institute, Tulane University.

Yoffee, N.
  1991   Maya Elite Interaction: Through a Glass Sideways. In *Classic Maya Political History: Hieroglyphic and Archaeological Evidence,* T. P. Culbert, ed., 285–310. Cambridge: Cambridge University Press.

Zuniga, A. E.
  1990   *Los modalidades de la lluvia en Honduras.* Tegucigalpa, Honduras: Editorial Guaymuras.

Index